Walkshaping™

Walkshaping™

Indoors or Out,
6 Weeks to a Better Body

Gary Yanker

With a Team of Medical Experts

SANDRA V. ABRAMSON, P.T.
DAVID AMUNDSEN, D.C.
JOHN BALL, M.D.
EDMUND BURKE, PH.D.
SUSAN CABLE, R.P.T.
DEEPAK CHABRA, M.D.
HOWARD FLAKS, M.D.
BARRY FRANKLIN, PH.D.
AVRUM FROIMSOM, M.D.
ROBERT GLICK, M.D.
HARLAN C. HUNTER, D.O.
JOSEPH KANSAO, D.C.
MARK LA PORTA, M.D.
MARK LANDRY, D.P.M.
KAREN P. LAUZE, M.D.
RUTH LERNER, PH.D.
RALPH MARTIN, D.O.

ROGER MAZLEN, M.D., P.C.
SARAH MILLER, PH.D.
KENNETH MURKOWSKI, D.C.
TOM ORMSBY, P.T.
TODD PELLESCHI, D.P.M.
KATHLEEN PETRILLO, R.D.
RONALD PONCHAK, P.T.
C. MALCOLM RICE III, M.D.
ALBERT ROSEN, M.D., P.A.
ALLEN SELNER, D.P.M.
PAUL SHEITEL, D.P.M.
ELIZABETH SILON, P.T.
TERRY SPILKEN, D.P.M.
JACK STERN, M.D.
JAMES D. THOMAS, M.D.
ROBERT E. TOMPKINS, D.O.
MARK YOUNG, M.D.

Quill · William Morrow · New York

It is the policy of William Morrow and Company, Inc., and its imprints and affiliates, recognizing the importance of preserving what has been written, to print the books we publish on acid-free paper, and we exert our best efforts to that end.

Library of Congress Cataloging-in-Publication Data

Yanker, Gary.
    Walkshaping: indoors or out, 6 weeks to a better body /
  by Gary Yanker; with a team of medical experts.
        p. cm.
    Includes bibliographical references (p.) and index.
    ISBN 0-688-14621-X
    1. Walking (Sports)   2. Physical fitness.   I. Title.
  GV502.Y365   1994
613.7'176—dc20   94-28834
                                                        CIP

Printed in the United States of America

First Quill Edition

1 2 3 4 5 6 7 8 9 10

BOOK DESIGN BY ALISON LEW

Preface

In the last ten years, walking has become the exercise of choice for many Americans. In 1985, walking surpassed jogging's 34 million participants with 55 million participants. By 1990, the number of walkers had grown to 70 million, and walking surpassed swimming to become the country's number-one recreation sport. Today, 77 million Americans say that they walk for exercise. Along with back pain, being overweight is the greatest health concern of Americans, 50 million of whom are either on a diet or say they want to lose weight. Walking offers the greatest hope for these two groups to stay active and is the best medicine for eliminating excess weight, as well as back pain.

The most common complaint among the 30,000 people who have attended my walking clinics in the last five years has been: "I'm walking three to five miles a day and I'm not losing weight." My quick answer is this: "If you measure yourself, you'll see that you've lost your girth or fat, even if the scale doesn't reflect a loss of weight. Your body has simply changed its composition: It may even be heavier, because muscle has replaced the fat."

Still, my students wanted more—having been exposed to the images of sculpted bodies such as those of Madonna and Jane Fonda, Arnold Schwarzenegger and Joe Piscopo. The standard for getting "in shape" has changed; the emphasis of health has shifted from feeling healthy inside to looking healthy, or rather, well built on the outside.

And although these walkers were otherwise satisfied with their walking program because it lowered their heart rate, blood pressure, and cholesterol levels (what I call the inside benefits), they still wanted more. If they were going to invest thirty to sixty minutes every day or every other day, they wanted a minor miracle—to transform their bodies as well.

I pondered this problem. There had to be a way to combine the substance of walking with the style of body sculpting. After all, walking had successfully challenged jogging by producing similar cardiovascular benefits without knee, back, and joint injuries. Now it was time for walking to take on bodybuilding.

I consulted medical experts in a variety of fields. I worked with hundreds of walkers individually and in groups in walking clubs and spas to develop a walking program that can really shape you up. I had my exercise models pose in bathing suits for "before" and "after" shots to show you the results. I also contacted the graduates of my beginner walking clinic and sought volunteers for what was to become the six-week Walkshaping program. They sent us their photographs before beginning the program, and at the end of six weeks they sent us their new bathing suit pictures.

For those who have never exercise-walked before or who have lost touch with exercising and staying in shape, rest assured: the Walkshaping program is good for beginners. It takes you step-by-step and arm-by-arm through the special Walkshaping techniques and exercises. Even in the first five minutes of practicing the posture exercise, you'll notice your figure improving immediately. Your thinner and shapelier appearance will help you visualize how your body will look after following the six-week Walkshaping program. With each progressive week, your appearance will improve dramatically, and your shaped-up body will quickly become a permanent fixture.

Contents

Introduction

Walkshaping

Millions of Americans have discovered a perfectly simple, perfectly astonishing form of exercise: walking. Now I have developed a revolutionary program that combines the aerobic benefits of walking with the most advanced body-sculpting techniques. The result is Walkshaping™—the easiest, most accessible, and most efficient way not only to lower your heart rate, blood pressure, and cholesterol, but also to burn fat and build muscle tone.

Developed with a team of medical advisers, Walkshaping is easy on the back and joints, so you'll avoid pain and injury. A series of comprehensive walking exercise routines—each incorporating a variety of weighted aids such as wrist and ankle weights, dumbbells, and ski poles—provides a total workout. I have designed a complete program specifically tailored to your age, fitness level, and schedule. You will learn a new way to walk—a whole-body workout that will work wonders in just six weeks.

With 150 photographs illustrating how to do the exercises for maximum effectiveness, *Walkshaping* shows you how to:

- set achievable goals and measure your progress each step of the way.

- outfit yourself with appropriate *and* inexpensive equipment.

- Select the Walkshaping routine—from 12 to 60 minutes a day—that's right for you.

- triple (even quadruple) the calories you burn and double the number of muscles you work out.

- increase your flexibility and the strength of your back and joints.

- compensate for interruptions in your routine.

- isolate ten major muscle groups, including thighs, chest, and abdominals, and sculpt them to your liking.

- master my 67 varieties of walking to combine Walkshaping with other activities.

Whether you work out in a gym on a treadmill or track, on the road, or on a beach, *Walkshaping* offers a safe, sure, and simple six-week solution to good health and a great body. It's as easy as a walk in the park.

WEEK ONE: Get with the program, learn the basics, select the routine that's right for you. And don't forget to take your picture—so you can see the difference in six weeks.

WEEK TWO: As you familiarize yourself with your routine, choose the muscle groups you want to concentrate on—for firmer thighs, a flatter stomach, or a sculpted physique.

WEEK THREE: You're making great strides. You begin to feel your hard body coming into focus.

WEEK FOUR: You see for yourself what you can accomplish. There's no stopping you now. You feel great, look even better.

WEEK FIVE: Start planning for the future. Decide whether you want to maintain your exercise level—or go even higher.

WEEK SIX: Take out your camera and take your best shot. Put the two photos side by side and they'll tell you all you need to know about what you have accomplished—your body of good work.

The Walkshaping™ Program promises to help you lose 2–10 lbs. or 1–5 inches of body fat every six weeks you are on the program, for as long as 54 weeks. It can be practiced indoors and outdoors. The claim that the Walkshaping techniques will burn 2–3 times (even four times) more calories than regular walking has been substantiated in calorie burn (VO2/Oxygen Consumption) tests at the Beaumont Hospital for Rehabilitation and Health Center in Detroit, under the supervision of Dr. Barry Franklin and his staff.

The secret to Walkshaping is its unique combination of body-shaping arm, leg, and torso movements with a new kind of dynamic walking action called the Stride Stretch and Arm Pump. While walking in place or on the move, Walkshapers practice 1–5 sets each of Upper-Body Shaping Routines and Lower-Body Shaping Routines.

The six-week Walkshaping Program was tested on (and vetted by) over one hundred participants, including over twenty medical experts, physical trainers, models, and actors. The current Miss New York and Mrs. New York graduated from the program before winning their titles.

Over 100,000 people have attended Gary Yanker's Walking School, which will now feature the Walkshaping Program. The Gary Yanker Walking Programs have shown that it is possible to lose from 5–10 lbs. in six weeks and up to 100 lbs. in one year.

Testimonials

Week One to Week Twelve

EILEEN HUNT, a 25-year-old pharmacist, lost 15 lbs. in 12 weeks practicing the Walkshaping Program. She started at 125 lbs. (Before: Photo 1). At the end of Week 6 (After: Photo 2), she had lost 5 lbs. and dropped from a 27- to a 26-inch waist. At the end of 12 weeks, she had lost an additional 10 lbs., to a final 110 lbs., and had a 25-inch waist (After: Photo 3).

CARLO FIORLETTA, a 33-year-old bank executive, lost 10 lbs. through Walkshaping. Carlo originally weighed 184 lbs., with a 37-inch waist (Before: Photo 1). After 6 weeks Carlo (After: Photo 2), had lost 6 lbs. and 3½ inches from his waist, while gaining 1 inch on his thighs and ½ inch on his biceps and triceps. After 12 weeks (After: Photo 3), Carlo had lost an additional 4 lbs. and 1½ inches from his waist, weighing 174 lbs. and with a 32-inch waist.

RENEE ROBERTSON, age 22, lost 4 lbs. in 6 weeks and became Miss New York. Renee started the 6-week Walkshaping program in preparation for the 1993 Miss New York contest (Before: Photo 1). In 6 weeks, she had lost 4 lbs., 2 inches from her thighs, 1 inch from her waist, and 1 inch from her calves. She also increased her shoulder, stomach, and buttocks tone significantly (After: Photo 2). Renee went on to win the 1993 Miss New York title.

BEFORE

Photo 1

AFTER 6 WEEKS

Photo 2
Eileen Hunt

AFTER 12 WEEKS

Photo 3

BEFORE

Photo 1

AFTER 6 WEEKS

Photo 2
Carlo Fiorletta

AFTER 12 WEEKS

Photo 3

CINDY MANION is a 34-year-old model who lost 2 lbs. in 6 weeks and became Mrs. New York (Before: Photo 1). She lost 2 lbs. and 1 inch from her chest and ½ inch from her hips. Cindy dramatically increased the muscle tone of her stomach, buttocks, and shoulders (After: Photo 2). She tripled the number of push-ups (10 to 30) she could do and doubled the number of sit-ups. Cindy went on to win the 1993 Mrs. New York Title.

DR. MARK LANDRY, age 43, is a podiatric surgeon in Overland Park, Kansas. At the start he weighed 250 lbs. and had a 42-inch waist.

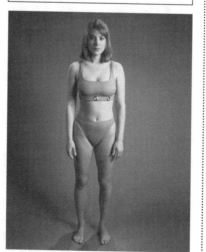

BEFORE

Photo 1

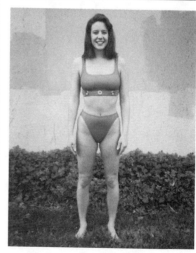

AFTER 6 WEEKS

Photo 2

Renee Robertson

BEFORE	AFTER 6 WEEKS

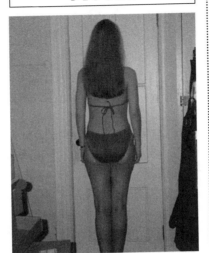

Photo 1   Photo 2

Cindy Manion

After 6 weeks, Dr. Landry had lost 4 lbs. and 2 inches from his waist, while achieving more of a V-cut torso and significantly diminishing the handles around the hips.

Week Twelve to Week Fifty-four

DOROTHEA BARNES, age 72, lost 32 lbs. on her walking program. Dorothea lowered her cholesterol from 260 to 199 milligrams, reduced blood pressure, and improved diabetic control in less than 9 months. Before she started her walking program, she couldn't walk two blocks without experiencing a pain in her heart, a "tight, choking pain." In 24 weeks, Dorothea could walk 2 miles, without stopping, at a moderate pace. In 36 weeks, she was walking 3 miles without stopping, at a pace of 4 miles per hour or 15 minutes per mile.

JAMES CHAPMAN, a 50-year-old engineer from Missouri, Texas, lost 35 lbs. (from 185 lbs. to 150 lbs.) in 52 weeks and reduced his blood pressure from 220/120 to 130/85.

LORI ROGERS, a 32-year-old walker from Oberlin, Ohio, lost the 30 lbs. she had gained during her pregnancy in 20 weeks.

EDMUND JOSEPH RIVET, age 43, lost 80 lbs. in 54 weeks. Ed walked an average of 15 to 20 miles a week in his program and has maintained an 80 lb. weight loss over 8 years.

CHRIS OEHLER, age 24, lost 30 lbs. in 6 weeks. Chris was already overweight before her pregnancy and had never done any sort of regular exercise program. She started walking 2 to 4 miles a day, six days a week, after she became pregnant. While she gained 30 lbs. as part of her pregnancy, she lost it all within 12 weeks afterward.

JIM WHITE, a 47-year-old Californian who started with 606 lbs. and a 66-inch waist, lost over 100 lbs. doing a variety of exercises in 6–8 months only to gain it all back again when he stopped exercising. But he also lost it again. Once he was down to 495 lbs., he decided to switch to the walking program. He built up his mileage from one block to 3 miles a day, and his speed to 11 minutes a mile. Jim has brought his weight down to 180 lbs., losing 315 lbs. on the walking program; and he has maintained his weight at 180 lbs. for over one year.

PAUL SPEAR, of Atlanta, lost 20 lbs. in 24 weeks by walking 12 miles a week and cutting out sweets and starches from his diet.

WALTER STEIN, age 46, lost 100 lbs. in 52 weeks and brought his diabetes under control.

STEPHEN WATKINSON, age 36, lost 100 lbs. in 52 weeks, quit smoking, and recovered from a heart attack. Stephen smoked 2–3 packs of cigarettes a day and was 100 lbs. overweight before he had his first heart attack. Twenty percent of Stephen's heart tissue was dead. After he had stabilized, doctors performed an angiogram. Two weeks later, doctors had to perform coronary bypass surgery. Stephen was put on a walk-rehabilitation program and lost 100 lbs. in one year. He can hike 2 miles up Squaw Peak near his home in Phoenix and has a resting heartbeat of 54 beats per minute.

Health and Medical Benefits

Physical Disabilities

JOE HUNTER, 52 years old, now can do 100-mile walking marathons with a complete right knee replacement. He injured his knee playing semiprofessional football.

Eighty million Americans suffer from disabling back pain. Robert Ross, a 64-year-old truck driver from Cedar Rapids, Iowa, says 80 percent of all truck drivers have bad backs. Robert severely strained a muscle in his back when he attempted to reach over and pull a pin on a truck wheel by hand rather than with a crowbar. He wound up hospitalized for many months. He was still on crutches when he started his walking program. Robert now walks 3–4 miles at a time.

Overrunning Life's Major Personality Traumas and Challenges

GAIL KIRSHNER RIGGS was 20 years old when her orthopedic surgeon told her she would be in a wheelchair by the time she was 50. But instead, her fiftieth birthday has been marked with a bronze medal in a national table tennis competition. Gail now walks, with four artificial joints, several blocks around the University of Arizona campus and once a week uphill.

Of the 40 million arthritis sufferers, 6 million suffer from the more serious rheumatoid arthritis like Gail. There is hope they can become mobile again or remain mobile through a walking program. Arthritis also affects 200,000 children.

JOAN SIMON, age 57, was diagnosed with breast cancer 10 years ago. She chose and could do the walking program for her comeback because it allowed her to exercise even when she didn't have a lot of energy. Now that she walks 3 miles four to five times a week, she feels energetic and has developed a positive attitude and a healthy life-style for a remarkable recovery.

When Marvel Svoboda found out her husband, Leon, had a malignant cancer on his tongue and had to have half his tongue removed, she asked him to join her walking program. Walking is by far the greatest reaction to major changes in our lives. It's been four years since Leon's operation and he can talk again. Leon and Marvel continue to maintain their 3-mile-a-day walking program.

Combating Compulsive and Addictive Behavior

JULIE MORRISON, age 35, had the eating disorder bulimia (binge eating) since she was 13 years old. Julie's binges were followed by crash dieting, and she was so obsessed with her weight that she weighed herself several times a day. As an adult, Julie sought psychological counseling (group therapy) at an outpatient treatment center for about six months. Although she learned a lot about herself and thought she had overcome her problem, she had not. Julie was not actively bulimic for twenty years, but she was always obsessive, and this showed up in an addiction to running. Julie also ran as part of her work—she had started a running magazine, *Running Journal*, with her husband. Running was a good workout, but not for Julie. She pushed herself to run up to 40 miles per week, often running until she felt nauseous. Running had become an obsession. Then she tried race-walking, but it too soon became an obsession as she competed to win races and walking marathons. It wasn't until Julie tried the noncompetitive walking program that she made her psychological breakthrough. At first, she gained 20 lbs., but that did not faze her. She understood that balanced mental and physical health was more important than weight perfection. The walking program did help bring her weight under control and made her less compulsive both in her eating and her exercise. She began to lose weight naturally and gradually. She maintained a 1–3-mile-a-day walk and lost 10 lbs. in 6 weeks. "If I realized what walking could do with a more balanced, less obsessive, controlled approach to exercise, I wouldn't have had the problems for twenty years!"

The man who walked and ran too much: Dr. William Farrell, a dentist in Atlanta, Georgia, walked and ran ultra marathons of 100 miles or more. His hundred-mile-a-week training schedule led to both physical and emotional stress. Dr. Farrell began experiencing flulike symptoms and walking pneumonia. His condition was diagnosed as chronic fatigue syndrome. The prescription was to cut his workouts back from 4–6 hours to 1–2 hours a day. His symptoms have disappeared.

Smoking

DOROTHY CHESTER, age 59, from Cedar Rapids, Iowa, decided to quit a forty-year-old, 1½-pack-a-day smoking habit after being diagnosed with high cholesterol. For the first six weeks, she practiced a 4-mile-a-day walk at her local mall instead of smoking. But then she became very irritable, fidgety, and restless. Her husband recently had gone into retirement. His being home all day added more stress to her withdrawal symptoms. Instead of reverting to smoking, Dorothy added an extra 2 miles to her daily walk and brought her symptoms under control. After one year, Dorothy no longer experienced withdrawal symptoms. Her friends at the Cancer Society had said she would experience those symptoms for up to two years as a smoker who had smoked most of her life.

Hope for the Heart-Attacked

ROBERT LITTKEY had a heart attack and underwent triple bypass surgery at age 45. Four and a half years later he had a stroke and was in a coma for twelve days, coming out of it half paralyzed and half blind. Over forty days, Robert embarked on a physical-therapy program that consisted of endlessly walking up and down halls and stairs. He completely recovered and has the physical condition of a man fourteen years younger (40) than his current 54 years.

HENRY HEATON had a heart attack at age 66. His doctor told him he was not strong enough to have bypass surgery, and he had only three months to live. He used the walking program to make an amazing comeback. Henry built up his daily walking mileage to 3 miles a day and was able to have triple bypass surgery a year later. He has logged 7,000 miles three years after his original diagnosis.

PART ONE

Welcome to the Club

CHAPTER 1

How Walkshaping Works

One August day, I happened to be trying out a new pair of weight sticks while I was pumping my arms and walking briskly through the beautiful parks of the Notre Dame campus in South Bend, Indiana. My mind drifted back to a challenging question that I'd been asked at the walking clinic that I'd taught just an hour before. A woman there complained that she had not lost enough weight on a six-week walking program and wanted to know if it would be possible to use walking techniques to reshape her body.

This request, coupled with the weight sticks I held in my hands, marked the beginning of a new way to walk. I started to mimic the weight-training moves I used on weight machines and free weights at my New York health club. At first, it seemed an awkward thing to do, and fellow walkers and joggers gave me strange sidelong glances as I passed them pumping out Flys, Press-Ups, and Overhead Arm Pumps, but I persisted.

I began developing a new type of walking step, which I christened Walkshaping. I noticed that simulating bodybuilding moves while walking made me change the pace and cadence of my walk, turning it into a full-blown bodybuilding routine. My exercise walking program was no longer a two-step affair with high and low arm-pumping motions to match. It went from a fox-trot to a variety of three- and five-step routines that resemble both a waltz and a country swing. Using three steps to complete an arm-pumping routine allowed me to integrate the bodybuilder's moves more fully into my repertoire.

Walkshaping: A Combination Aerobics and Body-Sculpting Program

The Walkshaping Program uses walking as its basic activity, then adds special calisthenic and bodybuilding movements. It offers you a new way to move. While you're taking a walk in the park, on the track, or stepping in place at home, you'll be reshaping your body.

You've probably already heard about walking's weight-loss and weight-control benefits; but have you also heard that, depending on the kind of walking you do, the results can take many months or even a year? Most people who are out of shape don't have the patience to wait that long; they want a visible result in a specific period of time. Walkshaping delivers visible results quickly because it provides a total-body workout. Not only does it engage all of the muscles in your body while you walk, it also provides routines that tone and strengthen muscles, changing the ratio of muscle to fat all over your body. With Walkshaping, every time you take a walk, you'll be burning up to two-to-four times more calories than if you were simply walking.

Putting More Muscle into Your Walking

The secret ingredient to my Walkshaping Program is putting more of your muscles to work while you're walking. Every other walking day, you'll do a series of exercises that concentrate on your upper, middle, or lower body. Muscles are the calorie-burning engines of the body, so why have a V-4 engine when you could have a V-8? Walkshaping helps you rebuild your engine and keep it revved up. Defining your muscles not only helps you look better, it also helps you burn more fat calories per movement. Building up your muscle reserves is the antidote to the fat reserves that you've accumulated. Muscle offers a line of defense against fat. Your new, more muscular body will burn more calories, not only when you walk, but when you're sitting, standing, or lying down.

A Sturdy Platform

Walking is the sturdy platform on which you can build a better body. When walking, your body, arms, legs, and torso are put through a full range of movements. It is just about the only activity in which you can safely combine aerobic calorie burning with weight training. You can load weight and add resistance without throwing yourself off balance. Joggers and dancers, on the other hand, who use weights while working out, multiply the injury rate to their knees, backs, and joints while also increasing the shock effect.

By definition, walking requires that you always keep one foot on the ground while moving the other forward, backward, or sideways. Since you always keep one foot on the ground, your other foot lands with only a quarter to a third of the impact that it would if you were running or jumping. Thus you minimize injuries caused by the high-impact movements used in other sports.

If you practice walking the old-fashioned way, your lower body is shaped at the expense of your upper body. People can tell if you're a frequent walker by the size and shape of your calf muscles, which get the most work from the regular walking action. If you're an "exercise walker," you will have well-developed arms, shoulders, and chest, because you pump your arms instead of swinging them. But if you're a Walkshaper, you'll also have well-developed buttocks, back, biceps, quadriceps, and hamstrings, because you'll be doing a series of calisthenic exercises while you walk. These exercises will involve ten major muscle groups rather than just the five used in regular fitness walking. As you can see, combining an aerobic workout with weight training saves time and maximizes the effectiveness of both.

In aerobic exercise, you focus on your heart and lung system; in bodybuilding, you focus on your skeletal muscles. By combining them with Walkshaping, you learn to put more muscle work into aerobic walking, to shape your whole body.

A Six-Week Solution

Professional athletes and models can afford to spend two to four hours a day working out and can eat like monks because they get paid to do just that. But for ordinary people it's difficult, if not impossible, to spend more than an hour a day exercising, even though we might want to. Some days we can't even afford more than a few minutes.

The Six-Week Shape-Up Program is designed to motivate you to start and get hooked on walking. With Walkshaping, I honor your schedule by providing both full-body and targeted exercise routines. I treat exercise like a healthy habit rather than an alternate career in competitive sports. You still have to be motivated to get started. But since you'll see results and feel good about them, staying with the program will be easy and effective.

The shock of seeing your own body partially nude is, perhaps, the best motivator of all, which is why I have you practice as much of our Walkshaping program as you can in the briefest possible bathing suit. You'll hate the idea at the beginning of the six-week program, but you'll love it in the end.

The Walkshaping program is results-oriented: you measure the results in inches and pounds. Here's what you can expect from Walkshaping:

- Lose 2–10 pounds of body fat in six weeks.

- Lose 1–5 inches from your waist, hips, and thighs. Achieve these results in as little as 12 minutes a day, but not more than one hour per day.

- Increase key muscle groups 1–3 inches, including biceps and triceps, chest, and calves.

- Develop shapely, well-balanced muscles.

- Increase your ability to burn off fat, burning as much as double or triple the calories you burn during a regular walk and the hours afterward.

- Eat more, in a health-conscious way, without gaining weight.

- Look thinner because of improved posture and muscle tone.

- Increase self-confidence, knowing your muscles feel and look pumped up and firm after every workout.

Other Exercise Programs

Walkshaping gives you a balanced approach to body development; it teaches you the best body mechanics not just for walking but for sitting and standing and even for running. Ninety percent of the population *can* achieve the well-shaped look of a Walkshaper.

If you're already a regular walker, Walkshaping is going to spice up your walking routine. If you're overweight, Walkshaping is the relatively easy and effective exercise program you've been waiting for. Walkshaping not only helps you lose weight in the easiest way (e.g., while walking), but it provides a long-term solution to your weight-control problem. Walkshaping will enable you to look and feel your absolute best—in just six weeks—for the rest of your life.

Indoors or Outdoors

But what if you're too busy, or even too embarrassed, to go out for a Walkshaping walk? You can practice the whole routine indoors. In fact, I recommend you start right now by Walkshaping, In Place, with this book open next to you in a small, five-foot-by-five-foot, space in your bedroom, basement, or living room. Once you've practiced the routines indoors you can take them outdoors, On the Move, and incorporate them into a daily walk. If you wish, you may stay indoors for all your exercise. Just remember, part of the fun of walking is enjoying the great outdoors.

With or without equipment, you can do the whole Walkshaping routine freehanded. The weight of your own arms, legs, and torso will supply the resistance. And you'll be able to do the walk anywhere. Of course you can also enhance the effect using the same program with hand-held weights, ski poles, and stretch cords. You can also practice Walkshaping on a treadmill, stepper, or ski machine. In fact, it will make the exercise machines more fun to use.

MULTI-DIRECTIONAL • Standard fitness walking programs have you walking in only one direction, forward. Walkshaping moves you in all directions, forward, backward, side to side, and even turning around. This, along with the variety of arm-, leg-, and torso-moving techniques, lets you sculpt all your body's muscles and develop the stature, body shape, alignment, and self-confidence of a physically fit and healthy person.

CHAPTER 2

Before and After Six Weeks

We often accuse fat of being our enemy, pinching angrily at it on our bodies and counting the grams of it in our food. Getting fatter, however is actually a natural part of the aging process. Our bodies experience a 2 percent decrease in metabolism for every decade over the age of 20; after we turn 25, most of us begin to notice that it becomes impossible to eat whatever and whenever we like without gaining weight, and we feel our clothes getting gradually tighter.

The Human Predicament: What We Do Know

Of course, a certain amount of fat gain may come from decreasing our physical activity over the years. The older we get, the more time we

Fig. 2–1 • Renee Robertson
Renee (Miss New York): Before

spend seated, either studying in school or working at desk jobs, and the less time we spend on playgrounds, in gyms, and on sports fields. But even those who work as physical laborers seem to gain weight with age. Whether we attribute this to the biological or social function, it's also true that our muscles atrophy and grow smaller with age. But as surely as we know this, we also know that a fat body and weak, small muscles can be brought back to life at any age, even after long bouts of inactivity. Yet we're all too familiar with how improvements in body shape can be lost, seemingly overnight, after stopping an exercise program. Like dieters, many exercisers yo-yo in and out of shape for years.

A certain amount of body fat is necessary, so using radical measures like surgery, liposuction, or crash diets to reduce your fat is counterproductive at best and dangerous at worst. The better approach is to learn to live with and manage the fat by eating nutritious foods low in fat and by increasing your amount of physical activity. It also pays to add muscle mass, since a more muscular body not only improves your shape by giving you more tone and definition, but also improves your ability to burn off excess calories, even those that have been stored as fat.

What Kind of Body?

Fig. 2–2 • Renee (Miss New York): After 6 weeks

To achieve high muscle definition like Linda Hamilton's or Sylvester Stallone's will require 3–6 hours of exercise a day. To be toned and sculpted like the model walkers you see in this book will require only 12–60 minutes of exercise a day. My program is more realistic and achievable for most people. Each "before" and "after" photo is marked with the amount of time (per day) that was used to achieve the result. The "before" and "after" photos are organized according to the amount of time our model walkers spent daily on the Walkshaping Program: you'll see everything from the 12-minute- to the 30-minute- to the 60-minute-a-day body. Walkshaping is a little like boiling an egg: the more time you spend on the program, the harder your body will become.

Over time, you'll develop a body that looks like a cross between that of a bodybuilder and a cross-country skier, runner, or race-walker. As you burn away fat, you'll also build up and tone muscle, but without the crash diets bodybuilders use to compensate for the low calorie-

Fig. 2–3 • Eileen Hunt
Eileen: Before

burning rates of weight training movements and without the injurious training techniques ("the pounding effect") of high-intensity aerobics.

Body shaping, or body sculpting, as practiced in the Walkshaping Program is really a new way to reconfigure your body by balancing fat loss with muscle gain. Results are faster and longer-lasting, because the method you use to reshape your body is also the most natural and comfortable way to stay active. You redistribute the aerobic work through the whole body, using more of your upper body to burn a large number of calories without making your legs do all the work. Instead of doing work that demands only a moderate effort from major muscle groups, you perform concentrated muscle contraction routines that help muscles to grow and become defined.

The Great Motivator

"Before" and "after" pictures are great motivators. We trust results that we're able to see. This book's gallery of "before" and "after" portraits show people who have successfully completed the Walkshaping Program (Gallery of Walkshapers—twenty photos, Figs. 2–1 through 2–29). I recruited and trained a team of twenty "model walkers," selected from over 500 applicants, to help me demonstrate these techniques. The profiles and testimonials that follow are from this group.

Renee Robertson (Figs. 2–1, 2) is a 22-year-old actress and dancer who started the program as an 8-mile-a-week walker, having used walking as a way to burn off fat and to firm the muscles of her legs and buttocks. Despite her "pre-25" status and her dancing career, weight control is a problem for her, and she had recently gained ten pounds while traveling in Europe. Her dancing roles are not consistent enough to serve as a regular exercise program. So when it came time for Renee to get in shape for the Miss New York contest, she started the six-week Walkshaping program. She lost 4 pounds, 2 inches from her thighs, 1 inch from her waist, and 1 inch from her calves. She went from doing 16 push-ups to 25 and from 28 sit-ups to 40. Not only that, she won the Miss New York title.

Eileen Hunt, age 25 (Figs. 2–3, 4), had gained 10 pounds over the last three years. By the end of Week Six of the program, Eileen had lost 5 pounds and dropped from a 27- to a 26-inch waist. She could also do 24 percent more push-ups and sit-ups than before starting

Fig. 2–4 • Eileen: After 6 weeks

Fig. 2–5 • Christina Lambertson
Christina: Before

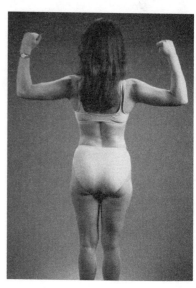

Fig. 2–6 • Christina: After 6 weeks

Walkshaping. By the end of Week Twelve, she had lost an additional 10 pounds and her waist measurement had dropped to 24 inches.

Christina Lambertson (Figs. 2–5, 6), a 32-year-old restaurant manager, had gained 25 pounds since her divorce. After six weeks on the program, she had lost 5 pounds. After twelve weeks, she had lost 10 pounds, as well as half an inch from her hips, 2½ inches from her thighs, and 2 inches from her waist.

Carlo Fiorletta (Figs. 2–7, 8, 9), a 33-year-old actor, lost 6 pounds and 3½ inches from his waist after six weeks. He'd gained 1 inch on

Fig. 2–7 • Carlo Fiorletta
Carlo: Before

Fig. 2–8 • Carlo: After 6 weeks

Fig. 2–9 • Carlo: After 12 weeks

Fig. 2–10 • Britt Kurtz
Britt (Mrs. New York Runner-Up):
Before

Fig. 2–11 • Britt (Mrs. New York
Runner-Up): After 6 weeks

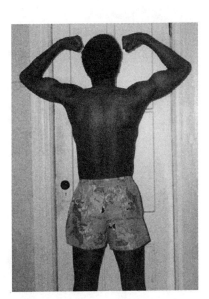

Fig. 2–12 • Derek Grier
Derek: Before

Fig. 2–13 • Derek: After 6 weeks

his thighs and half an inch on his biceps and triceps, and he could do 13 additional push-ups and 8 additional sit-ups.

Britt Kurtz (Figs. 2–10, 11) is a 30-year-old model. When she started the Walkshaping program, she had already lost 20 pounds with the help of a 30-mile-a-week walking routine. Walkshaping let her cut her mileage back to 15 miles a week, with the same weight-control benefits, and it gave her new posture, shape, and poise. Britt also

Fig. 2–14 • Avis Boone
Avis: Before

Fig. 2–15 • Avis: After 6 weeks

Fig. 2–16 • Pam Kobrin
Pam: Before

Fig. 2–17 • Pam: After 6 weeks

gained half an inch on her biceps and triceps and a 50 percent increase in the number of push-ups she could do.

Derek Grier (Figs. 2–12, 13) is a 36-year-old professional actor and former boxer and stuntman. Unlike many on the program, Derek's goal was to gain pounds and inches. After six weeks, he'd gained 7 pounds, and while his waist measurement remained the same at 30 inches, he increased his neck, chest, and thigh measurements by half an inch each.

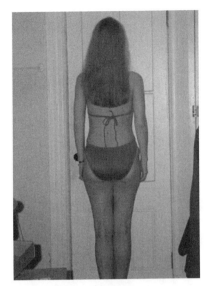

Fig. 2–18 • Cindy Manion
Cindy (Mrs. New York): Before

Fig. 2–19 • Cindy (Mrs. New York):
After 6 weeks

Fig. 2–20 • Zoie Michaels
Zoie: Before

Fig. 2–21 • Zoie: After 6 weeks

Avis Boone (Figs. 2–14, 15), age 30, an actress and model, lost only 1 pound in six weeks but, more important met her goal of shaping her inner thighs. She lost 2 inches from her thighs and gained half an inch on her triceps and biceps. She also doubled her upper body strength.

Pam Kobrin (Figs. 2–16, 17), age 30, is a part-time model and pharmaceutical worker. She lost 1 inch from her thighs and 2 inches off her hips. She could do 50 percent more push-ups and 25 percent more sit-ups after six weeks.

Cindy Manion (Figs. 2–18, 19), a 34-year-old model and mother, took up Walkshaping to lose weight and shape up after a serious ski injury sidelined her for months. By her third week on the program, she had already lost 2 pounds, an inch off her chest, and a half inch off her hips. Cindy tripled the number of push-ups she could do from 10 to 30 and doubled the number of sit-ups from 20 to 40. Cindy went on to win the Mrs. New York title.

Fig. 2–22 • Nancy Mulholland
Nancy: Before

Fig. 2–23 • Nancy: After 6 weeks

Fig. 2–24 • Alexa Servodidio
Alexa: Before

Fig. 2–25 • Alexa: After 6 weeks

Thirty-five-year-old actress Zoie Michaels (Figs. 2–20, 21), wanted to lose 5 pounds. At the end of six weeks, she'd lost 2 pounds and a half inch from her waist; after twelve weeks, she had lost the 5 pounds.

Nancy Mulholland (Figs. 2–22, 23), age 36, lost 1 inch from her thighs, and her weight stayed the same, at 111 pounds.

Alexa Servodidio (Figs. 2–24, 25), a 20-year-old law student and part-time model, wanted to lose 5 pounds. She lost 6 pounds in just

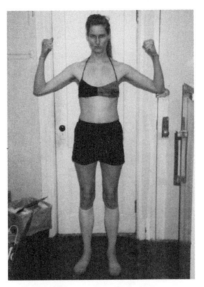

Fig. 2–26 • Marian Voetberg
Marian: Before

Fig. 2–27 • Marian: After 6 weeks

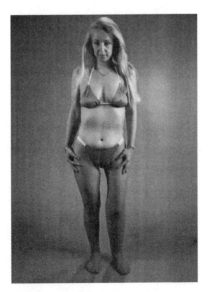

Fig. 2–28 • Juliane Feuerstein
Juliane: Before

Fig. 2–29 • Juliane: After 6 weeks

six weeks, going from 114 to 108 pounds. Her waist shrank from 26 to 24 inches, her hips from 32 to 30 inches, her thighs from 21 to 20 inches, and her chest from 32 to 30 inches. She also increased her push-ups to 23 (up from 15) and sit-ups to 39 (from 30).

Marian Voetberg (Figs. 2–26, 27), a 35-year-old actress, lost half an inch from her waist, 2½ inches from her hips, and 2 inches from her thighs. Her weight remained the same.

Julianne Feuerstein (Figs. 2–28, 29), a 26-year-old actress and model, met her goals when she lost 3 pounds and half an inch from her hips.

CHAPTER 3

Mental Gymnastics

Are you a highly motivated person who sets goals and works to achieve them step by step? Or do you need a personal coach, a taskmaster, to keep you going? Or perhaps you work best when others around you are supporting and participating in your efforts.

I've met each of the above types in my walking classes, and each one can succeed with Walkshaping. Some work from our program manual to practice the program on their own time. Others join Walkshaping groups or start their own group in their neighborhood, community center, health club, or local mall. Still others enlist their personal trainer, athletic friend, or spouse to act as their coach, helping them stick to the program. Whatever your preference, you can adapt the Walkshaping program to your individual and social needs. And if time is a constraint, you can practice the exercises in shorter intervals throughout the day to meet the demands of a busy schedule.

Remember: you carry your own walking gym with you wherever you go!

Now let's take a look, in the mirror, at your future. No words of encouragement or stern reprimands will ever motivate you as much as will standing naked or in your bathing suit in front of the mirror. The Posture-Correction Exercise gives you a preview of the body you can expect to have in just six weeks.

Put your book down, leaving it open to this page.

"New You" Posture-Correction Exercise

Fig. 3–1 ● Knees slightly bent, pulling in stomach, breathe from chest.

Put on your bathing suit or underwear and stand in front of a full-length mirror. If possible, place another mirror behind you. Place your feet hip-width to shoulder-width apart, choosing the stance that feels most comfortable. Your arms should hang loosely by your sides, with the elbows slightly bent. For example, try bending them to 160-degree angles (fully straightened is 180 degrees.) Bend your knees slightly, and straighten up your body by pulling your stomach in and holding it there. Don't hold your breath, but try to breathe slowly from your chest rather than your stomach (Fig. 3–1). Next, squeeze your buttocks together as you tilt your pelvis under your trunk and flatten out your back. Sink a little further into your knees, if you have to, in order to center your balance. Put your head and shoulders back (like a marine stance). Now, clench your fist (if you have hand pain or an injury, keep your fingers unclenched, but curled slightly inward). Extend your arms, either by pushing behind your body and tensing your forearms and triceps, or raising them up over your head with your elbows slightly bent. Push slightly as you tense your tricep, forearm, and shoulder muscles. Tuck your chin into your neck, and take a deep breath, filling and expanding your chest with air (Fig. 3–2). At the same time, straighten your legs and flex or tighten your thigh muscles. Pull your stomach in further.

Now you can see the front view of yourself as you will look in six weeks—only then you won't have to suck in your stomach, raise your arms, or squeeze your muscles as tightly. Your body will be trimmed and tucked in without exerting this much effort or assuming a special pose.

Fig. 3–2 • Tense Triceps

Fig. 3–3 • New You: Muscles Squeezed from Behind

Fig. 3–4 • New You: The Side Posture Realigned

Look over your shoulder and into the mirror to see your image. As you do this, squeeze your shoulder and upper back muscles, and also straighten your legs as you squeeze your thighs and buttocks/hips muscles. You'll get a "new you" view of yourself from behind (Fig. 3–3).

Now, turn one quarter rotation sideways to your left, so that your right side is facing the mirror. With your arms lowered against your sides, assume the same pose as before: feet hip-width apart, stomach pulled in, and buttocks/hips muscles squeezed. Hold your shoulders back as you tuck your chin straight into your neck. Here's how you will look after you've realigned and straightened up using the Walkshaping system (Fig. 3–4). Now, grab the top of your right wrist with your left hand so that your left arm is hugging the bottom of your chest. Again, put your shoulders back and tuck your chin into your neck. Flex your biceps, put your right foot back, and tighten your calf and buttocks/hips muscles. Here's the side view of you in six weeks: Your upper arms and shoulders will be tighter, and your buttocks and calves will be firmer. Now, face the mirror and resume your old relaxed position for a quick comparison. Figures 3–5 through 3–10 show how our model Walkshapers did their instant makeover before starting the program.

Do the posture exercise again. This time, visualize the six stages your body will go through in the next six weeks by taking six short breaths as you slowly pull in your muscles and align your posture.

STEP 1 (Fig. 3–5) • Breathe in and count, "1 and 2 and." Hold your breath for 2–5 seconds. Now, visualize: by the end of Week One, your posture will have improved and you'll be able to hold your body in a properly aligned, upright position whether sitting, standing, or walking. Even though you'll have lost only a half a pound of body fat and maybe 1–2 pounds of water, your new posture will make you look 5–10 pounds thinner. You'll also look better when you move and walk because you'll be able to maintain your new posture throughout the day. Your body will look dramatically different, especially when walking. You'll look more energetic; you'll have a bouncier step and a longer stride, and your arms will move with vigor and purpose. As a result, you will soon see yourself as a livelier and more energetic person. Exhale.

STEP 2 (Fig. 3–6) • Breathe in and count, "1 and 2 and." Hold your breath for 2–5 seconds. Now, imagine: by Week Two, you'll start to feel your muscles more. Your body will feel firmer and your muscles more pumped up after every workout. Exhale.

Fig. 3–5 • Step 1 one breath: ⅙ improvement

Fig. 3–6 • Step 2 two breaths: ⅓ improvement

Fig. 3–7 • Step 3 three breaths: in ½ improvement

STEP 3 (Fig. 3–7) • Breathe in and count, "1 and 2 and 3 and." Hold your breath again for 2–5 seconds. Picture yourself by the end of Week Three. You'll be able to walk faster and burn two to three times more calories during each workout session than you did at the start. You'll notice that your pants feel looser and that your thighs, buttocks, and stomach feel firmer even when you're not exercising. By now you'll be able to do extra sets of exercises on body parts that you want to really shape up. Exhale.

STEP 4 (Fig. 3–8) • Breathe in while counting, "1 and 2 and 3 and 4 and." Again, visualize how you'll look and feel by the end of Week Four, when Walkshaping will have become a daily habit. You'll look forward to the pumped feeling you get from your workout. By now, many of you will have experienced a drop in weight of 2–5 lbs. While most of this will be water weight, it will be coming off because you will have exercised the equivalent of up to 3 lbs. of body fat. Breathe out.

STEP 5 (Fig. 3–9) • Breathe in while counting to yourself: "1 and 2 and 3 and 4 and 5 and." Be sure to keep your stomach in and buttocks tucked under. This is what your body will look like at the end of Week Five. But your gains will be much more than cosmetic. You'll be developing a level of cardiovascular fitness that allows you to burn a higher number of calories in a shorter amount of time. With your newly developed muscles, you'll be able to do up to four or five sets

Fig. 3–8 • Step 4 four breaths: in ⅔ improvement

Fig. 3–9 • Step 5 five breaths: in ⅚ improvement

Fig. 3–10 • Step 6 six breaths in ⅚ improvement

of each exercise in the 45 to 60-minute exercise period. Now, breathe out.

STEP 6 (Fig. 3-10) • At this point, you should be standing up, with your book on the sink or a chair in front of you. Breathe in slowly while counting, "1 and 2 and 3 and 4 and 5 and 6 and." Pull in your stomach as far as you can. Expand your chest and raise your arms, making your waist appear thinner. Concentrate on flexing all of your muscles. This is what you'll look like at the end of the sixth week. Soon you'll be comparing your own "before" and "after" photos. Now, breathe out.

Your progress won't match exactly what the pictures show: it may be better or worse. It will, however, be within the framework I've outlined for you.

About All of Those Interruptions . . .
(Or, What Happens If You Cheat?)

Ideally, Walkshaping is a daily exercise program. But human nature and busy schedules will cause some of you to fall off the wagon. Promise me and (more important) yourself, right now, that you will not use a missed day or two of exercise as an excuse to give up completely. Just pick up where you left off and add your days off to the end of the six-week period, or else try to do some makeup workouts on the weekend or interspersed among the weekday workouts. Remember, with Walkshaping every step counts. Your walking program should become as basic and as central to your daily life as taking a shower or brushing your teeth.

When you don't feel like exercising, try pushing yourself before you throw in the towel for the day. If you're indoors, start with just a few steps. You've got nothing to lose, since you've already decided you aren't going to do it. If you're outside, just consider yourself taking a leisurely walk to the corner store or around the neighborhood. If after few steps you still don't feel like doing the day's Walkshaping exercises, try later. Or tell yourself that at least you gave it a try: "I need this break, and tomorrow's another day." If you skip a workout or have to stop and start again, just make sure that you complete your quota of miles and repetitions for that day or for that week. Think of it as having to stop the VCR in the middle of a movie when the telephone rings: you'll pick up the program again later where you left off.

Why Have You Failed Before?

People have a myriad excuses for abandoning exercise, such as:

1. **Exercise is too time-consuming.** Walkshaping gives you a choice of workouts, ranging in length from 12 to 60 minutes a day. This leaves you plenty of time to do other things, including sports, reading, or even a bodybuilding workout.

2. **Exercise is too expensive or complicated.** Your walking body will be your major piece of equipment—and you already carry this around wherever you go! If you do choose to add accessories, they'll be much cheaper than a health club membership.

3. **The results are disappointing.** You've tried an exercise program and have not seen any results, or at least not the results that you wanted. I won't kid you: exercise does require effort, and even more effort if you want to see and feel dramatic results. The gallery of "before," "during," and "after" photos is accompanied by a pricetag measuring the amount of time and exercise that a particular transformation costs.

4. Exercise requires "athletic" or other special skills.   With Walkshaping, you won't have to run a seven-minute mile, show off your dance steps, or feel like you're part of the third string. Shy people, showoffs, and everyone in between can participate—and reap all of the benefits.

5. Exercise requires too much motivation.   Walkshaping is not a boot camp or an ashram for out-of-shape people. No one will call you to early-morning reveille or look over your shoulder as you're exercising. You're on your own, and on your honor. You can do it at your own pace: slow, moderate, or fast and intense if you're gung-ho. Find what works for you. Perhaps you need to start slowly, then graduate to a higher-intensity workout when you're ready.

6. Exercise is too painful and strenuous.   I've saved the number-one reason for last. Should exercise be work or should it be fun? Here's the short answer: it should be like a job or a career you love. You've heard movie stars, CEOs, novelists, and artists describe the long hours they spend doing their work; if they don't seem to mind, it's probably because their work is something that they love to do. When you're enjoying yourself, the time you spend working seems to go faster. This is the appeal of doing your favorite sport to stay fit, and also the joy of spending time outdoors, in nature. I've made Walkshaping into just this kind of enjoyable exercise: you can do it at the beach, in a park, or nearly anywhere, whether you're alone or with a group of friends. And there is no pain involved because the stress of the workout is shared by the whole body.

Walkshaping uses both art and mathematics. The math is used to count steps and arm pumps, then to see them add up to your quota. The art is in sculpting. You'll be applying movement techniques that will make certain parts of your body grow and others shrink. Your tools will be your arms, legs, and torso; the putty will be your fat and muscles.

You're Still Not Convinced?

Dieting and exercise program dropouts now number in the millions. Many have started and then dropped out two, five, ten, or more times. There are yo-yo exercisers, who are much like yo-yo dieters. If you are one of these or worry about becoming one, we say, "Welcome. Welcome to the club." You are in the process of becoming a lifetime walker. You are going to learn the techniques and gain the tools for getting back in shape whenever you want. It's as simple as taking a walk.

Based on studies of dropout rates of competitive versus noncompetitive exercise, there's a 60 to 90 percent chance that if you finish the Walkshaping Program, you'll like your new body so much that you'll keep walking. Walking programs have such a high adherence rate because they are more accessible, less stressful, and less injurious than any other exercise programs. If you are a gung-ho but injured athlete (e.g., jogger or bodybuilder), I suggest that you try Walkshaping in stages. Don't switch completely from your old routine to our new one until you feel that ours will give you enough to let go. You know you must do something new, because your back and joints can't take too much more abuse. So give my six-week program a try.

PART TWO

The Shape of Things to Come

CHAPTER 4

Starting Measurements

Ⓑefore you start your Walkshaping program, take a series of "before" photos and body measurements, so that you'll have them to compare to "after" shots and measurements at the end of Week Six and, if you go on, with those from Weeks Eight and Twelve. Record these on the Before and After Chart on page 44, and tape your photos over those in the book. This is an important part of motivating yourself to start and stick with the program, as it will help you document your results. You'll need a camera. You'll also need a measuring tape, scale, and a watch with a second hand.

Before You Start

Before you start, take your resting pulse. Be sure that you have not done any physical activity, including walking, in the last 15 minutes.

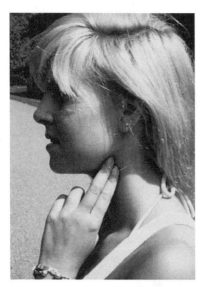

Fig. 4–1 • Taking pulse at neck

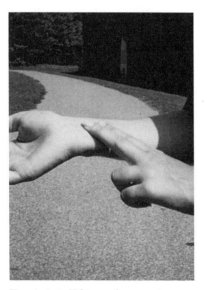

Fig. 4–2 • Taking pulse on wrist

You can take your pulse at the carotid artery, on your neck (Fig. 4–1), or at the radial artery, on your wrist (Fig. 4–2), depending on where you are able to feel the most steady beat. Place your index and middle fingers against the blood vessel where you feel the pulse. Count the number of beats you feel in fifteen seconds, and multiply that number by four for your sixty-second pulse rate.

Walkshaping strengthens your heart muscle and, consequently, lowers your resting pulse by a few beats. Be sure to make a note of which artery you used for your measurement and take subsequent measurements at the same spot.

Now you're ready to take your "before" and "after" photos. It's best to have a friend or spouse take these pictures and measurements, but you can take them yourself if you have to. Take "before" shots wearing as little clothing as possible. Use a Polaroid or automatic camera with a flash, and take the pictures against a solid-color background. Be prepared to use the same background and "outfit" for your "after" shots. This will give you the best visual comparison.

We've used 4 × 6-inch photos to show you the proper pose, but you can use any size you wish. Stand five feet from the camera, and be sure the middle of your body is at the center of the frame.

NOTE: For an accurate measurement of a relaxed muscle, all measurements should be taken before any muscle is tensed. This is because a fully contracted muscle takes a while to relax again completely. When this is completed, you may proceed with the tensed poses.

POSE 1

Full-Figure Front View: Muscles Relaxed

| BEFORE (Fig. 4-3) | AFTER (Fig. 4-4) |

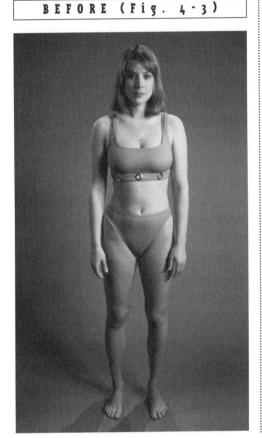
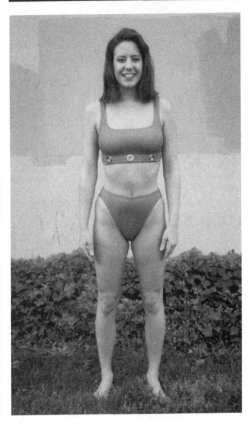

Pose: Stand with your feet hip-width apart. Bend your knees slightly. Keep your shoulders, chest, stomach, and legs relaxed. Let your arms hang loosely by your side.

Relaxed Girth Measure: Have a friend tape-measure your neck, chest, waist, hips, thighs (right and left), and calves (right and left).

Tape your photos over these for your own personal record. Photos are, preferably, taken in black and white, so that muscle definition will be shown with the shadow. You may also apply suntan oil to your body to further enhance definition, but be sure to do it for both your "before" and "after" shots.

POSE 2

Full-Figure Back View: Muscles Relaxed

BEFORE (Fig. 4-5)

AFTER (Fig. 4-6)

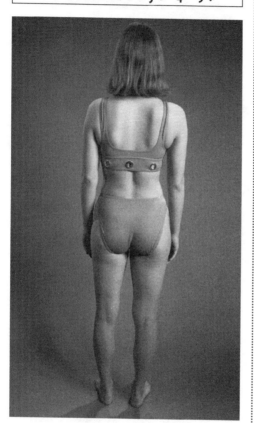 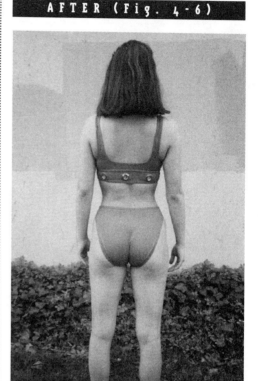

Pose: Stand with your feet hip-width apart and parallel to one another. Bend your knees slightly. Bring your shoulders back slightly, and let your arms hang loosely by your sides. Don't tense any muscles.

Measure: Have a friend measure your neck, chest, waist, hips, buttocks, right and left thighs, and calves. Be sure to keep your muscles relaxed during these measurements.

You may also want to take a close-up photo of your buttocks/hips.

POSE 3

Full-Figure Side View: Muscles Relaxed

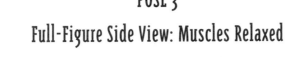

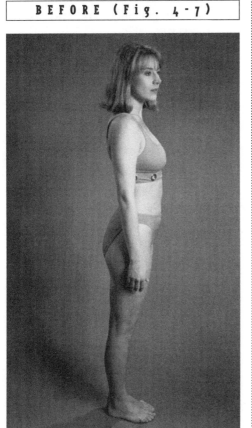
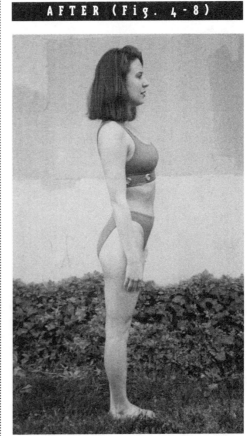

Pose: Place your feet hip-width apart, arms by your side. Don't let your arms block the view of the stomach or buttocks/hips. Keep your muscles completely relaxed.

You may want to shoot a close-up of your stomach and buttocks/hips.

POSE 4

Full-Figure Front View: Muscles Tensed

BEFORE (Fig. 4-9)	AFTER (Fig. 4-10)

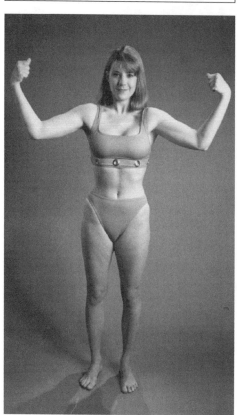

Pose: From the Pose #1 position, (1) Raise your arms to shoulder height and bend them at the elbows. Make a fist and curl your arms in until both of your biceps are tense. (2) Now, tense your whole upper body in the front by bringing your elbows slightly forward, expanding your chest with air, and squeezing your chest (pectoral muscles). Tighten your neck muscles by jutting your jaw forward and bringing your lower teeth in front of your upper teeth. (3) Don't let your teeth touch, but leave your mouth open slightly. (4) Suck in your stomach. (5) Straighten your legs and tighten your quadriceps (front thighs). Hold this fully tensed position for the photo.

Measure: Do each of the poses again, but separately for each body part, and have your partner take a tape measurement of each of the five muscle groups. For example, when measuring a limb such as arm biceps curl, be sure it is stretched horizontally so that the tape is in a line perpendicular to the ground. When measuring a limb vertically such as the front thighs, be sure that the tape is parallel to the ground. Record this measurement on the Before and After Chart on page 44.

POSE 5

Full-Figure Back View: Muscles Tensed

BEFORE (Fig. 4-11)

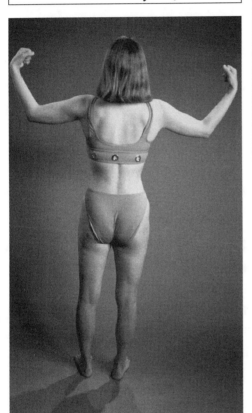

AFTER (Fig. 4-12)

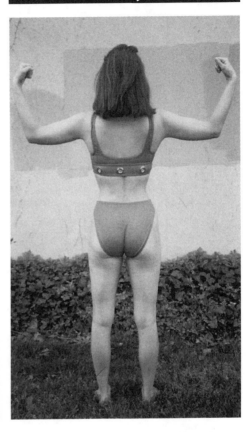

Pose: (1) Raise your arms to shoulder height. (2) Bend both arms at the elbow for the Biceps Curl. (3) As you curl, raise your shoulders, slightly tensing the back of your deltoid (shoulder). (4) Move both arms back, creating a crease down the center of your back and showing your shoulder blades protruding. (5) Lower your arms so that your back muscles contract. (6) Bend your knees slightly as you squeeze your buttocks. (7) Curl your toes up as you contract your calf muscles.

You may want to take a close-up photo of your tensed buttocks/hips muscles or your upper and lower back.

Muscle Imbalance

In Walkshaping, the calf and shin muscles get the most use for their relative size. That's why you should stretch these muscles more often than any others. Abdominal, gluteal, and quadriceps muscles are the hardest to overuse and therefore are less frequently injured. Still, it is not a good idea to exercise a muscle group without exercising the antagonistic, or opposite side, muscle group. Overexercising your pectoral muscles, for example, can pull your shoulders, causing your posture to suffer. Likewise, if your calves get overworked, they can overpower the shins, causing inflammation, a condition known as shin splints.

When weaker muscles are pulled at by stronger muscles, they get stretched out—this occurs even when the muscles are at rest. Because the muscles cannot relax properly, they can become strained. Finally, muscle imbalances can be a prelude to injuries such as pinched nerves. To avoid strain, injury, and fatigue, muscles should be developed in a balanced fashion, equal repetitions of weight training. If this isn't possible, stretching the overtrained muscle will relax it, thereby preventing it from pulling against its antagonist.

Balanced muscle development is also healthier because it produces a better aligned, injury-resistant body. Walkshaping exercises have been developed for both aesthetic and health purposes.

Muscle-Groups Breakdown (see also Figs. 4–13, 14, 15, 16 for muscle ID)

Upper Body

1. Shoulders and Neck
   A. Neck
   B. Deltoids (*Three heads: Front, Middle, Rear*)
   C. Trapezoids

2. Chest
   A. Pectorals
      1. Clavicular (*Upper*) Portion
      2. Sternal (*Lower*) Portion
   B. Deltoids
   C. Serratus anterior
   D. Intercostals
   E. Latissimus dorsi (*Front view*)
3. Upper Back
   A. Trapezius

B. Latissimus dorsi (*Upper/Middle*)
C. Rhomboids
D. Teres Major
E. Infraspinatus

4. Biceps and Forearms
   A. Biceps (*Two Heads: Outer/Inner*)
   B. Forearms

5. Triceps
   A. Triceps (*Three Heads: Outer, Middle, Inner*)

Lower Body

6. Buttocks and Hips
   A. Gluteus Maximus
   B. Gluteus Medius
   C. Hip Extensors

7. Thighs
   A. Quadriceps
      1. Outer
      2. Middle
      3. Inner
   B. Hamstrings
      1. Outer
      2. Middle
      3. Inner
   C. Iliotibial Tract
   D. Pectinus
   E. Tensor fasciae latae
   F. Adductor longus
   G. Sartorius
   H. Adductor magnus
   I. Gracilis

8. Abdominals
   A. Rectus Abdominis
      1. Upper
      2. Middle
      3. Lower
   B. External Obliques

9. Lower Back
   A. Spinal Erectors
   B. Lower latissimus dorsi

10. Calves and Shins
    A. Calves—gastrocnemius
       1. Outer Head
       2. Inner Head
    B. Soleus
    C. Achilles Tendon
    D. Tibialis anterior

Levels of Exercise and Walkshaping Skills

Your ability to do the Walkshaping exercises skillfully and without stopping for too many rests will serve as a measure of your progress. First, however, start by assessing your general level of fitness. I've graded fitness levels from I to V. Once you determine your level, you'll know how skilled you are to practice the Walkshaping exercises. Determining your level also ensures that you won't start off too aggressively, which is a sure way to cause injury and/or discouragement.

Ideally, you should progress one level for every six-week practice period. Each level represents a potential 2 to 10 pounds of weight loss, 1 to 3-inch loss of body fat, and a 1 to 3-inch increase in your muscle mass.

Level	Time it takes to get there or stay there:
I	**12 minutes a day:** You've been inactive for more than six months, and are in poor shape.
II	**20 minutes a day:** You walk less than a mile a day, and are in fair shape.
III	**30 minutes a day:** You're in good shape. Most people should strive to get to and maintain this level, which is really for people who want to be fit and healthy but don't want to spend a lot of time doing it.
IV	**45 minutes a day:** You're in very good shape. This is for people who want to be extremely fit.
V	**60 minutes a day:** This is the gung-ho level. You're willing to devote lots of time and energy to your body.

Identify the level you are at now; this is important, since it's the only way that you can see where you'll be going from here. As you get stronger and more motivated, you will increase the number of miles and minutes you walk, the number of strengthening and stretching repetitions you do, the counts that you hold per second, and the number of sets of exercise you complete. But you should progress one level at a time—don't jump ahead or you will strain yourself. This doesn't mean that when an exercise routine becomes too easy for you to do, you shouldn't advance to another level. It does mean that once you're within a level, you should progress according to the exercise prescriptions given for that level. Don't yo-yo from level to level by overdoing it on one day, then underexercising on the next day. When you strain or injure yourself, you lose valuable days recovering. Also, some injuries can be disabling.

Rate Your Fitness to Do Walkshaping Workouts

You should be reasonable about setting your Walkshaping progress goals. The five programs correspond to five levels of fitness.

You can have your fitness level precisely tested by a certified physical trainer or a sports-medicine doctor. Be sure to test your muscular and cardiovascular fitness.

If you are rating your own fitness, it is still important to seek a doctor's advice, especially if you have never exercised, are over 35 years of age, or have not been physically active for more than three months.

Your Aerobic Fitness

Rate your heart/lung fitness by your ability to walk a mile in a specific time period.

Level	Distance Covered	Minutes per Mile
I (Poor)	0–1 mile	60–30 min.
II (Fair)	1–2 miles	29–20 min.
III (Good)	2–3 miles	19–15 min.
IV (Very Good)	3–5 miles	14–12 min.
V (Excellent)	5–10 miles	12 min. or faster

NOTE: If you are unable to walk a mile without having to rest, you definitely fall within Level I. When taking the walking test, walk as fast as you comfortably can without losing your breath.

Rating Your Muscular Strength

Rate the strength of your upper and middle body by carefully testing your arms, abdominals, shoulders, chest, and back.

ARMS (BICEPS CURLS)		
Level	No. of Curls	Weight
I (Poor)	0–11	0–½ lb.
II (Fair)	12–14	½–2 lbs.
III (Good)	15–18	2–3 lbs.
IV (Very Good)	19–24	3–4 lbs.
V (Excellent)	25 or more	4 lbs. or more

ABDOMINALS (SIT-UPS PER MINUTE)		
Level	Men	Women
I (Poor)	0–19	0–15
II (Fair)	20–29	16–19
III (Good)	30–39	20–29
IV (Very Good)	40–49	30–39
V (Excellent)	50 or more	40 or more

SHOULDERS/CHEST/BACK (PUSH-UPS—NO TIME LIMIT)		
Level	Men	Women
I (Poor)	0–9	0–4
II (Fair)	10–14	5–9
III (Good)	15–19	10–14
IV (Very Good)	20–29	15–19
V (Excellent)	30 or more	20 or more

NOTE: Full or half push-ups may be done. Half push-ups are done with knees touching the ground.

Rating Your Overall Fitness

Take an average of your fitness scores, then start at your average level if they are only one level apart. If you are two or more levels apart, you should start to practice at the lower level until your scores even out. Give yourself 1, 2, 3, 4, or 5 points corresponding to each of the fitness levels in which you scored in the above five fitness tests: Aerobic, Arms, Abdominals, and Shoulders, Chest, and Back. For example, if you scored Level II on the Aerobic Fitness test, give yourself 2 points. Total your points for all the tests you completed and divide by the number of tests. If you scored 25 points on 5 tests, your overall score is 5 and your overall fitness level is V.

Setting Your Overall Goals

A six-week goal of losing 2–10 pounds and 1–3 inches is a reasonable one. But the amount of fat you lose and muscle you gain will depend primarily on two things: the calories you burn (based on the number of times you repeat the body-shaping exercise), and the extra weight or resistance that you use. Since between 100 and 300 calories are burned per mile walked, you'll have to walk 12 to 35 miles to lose a pound.

Getting Hungrier from Exercising

But won't doing extra exercise make me want to eat more? Not necessarily. Exercising before mealtimes tends to suppress appetite, possibly because the blood in your stomach is drawn to your skeletal muscles. Many people find that they actually have less of an appetite after exercising and thus eat less. Also, by exercising at a moderate level of intensity as you warm up, you will avoid the hungry, weak feeling that comes from burning off too much blood sugar and not enough stored fat. If you find that low blood sugar is still a problem, eat something sweet but not fatty (fruit, not chocolate). This will help you quell the feeling of hunger that you experience during or right after exercising.

Eating Less, Naturally

Rather than eating more because you're on an exercise program, you may find that you eat less. First, you'll have one less hour per day to eat, since you'll be exercising. And most important, you'll be motivated to eat less because you'll see that by doing so, you'll have less fat to burn off later.

Walkshaping and Dieting

The only safe and healthy weight-loss diet is to cut back on calories. All other diets should be avoided, or at least done under the supervision of a doctor.

The more body fat or weight you want to lose, the more miles you'll have to walk or, if you're fit enough, the more sets of body-shaping exercises you'll have to do. The good news is that the more you need to lose, the easier it will be—initially, at least. A large amount of extra weight acts very much like extra resistance, and it helps burn calories. Thirty pounds of extra weight on a 100-pound frame adds up to 30 percent more calorie burn. The fatter you are, the more calories per minute of exercise you'll burn. So if you're overweight, you'll be able to double or triple your burn and work rate with Walkshaping, without straining your muscles or joints.

With regular walking, you must walk 350 miles to lose 10 pounds in six weeks. That's 58.4 miles per week. But with Walkshaping, you burn up to two to three times the calories with every mile, so weight comes off with one half to one third of the mileage, or 20–40 miles per week. Of course, these are only the calories burned while exercising. By exercising daily, you also raise your daily metabolic rate, which determines the number of calories that you burn while sitting, standing, or resting. This gives you the advantage of having to devote fewer miles per week to burn the same number of calories. If you devote one hour a day to Walkshaping, you'll be able, reasonably, to finish 3 miles a day, or 21 miles a week. As you become more skilled at walking, you'll increase your speed to 3½, 4, and even 5 miles per hour. You will then be able to choose: maintaining your weight, cutting your workout time back to 30–40 minutes, or continuing to work out for the full hour and increasing the rate at which you lose weight.

Setting Your Body-Shaping Goals

Both men and women can practice the Walkshaping exercises using the same movements. But you can choose exercises based on the body shape you desire. Many women body sculptors focus on the thighs and buttocks. These areas contain more fat and less muscle and get less exercise from daily living than, for example, calves do from standing or forearms do from holding, pushing, and lifting. Men are often more interested in shaping their chests, biceps, and shoulder muscles. It's fine to give a particular muscle group more attention as long as all the individual muscles in that group are given equal attention. You don't want to train the gluteus maximus (larger gluteal muscle) at the expense of the gluteus medius (smaller gluteal muscle), or the inner and outer thigh at the expense of the middle thigh or the hamstrings.

Overall, many people tend to train the front of their bodies more than the back, because that's what we see when we look in the mirror. As a result, we often neglect our back muscles, even though they can be seen by anyone who walks behind us.

Setting Your Goals/Charting Your Progress

Taking Stock

The following Before and After Chart will monitor your progress. You'll need a measuring tape, a scale, and a watch with a second hand. Your chart may be your most powerful motivator for sticking with the program. As you become more fit week by week, you'll also have a tangible record of your progress.

BEFORE AND AFTER CHART					
	Start (Baseline)	Goal***	Week 6	Week 8	Week 12
Resting Pulse* (per min.)					
Weight (lbs.)					
Body Fat (%)					
Girth (inches)					
Waist					
Neck					
Chest					
Hip					
Thighs					
Calves					
Biceps					
Triceps					
Strengthening (repetitions)					
Push-Ups (without stopping)					
Full (hand to foot)					
Half (hand to knee)					

BEFORE AND AFTER CHART (CONTINUED)				
Start (Baseline)	Goal***	Week 6	Week 8	Week 12

	Start (Baseline)	Goal***	Week 6	Week 8	Week 12
Sit-Ups					
30 Seconds (beginning)					
60 Seconds (advanced)					
Endurance					
Miles per minute**					
Miles per hour					
Total miles walked					
per day					
per hour					

*While seated, count your pulse for 15 seconds and multiply by 4.

**When you're outside, record your walking speed using the -same ⅟16-, ⅛-, ¼-, ½-, or one-mile course for "before" and "after" walking.

***Place an asterisk next to areas you want to improve and put your six-, eight- to twelve-week goal, indicating amount of other improvement (e.g., inches, pounds, seconds) and weeks needed to achieve it in parentheses afterward.

Fitness Log

A good measure of progress is your improved performance in both ordinary and power-walking. As you become more fit, you'll be able to walk more miles at a faster pace and incorporate more repetitions of body-shaping exercises. Use the log below to record your progress by Levels I (Poor) through V (Excellent). Make six to twelve copies (one for each week) of the Sample Log Sheet. Each level also represents your levels of fitness and skill in the special walking techniques.

🥿 Sample Log Sheet 🥿

Name: _____

WEEK (circle one):   1   2   3   4   5   6   7   8   9   10   11   12

LEVEL (circle one):   I   II   III   IV   V

SESSION INFORMATION

	Duration and Miles	Body Shaping Routines (Repetition/Sets)	Stretching Routines (Counts Held/Sets)
MONDAY			
TUESDAY			
WEDNESDAY			
THURSDAY			
FRIDAY			

Miles per Minute Walking Speed at beginning of Week _____ ; end of Week _____ .

Weight at beginning of Week _____ (lbs.); end of Week _____ .

Resting Pulse at beginning of Week _____ ; end of Week _____ .

Tailoring Your Program

While your overall body-shaping goals should be to strengthen and shape all ten muscle groups in a balanced way, you'll still want to do extra work on areas you consider flabby.

Fill in here which one, two, or three area(s) you consider the weakest or flabbiest:

1. _____   2. _____   3. _____

It will be difficult to identify certain muscles on your own body at first because they're covered by fatty tissue. But if you flex the muscle, you'll be able to see its outlines. Figures 4–13 through 4–16 will help you identify what the various muscles or muscle groups look like.

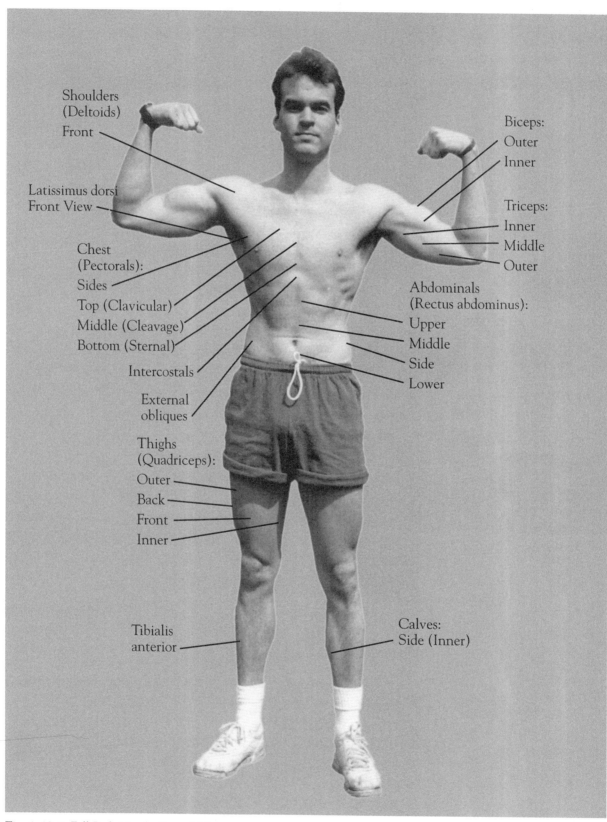

Shoulders
(Deltoids)
Front

Latissimus dorsi
Front View

Chest
(Pectorals):
Sides
Top (Clavicular)
Middle (Cleavage)
Bottom (Sternal)

Intercostals

External
obliques

Thighs
(Quadriceps):
Outer
Back
Front
Inner

Tibialis
anterior

Biceps:
Outer
Inner

Triceps:
Inner
Middle
Outer

Abdominals
(Rectus abdominus):
Upper
Middle
Side
Lower

Calves:
Side (Inner)

Fig. 4–13 • Full-Body Muscles Front: Male

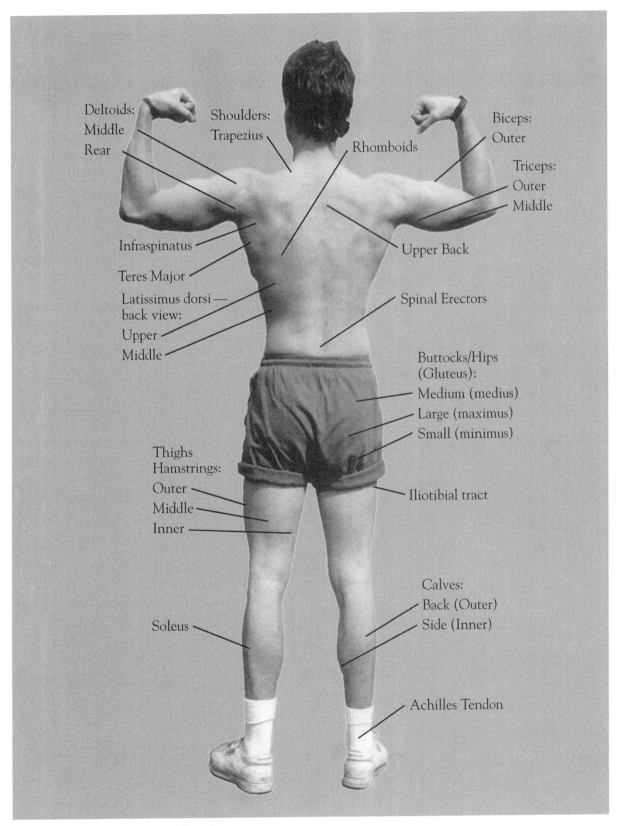

Deltoids:
Middle
Rear

Shoulders:
Trapezius

Rhomboids

Biceps:
Outer

Triceps:
Outer
Middle

Infraspinatus

Teres Major

Latissimus dorsi —
back view:
Upper
Middle

Upper Back

Spinal Erectors

Buttocks/Hips
(Gluteus):
Medium (medius)
Large (maximus)
Small (minimus)

Thighs
Hamstrings:
Outer
Middle
Inner

Iliotibial tract

Calves:
Back (Outer)
Side (Inner)

Soleus

Achilles Tendon

Fig. 4–14 • Full-Body Muscles Back: Male

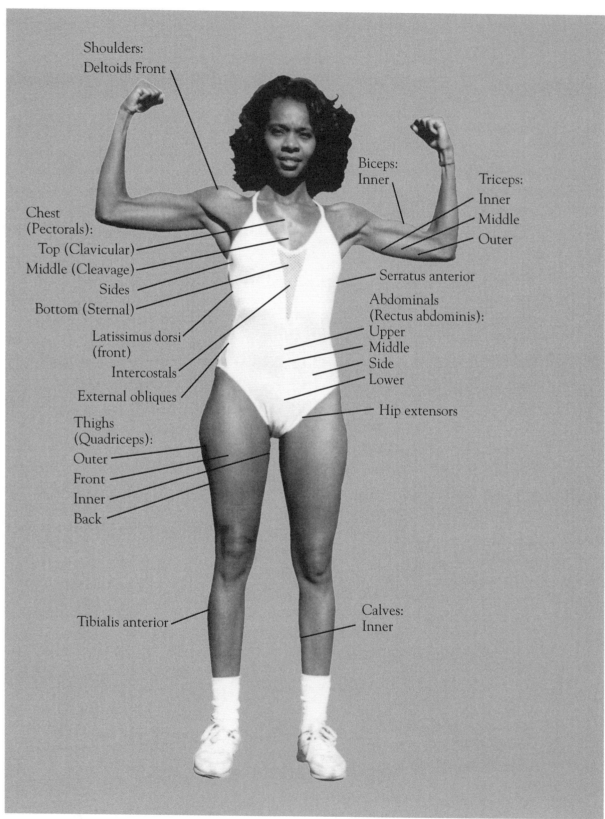

Fig. 4–15 • Full-Body Muscles Front: Female

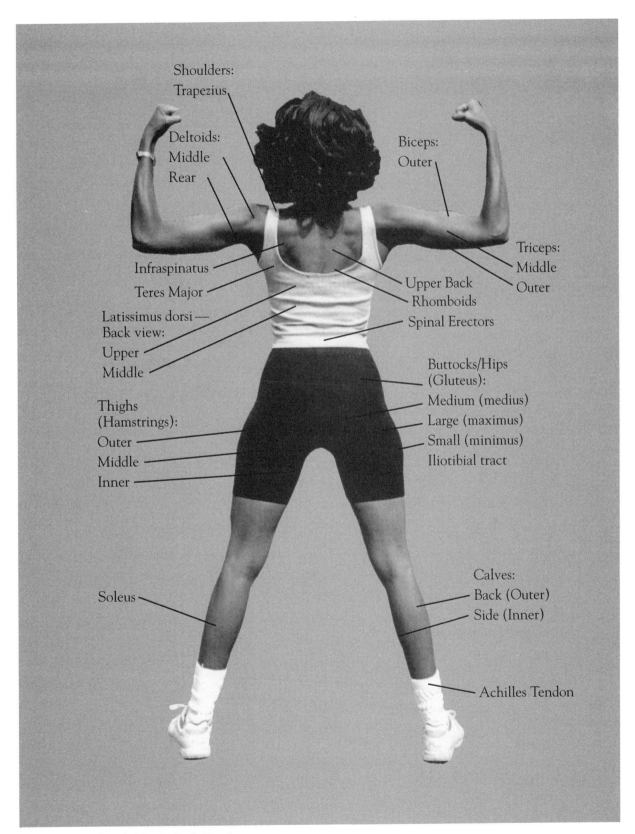

Shoulders:
Trapezius

Deltoids:
Middle
Rear

Biceps:
Outer

Triceps:
Middle
Outer

Infraspinatus

Teres Major

Upper Back
Rhomboids

Spinal Erectors

Latissimus dorsi
Back view:
Upper
Middle

Buttocks/Hips
(Gluteus):
Medium (medius)
Large (maximus)
Small (minimus)
Iliotibial tract

Thighs
(Hamstrings):
Outer
Middle
Inner

Soleus

Calves:
Back (Outer)
Side (Inner)

Achilles Tendon

Fig. 4–16 • Full-Body Muscles Back: Female

CHAPTER 5

Your New Walking Gym

Your walking body is your own personal piece of gym equipment. Unlike heavy exercise machines, though, your body has the advantage of being portable, weather-resistant, and compact. You can add accessories such as shoes, weighted packs, and hand weights to it easily and can quickly set up your "walking body machine" in your living room, hotel room, aerobics studio, gym or on a running track or hiking trail.

Resistance can help you achieve an increase in physical activity. Work, and therefore exercise, is measured by multiplying the force you exert by the distance over which you maintain the exertion. The greater the force resisting you, the more force you have to exert to work against it. It's more work to move against gravity (up and down or away from the ground) than to move sideways or parallel to the ground. When you walk, gravity and resistance from surface friction are also working against you, but with Walkshaping, resistance actually works for you. The exercise value of Walkshaping equals the weight or the resistance times the miles walked times the range of motion of the arms and legs against gravity (translation: how high you pump your arms or raise or extend your step times how fast you walk or move your legs per minute). All of these variables help to determine the number of calories of fat you burn and the concentration of repetitive forces on your muscles.

Resistance Systems

I've divided the descriptions of the weight systems that follow into Your Own Body Weight, Upper-Body Devices, Lower-Body Devices, and Trunk-Loading Devices.

Of course, Walkshaping exercises can be practiced without added weights or resistance devices, taking advantage just of your own body weight. But for those who want quick or enhanced results, I've designed the exercises to be done with almost any weight or resistance device.

Walkshaping is for body sculpting, not bodybuilding. Therefore, Walkshapers use light weights and medium-resistance devices (generally under 10 pounds for hand and leg weights and under 30 percent of body weight for torso added weight). By contrast, bodybuilders use two to three times as much weight. This makes their muscles bigger and bulkier; they burn fewer fat calories.

Follow the schedule below:

FIRST WEEK • Do the Walkshaping routines without resistance devices.

SECOND WEEK • Introduce one light-weight resistance device, such as ski poles or stretch cords.

Also, if you are doing a walking-in-place routine, you can add secondary devices like ankle weights and a step-up bench to this week's routine.

THIRD WEEK • Add a second resistance device. Weights are preferable since they are more versatile than stretch cords. Begin doing the whole routine, using one device on one day and another device on another day.

FOURTH WEEK • Add the third resistance device, the stretch cord or ski poles. Divide each week into three alternate days, each with a different device. When walking in place, divide your workout routine into thirds, each using a different device.

FIFTH WEEK • You can add secondary resistance devices like ankle weights and weight vests to the on-the-move routines for extra muscle shaping and calorie burning.

SIXTH WEEK • Continue with your Week-Five program.

Your Own Body Weight

Your body is the first and primary resistance device you'll use for Walkshaping. Based on a body weighing from 100 pounds (small) to 200 pounds (large), with 150 pounds being the midpoint, your two arms together represent approximately 20 percent of your body weight, or about 10 to 20 pounds each. Your legs represent 30 percent, or 20 to 40 pounds each. Your head is 10 percent, or 10 to 20 pounds. Excluding your arms, your upper torso represents 20 percent of your body weight, or 20 to 40 pounds. Including your arms and measuring only from your belly button up, it is then about 40 percent. Your lower torso alone is 10 percent, and 40 percent with your legs included. So, particularly at the beginning, when you're the most out-of-shape, your own body weight works as a kind of built-in resistance, contributing significantly to the exercise value of Walkshaping. That's why we start by doing all of the exercises without weighted aids.

For example, when you do a Biceps Curl without a weight, you're really using your biceps muscle to lift the weight of your hand and forearm, which together equal 5 percent of your body weight, or 5–10 pounds on each arm. When you do the basic Arm Pump, you're using your shoulder muscles to lift your arm to the height of your head, doubling the distance the weight of your arm would travel. Most walkers swing their arms in a 45-degree arc, or a distance of about one foot. Arm-pumping walkers move their arms 90–180 degrees, for a total of twice the distance and at least twice the work. By increasing the arc in your arm pumping, you not only increase the weight of your body and the distance that you travel, you also move half of that distance away from the ground against the force of gravity. This amounts to two or three times the work that would result from moving the weight parallel to the ground. Likewise, when you stretch your stride from one-foot-long to two-foot-long steps, you also double the number of calories that you burn as you walk, because you double the distance each leg (carrying 20 lbs. of weight load) must travel. Of course, if you're one of the many people who start with a step length of 2 feet, increasing your stride length by 3 to 12 inches will increase the exercise value of your walk by 30 to 75 percent, but it really amounts to more than that. Increasing your step length involves more muscle-controlled action and less of a throwing action in the movement of your legs.

Upper-Body Devices

Fig. 5–1 • Strong-puts

The upper-body devices will be your primary or basic resistance devices. These consist of:

1. **The weight of your arms—** called freehanded exercise.

2. **Weights**—added to each of your hands.

3. **Sticks or Poles**—held and pumped singly or doubled-up to work like a barbell or exercise stick. These add balance as well as resistance.

4. **Stretch Cords or Rubber Tubing**—add resistance to the arm action as you pull or stretch out the cord and gradually let it contract again.

These devices can be used separately or combined for your most effective workout.

Rather than concentrating on a single type of weighted device, Walkshaping allows you to alternate your hand weights, taking maximum advantage of their special construction by using certain aids to work certain muscle groups. For example, torso-twisting exercises and exercises that train your back muscles can be done more easily while you use ski poles. Or, use dumbbell-style weights when training your biceps, triceps, and shoulder muscles for a more thorough workout.

Varying the equipment, like varying the exercises themselves, helps you avoid overstraining a joint or muscle. Walkers who train with just one device can put too much stress on a particular joint. For example, if you just use dumbbells for your upper-body workouts, you risk overstraining your elbow or shoulder joints, especially if you have a tendency to swing or throw the weights rather than pump them—a

Fig. 5–2 • Air Weights

Fig. 5–3 • Swing Weights

Fig. 5–4 • Create a special grip with rubber bands or bungee cords

Fig. 5–5 • Selective thumb and middle finger grip

mistake often made by beginners—or by anyone else when fatigue sets in. When you alternate between dumbbells and ski poles, the stress on these joints is transferred to the back muscles and abdominal muscles, since the poles involve both a pumping and a pushing motion.

Choosing the Right Device

Ski poles are the best device for doing Lunge and Squat Steps, Double Arm Pumps, Torso Twists, and a variety of back exercises. For biceps, triceps, shoulder, and chest work, use dumbbells, short sticks, and other compact hand devices. Wrist and ankle weights are useful, but they don't allow you to add as much weight and have the additional disadvantage of cutting off circulation, thereby reducing mobility. The major advantage of wrist weights is that you can keep your hands free, and even outstretched. Freed from the exhaustion that eventually ensues from gripping something, you are able to do more repetitions of an exercise. Resistance cords are excellent for working the chest.

Hand-Held Weights

If after using only your own body to work out with the Walkshaping exercises you decide to incorporate weights and devices into your routine, you'll first add hand-held weights or wrist weights, starting as early as the second week. Hand weights are perhaps the broadest category of weighted devices; they include standard dumbbells, wrist weights, weights with special hand grips, weighted sticks, weighted ski poles, and weighted balls. Since regular walking is primarily a lower-body exercise, you'll want to start by adding more resistance work to the upper body. Your hands are the best place to start, since they can carry or hold the weights while guiding the movements (see Figs. 5–1, 2, 3).

I recommend that you use a hand-weight device with a built-in grip that allows you to maintain a loosely clenched fist. If you don't have this type of device, you can tie or otherwise attach a bungee cord or rubber tubing to your weight at either end, then strap the weight around your hand (Fig. 5–4 shows you how to create a grip). If you're stuck without a special grip, try shifting your grip between different fingers. For example, start by gripping with your thumb and index finger. Next, change your grip to your middle finger and thumb

(Fig. 5–5), ring finger and thumb, or pinkie and ring finger and thumb. This method lets you relax your hand a bit.

Strong-puts are shaped like a shot-put ball and can be pumped with an open hand. *Air weights* are tightened all the way around your hands with an air pump. Since the weight does not just rest on your palms, you can keep your hands open. *Swing weights* are weight sticks that convert from 1-pound to 3-pound weights, depending on which one of the three possible positions you use to grab the sticks.

Weight Loading

Using Hand Weights

The standard dumbbell comes in all weights and sizes, but the ones used in walking on the move should weigh no more than 10 pounds, and for walking in place, a maximum of 20 pounds. Limiting the weight you add allows you to do more repetitions than a bodybuilder does in his or her workout. As you become stronger, you'll increase the amount of weight you use. If your total body weight is below 100 lbs., you'll need ½-pound weights. If you weigh more, you'll be able to progress in one-pound increments. The goal is to pump rather than swing through the weight.

Because of their compactness, hand weights allow you to move your arms easily in a variety of directions, or even to change directions after only a few repetitions. You can also create wider, longer arcs more easily by bringing your hands together for Double Arm Pumps, forward and back, across your body, away from your body, and over your head.

The Loosely Clenched Fist

Many of the arm actions in Walkshaping require you to tighten and loosen your grip. With curl-up or push-up movements, you will keep a "loosely clenched fist."

Form the loosely clenched fist by touching your thumb and middle finger together lightly. Then, curl your other fingers alongside the two that are touching. A variation is to alternately touch your thumb to each one of your other fingers; the object is to hold something lightly in your hand.

To clench and unclench your fist, pretend that you are reaching out for something. First straighten out your fingers and reach toward the object (e.g., pole, bar), then curl your fingers around it. Pull down or back as you tighten your grip. At the end of the pulling motion, loosen your grip again. If you do not have an object to grip, you can simulate the action by fully extending your fingers, then closing them into a loosely clenched fist, and finally, by tightening your grip into a clenched fist.

If you have arthritis, hand injury or pain, or high blood pressure, maintain either a loosely clenched fist or loosely straightened fingers while doing the exercises.

Later, I will introduce you to several exercises that will use the loosely clenched fist. Your ability to loosen your grip will be important in order for you to carry out the prescribed number of repetitions for each exercise.

Ski-pole straps and wrist weights allow you to keep your hand open, loosely curled and open, loosely gripped, or alternately opened and closed.

Ski Poles

Ski poles or walking sticks are the most versatile of all the walking aids, especially for outdoor walking. Using them allows you to incorporate the lifting and lowering action of weights with the pushing and pulling action of cords. The poles help you extend your stride, and the sound of the poles dragging reminds you to keep your arms pumping.

Europeans, especially Germans, have substituted ski poles for walking sticks on their hikes for many years and can be seen trekking through the mountains of Germany, Austria, Switzerland, Italy, and Greece with their ski poles proudly in hand. In the U.S., skaters have started to use ski poles, both for increased stability and as a way of working more of the upper body by using both the arm and shoulder muscles. They're also used by roller skiers to help simulate the cross-country ski motion.

When you walk, ski poles can help to propel you up inclines and also to slow your descent on the downhill walk. For Walkshapers, the poles provide more balance, enabling you, for example, to sink lower with each step, thereby working the thighs and gluteus. The act of pushing the poles against the ground while you walk also adds resistance. In addition, you can use the poles to strengthen your abdominal and back muscles by rotating your torso as you walk.

Fig. 5–6 • Ski poles enter loop from underneath

The poles are less versatile for indoor walking and walking in place, except when you take deep sinking steps like Lunge Steps and Stretches, which allow you to use the poles to balance yourself and to lower and raise your body. They are also less versatile for chest and shoulder work, and in any movement in which a final wrist turn is required.

Collapsible Power Poles (available through WALKING WORLD, p. 246) offer greater versatility and convenience.

Using Poles/Sticks

Insert your hand into the loop of the strap from underneath (see Figs. 5–6, 7). Once the loop is across your wrist, grab the two ends of the strap and the pole grip simultaneously. To loosen your grip, spread out your fingers, but maintain the contact between your thumb and middle finger.

At the same time, push down with the palm of your hand until the strap becomes tighter around your hand (i.e., the two ends in your palm and the loop around your wrist). This way, you will be able to control the pole without gripping it fully. To lift and guide the pole, use a two-finger grip. To push down and through with the pole, apply pressure on the straps with the palm of your hand instead of gripping and applying pressure to the pole.

To lift the pole, tighten your grip and bend your wrist back. Then, as you plant the pole, loosen your grip and begin to press down on the straps with your palm, which should be facing down. Since the strap is attached to the grip, this will transfer the downward pressure to the pole and grip. As you push back, continue to put pressure on the strap with your palm. Only begin to tighten your grip as you are ready to lift the pole and bring it forward again, and even then, you don't have to clench your fist fully.

Stretch Cords (or Rubber Bands)

Fig. 5–7 • Grab two ends of strap and pole simultaneously

Stretch cords are best for walking in place. These can also be used for both Upper- and Lower-Body Routines. The cords are made of rubber tubing; the thickness of the tubing determines how much resistance they provide. A waist cord approximately ¼-inch thick and 1 to 3 feet long, or a body-length cord, is equivalent to a 1- to 3-pound hand weight. A cord approximately 3 to 5 feet long and ½-inch thick is

Fig. 5–8 • Cord wrapped around waist

equivalent to a 3- to 5-pound hand weight. For example, to perform the shoulder exercise Clean and Press-Up (Shoulder Set #4, page 154, see Fig. 9–47), you would stretch a 3-foot cord an additional 1½ feet. This will produce the same resistance as if you were pumping a 5-pound weight in each of your hands.

Using Your Cords/Rubber Bands

Cords work well for walking-in-place exercises where you can anchor cords to your body, the floor, or around a door or when they are covered over by your step-up bench. When you are walking in place, they work best attached to your waist (Fig. 5–8) or wrapped around your back (Fig. 5–9). You can attach rubber stretch cords (or surgical tubing) around your arms, wrists, hips, legs (above your knee joints), ankles, feet, or below your gluteals.

If you don't have a ready-made device, simply use your belt and belt loops to anchor the cords to your waist. From here, it will be much easier for you to do shoulder and arm exercises. For chest and back exercises, hold a cord in each hand, positioning your hands like you would with hand weights (Fig. 6–9).

Lower-Body Devices

Fig. 5–9 • Cord wrapped around back

After you have learned the routines and integrated the upper-body-resistance devices, you are ready to add lower-body-resistance devices.

Since you already carry the weight of your body on each of your legs, adding weights to your legs is of secondary importance. Although your legs make up 20 percent of your body weight on their own, strategically located weights can enhance the toning effects on thighs, buttocks, and even calves. Many of the lower-body routines can be enhanced further with devices like thigh and ankle weights, stretch cords (known as exercise bands and used around your ankles), and step-up benches.

Ankle Weights/Ankle Bands

Ankle weights or bands are usually used for walking in place. In regular walking or power-walking, ankle weights for walking on the move

Fig. 5–10 • Ankle Bands

can be dangerous, for they can put extra stress on your knee, hip, and ankle joints during the leg-swing phase.

However, Walkshaping's leg movements guide and proceed more slowly under continual muscle control, so you can safely use ankle weights for the Lower-Body Routines. Do not use ankle weights or bands for the Upper-Body Routines or for any exercise that requires continuous forward motion at a pace greater than sixty steps per minute. This means that while wearing ankle devices you will have to avoid any "transition exercises" that use the Pump 'N Stride technique for the Lower-Body Routines (see Fig. 5–10).

Thigh Weights

Power Pants are bicycle pants with pockets for added weights built right into the thigh coverings. This is a great way to work on your thighs without straining your ankles.

Step-Up Benches

If you don't want to invest in a custom step (available in fitness stores), you can substitute a sturdy kitchen stool or staircase or any other sturdy block system that is at least 2 feet long, 2 feet wide, and 6 to 18 inches high. Since step-up benches and ankle weights can overstress the knee joint by overbending it from the same angle, exercises that include these devices should be interspersed with leg lifts using ankle weights. With ankle weights, the whole body's weight is not brought to bear on each knee-bend, as it is with step-up benches. Use ankle weights when using the program to walk about; step-up benches are useful for doing the walking-in-place version of the program.

Trunk-Loading Devices

Devices in this category include backpacks, weighted vests, and weight belts. Although trunk-loading devices do very little for concentrated muscle shaping, they do increase the number of calories you burn. To calculate how many extra calories you will burn: weight added plus weight of your device divided by body weight.

Backpacks

Backpacks are a very useful way to tote your weights, but be sure to use a pack with a frame and waist belt.

The safest and most secure place on your body to add weight is your torso and trunk. Adding weight here is like walking in the body of a heavier person. Many people (hud carriers in India or Olympic weight lifters, for example) are able to walk while carrying weights equal to or greater than their own weight on their shoulders, with frame packs held close to their stomachs. Safety limits dictate that you not carry anything that weighs more than 60 percent of your own body weight, and even then, only after achieving a Level V in strength and fitness. When adding weight to your trunk, the weight pack or other item should be secured so that the weight rests over your hips or girdle rather than your shoulders. Even a backpack hanging from the shoulders should have a frame and waist belt to transfer most of the weight off of your shoulders and onto your hips.

For Walkshaping, I recommend that you use only external or internal framed packs, especially when carrying over 15 pounds. A backpack without a frame or belt can be converted into a frame pack by using a belt to cinch the pack to your waist.

Carrying weight from your shoulders is ill-advised because it pulls at your shoulder joints, where there are no muscles to pull the shoulders back into place. Be sure to adjust the pack by loosening the shoulder straps; this will transfer the weight from your shoulders to your hips. Furthermore, heavy weights squeeze the vertebrae in the neck, which also has no muscle to counterbalance it. Resting weight on your hips moves it closer to your body's own center of gravity and off of your spinal column. While it's not bad to put weight on your spinal column from time to time as you do when pumping your hand weights, straining it continually keeps your vertebrae compressed and can lead to pinching of the nerves and permanent nerve damage.

Weight Vests

Weight vests or jackets with pockets in which you can insert weights have advantages and disadvantages over framed backpacks. The advantages are that the weight is distributed throughout your body, not just at your back. This makes it easier to hold your proper posture while walking. The vests also have pockets that allow you to add or subtract weight easily. Of course, the weighted vests should also be firmly secured around your waist so that the weight rests on the hip and not on the shoulders. The main disadvantage of the vests is that they make you sweat more than you have to, since some are made of neoprene or other rubberlike materials. Although this can be very uncomfortable, you may burn more calories. (This is a point of controversy; some experts say that since vests hinder the release of heat, you may in fact burn off fewer calories.)

Weight Belts

Weight belts are strapped around your middle, just as ankle weights are attached to your ankles, and offer a very safe way of adding weight to your body. Ask a reputable dealer for advice on weight belts of more than 20 pounds, since the quality of these devices varies greatly.

Rules for Adding Weight

Walking with weights, or against resistance measures, requires both muscular strength and cardiovascular endurance. You don't merely lift and lower the weight while your body remains in a static position; you

LEVELS OF STRENGTH/ENDURANCE—ADDED WEIGHT					
	Level				
	I	II	III	IV	V
Hand	0–½ lb.	½–1 lb.	2–5 lbs.	5–10 lbs.	10–20 lbs.
Waist	5–15 lbs.	15–25 lbs.	25–50 lbs.	50–75 lbs.	75–100 lbs.
Thighs	½–1 lb.	1–2 lbs.	2–3 lbs.	3–5 lbs.	5–10 lbs.
Ankles	½–1 lb.	1–2 lbs.	2–3 lbs.	3–4 lbs.	4–5 lbs.
Backpack or Weight Vest	10–20 lbs.	20–30 lbs.	30–50 lbs.	50–60 lbs.	60–75 lbs.

NOTE: These are maximum suggested weights. Of course, you can always use less weight, or none at all.

CORD–WEIGHT LOAD EQUIVALENTS (STRETCHED 1–3 FEET)		
	Weight	
Thickness	(1–3 ft. Range)	(Midpoint)
5/16"	0–5 lbs.	3 lbs.
3/8"	0–8 lbs.	4–5 lbs.
7/16"	0–12 lbs.	6½–8 lbs.
3/4"	0–17 lbs.	10–12 lbs.
1"	0–20 lbs.	15–18 lbs.

NOTE: Midpoint refers to the average resistance offered for any cord.

RUBBER-BAND-WEIGHT-LOAD EQUIVALENT		
	Weight	
Thickness	2 x length	3 x length	4 x length
1/4"	1 lb.	3 lbs.	6 lbs.
3/8"	2 lbs.	4 lbs.	9 lbs.
5/8"	6 lbs.	10 lbs.	18 lbs.
3/4"	8 lbs.	20 lbs.	28 lbs.
1"	13 lbs.	22 lbs.	36 lbs.
1½"	19 lbs.	34 lbs.	55 lbs.
2"	24 lbs.	42 lbs.	60 lbs.

move your whole body at the same time. This requires endurance as well as strength. Use the following table to determine how much weight you can safely and comfortably carry.

Footwear

Don't Walkshape barefoot. As a rule, you should always wear good walking shoes to do the exercises. There are two exceptions: when you exercise in sand or water. You can do the Walkshaping exercises barefoot in soft sand or in deep water. However, if the sand is hard or packed, wear walking shoes with good arch support. Walking barefoot in soft sand adds extra resistance to each leg repetition. For example, Heel Digs (see Buttocks/Hips Set #1, page 176) are particularly effective because your heel-strike digs deeper into the surface, thus allowing your foot and ankle to go through a fuller range of motion. Walkshaping exercises can be done in knee-to-shoulder-deep water. Water shoes are recommended when walking in knee-deep water, since they will keep you from slipping on a swimming pool's slick surface or cutting yourself on rock and shells in the ocean. But if you're exercising in deeper water you needn't worry; since the water provides buoyancy, foot support is no longer a major factor.

Back on dry land, the shoes you use for Walkshaping should be flexible, allow aeration, and firm in the soles and heel cup. I recommend high-top jogging shoes or low-cut hiking boots, many types of cross-training shoes, or shoes that you can make firmer by pumping in air or liquid. Some standard walking, race-walking, and running shoes may not qualify because they're too soft and flexible to support extra weights. Weight-training shoes aren't good either, because they're not built for walking and active side-to-side motion. Firmness and foot coverage are of particular importance when wearing ankle weights, since they rest partially on the tops of your shoes.

Finally, I suggest that you have at least two pairs of walking shoes. This way you can alternate the pairs, letting one air out while the other is in use.

Clothing

While there is a great selection of specialized clothing available, Walkshapers need not be slaves to clothing fashion. I like to exercise in loose-fitting walking shorts and T-shirts, whether I'm working out indoors or outdoors. Tight-fitting clothing restricts your movement and can even cut off your circulation. No clothing feels cooler than that with gaping openings for arms and legs, through which air can circulate freely. Also, you may want to wear layers of clothing that can be easily added or removed depending upon the weather and environment.

Specialized padded walking socks are good for cooler weather, and they can help keep your feet warm while providing extra cushioning. Many walking shoes have built-in padding, so a pair of thin cotton socks will keep your feet dry and cool and allow for more air to pass in and around your feet. If you like "sport socks," choose those made with acrylic.

CHAPTER 6

Your New Way to Walk

Although the Walkshaping routines may seem more complicated than the average fitness routine, they aren't once you know a few basics. You can make them easier to do by incorporating a variety of the basic leg, arm, and torso movements into your daily walking routine.

This chapter defines the new ways of walking and moving you'll use in the Walkshaping Program. Turn to this section anytime you find a particular move confusing. Notice that the Walkshaping exercises are really just extensions of everyday movements, combined with walking.

Steps (Leg Moves)

We all know how to walk by putting one foot in front of the other. And we all know to march by lifting our legs straight up as we bend our knees. Most of us have also stepped up and to the side. With Walkshaping, you will progress from these basic steps and learn to build on them by taking bigger steps, steps with a straightened leg, and steps that bend and extend the leg in a concentrated fashion. These new steps go by the name of Lunge Steps, Heel Digs, Push-Back Steps, etc. You must take greater care when doing these because they will work your muscles harder and place more pressure on your knee, ankle, and hip joints. But don't worry. It won't be the kind of stress you experience when jumping or jogging. Regular walkers work mostly their calf and upper-thigh muscles. Walkshapers work their buttocks/hips and inner- and outer-thigh muscles as well.

Basic Steps

WALK (OR WALKING) • In Walkshaping, to "walk" means to move in any direction while always keeping one foot on the ground. Walking can be done in place or on the move.

WALKING IN PLACE • Walk in place by lifting your feet straight up and down. Also, step in place by taking fewer than three steps in any one direction forward and back and side to side. Because this allows you to complete your walking program in a 5-by-5-foot (or 25 square-foot area), use it to practice your walking exercise program in your home or in an aerobics studio.

WALKING ON THE MOVE • This is actual walking. All of the Walkshaping routines can be performed either in place or on the move.

DIRECTION OF TRAVEL • All the Walkshaping moves are described with reference to the direction you walk: forward, backward, and sideways. This is represented by an imaginary line which bisects the center of your body, and continues in the direction you are walking.

DIRECTION OF TRAVEL FORWARD AND BACKWARD • This is an imaginary line bisecting your belly button. When you place your legs hip-width or shoulder-width apart, you are straddling this line with your feet parallel and equidistant from it.

DIRECTION OF TRAVEL SIDEWAYS • An imaginary line that bisects your hip joints. Various steps to the sides, left and right, are done along this line. Plant your feet so the line intersects the middle of your foot by the arch (see also Grapevine Steps).

STANCE • This is the basic starting position for your feet. For walking in place, feet start side by side; for walking on the move, feet start in the Forward Step or Stride Stretch position. "Hip-width" stance means that your feet are hip-width apart and parallel to each other; "shoulder-width" stance means that your feet are shoulder-width apart. These two stances are preferred in Walkshaping because they provide greater stability.

HIP-WIDTH STANCE • (See Stance.)

SHOULDER-WIDTH STANCE • (See Stance.)

STEP • Any movement of your left or right foot in any direction; this includes all movements in which the foot leaves or touches the ground.

Super Steps

BACK CROSS-OVER STEP • An exercise for your inner thighs as well as your hamstrings, buttocks/hips, and lower-back muscles. Starting with your left leg, step back, crossing behind your right leg and plant your left forefoot to the rear and outside of your right. (See page 199, Alternate Lower-Back Set #4A—Back Cross-Over Steps—for a detailed description.)

BACK LUNGE STEP • (See page 167, Thighs Set #1—Lunge Steps.)

BACK STEP • When you step back, you push off with the ball of your foot and you also land on it. An exercise for buttocks/hips, hamstrings, and lower back. Standing with your feet at hip width, simply take a step straight back. You may also cross one leg behind the other. To exercise your shin muscles, lift your toes up to make sure your foot clears the ground. To exercise your calf muscles, step forward again. (See also page 197, Alternate Lower-Back Set #3A—Back Steps.)

COUNT STEP • Count the number of steps you take during each movement to synchronize your steps with your arm and torso movements. A Two-Count Step is one left step per one right-arm or right-direction torso move and one right step per one left-arm or left-direction torso move. For a Three-Count Step, take two steps during the most difficult part of the arm/torso move (the part where you breathe out and exert your muscles the most) and one step during the easiest part. For a Five-Count Step, take three steps during the most difficult part of the move and two steps during the easiest part.

CROSS-OVER STEP • An inner- and outer-thigh exercise that is done by "side-stepping,"—crossing one foot in front of the other. (See page 169, Thighs Set #2—Cross-Over Steps, and also Side-to-Side Cross-Over Steps.)

FIVE-COUNT STEP • (See Count Step.)

FLAT-FOOTED STEP • (Also called Flat-Footed Walking.) A method of stepping that resembles Frankenstein's stiff-legged walk. Let your leg drop to the ground, landing flat-footed on the sole. In this this step, you use very few muscles; when landing, it is better to roll from heel to toe or forefoot to heel.

FOREFOOT-RAISED STEP • (Also called Forefoot Raise and Toes-Raised Walk.) This is like going up on your toes every time you take a step. It is a shin exercise in which you shift your body weight to your heels and raise your forefoot 15–45 degrees as you take a step. (See page 203, Calves and Shins Set #1—Toes-Raised Walk.)

FOREFOOT STRIKE • This is walking when landing your forefoot first; it is a calf muscle exercise. Plant the ball of your foot and shift your body weight onto that foot. Forefoot Strikes are generally used for Step-Back Steps (and walking backward), Step-Ups, and Step-Downs. To do the Forefoot-Heel Roll: after planting your forefoot, roll your foot down to the heel until it's fully flattened, then roll it back up to your forefoot before taking the next step. If you don't shift your weight, it's called a Forefoot Touch.

FORWARD LUNGE STEP • (See page 167, Thighs Set #1—Lunge Step.)

FORWARD STEP • This is the basic walking step. Also called a Swing Step or Stride Stretch Step, this is something you do in everyday walking. Swing your leg forward before placing your foot on the ground. Because each exercise in Walkshaping starts with the left foot, your first step will always be a left one. Although mainly a quadricep and calf exercise, this also exercises your shins (when you lift your toes to strike with your heels) and your calves, hamstrings, and buttocks/hips muscles (when you push off with your back leg to take the next step).

GRAPEVINE STEP • Here's a fancy way to walk diagonally (forward and to the side while facing forward). While walking on the move, this outer- and inner-thigh exercise combines Cross-Over Steps and Side Steps. Make a quarter turn to your left so that the right side of your body faces the direction of travel. Take a right Side Step, then a left Cross-Over Step. Then take another right Side Step, followed by a left behind Cross-Over Step. Repeat this front-back step series 12 times. Then turn 90 degrees to the right so that your left side faces the direction of travel. (See also Cross-Over Step and Side Step.)

HEEL STRIKE • Avoid walking flat-footed. Land on your heel first and roll forward from there. The opposite of a Forefoot Strike, this shin exercise is generally used when stepping forward. You do it by raising your toes off the ground when taking a step so that your heel strikes first. Be sure to shift your body weight to the striking heel (otherwise, it's a Heel Touch). From the Heel Strike, you can continue with the Heel-Toe Roll. (See page 203, Calves and Shins Set #1—Toes-Raised Walk; page 205, Set #3—Heel-Toe Rock; and page 206, Set #4—Toeing-Out and -In.)

HEEL DIG • A variation of the Heel Strike that exercises the buttocks/hips, hamstrings, and shins. Instead of heel-striking and then rolling forward to your toes, keep your weight on your heels longer by pressing your heels into the ground. To do this, straighten out your leg and push with your buttocks/hips and hamstring muscles. (See page 176, Buttocks/Hips Set #1—Heel Digs.)

HEEL-RAISED STEP • (Also called Heel Raise and Heels-Raised Walk.) In this calf-muscle exercise you raise your heels off the ground, placing your body weight onto your forefeet. (See page 204, Calves and Shins Set #2—Heels-Raised Walk and page 208, Set #5—One-Leg Heel Raise.)

HEEL-TOE ROLL • As you land, strike with your heel and roll onto the ball of your foot. This prevents flat-footed walking, uses more leg and midriff muscles, and contributes to smoother and more rhythmic walking steps, allowing you to move at a faster clip. This is essentially an ankle exercise that also works your calves, shins, quadriceps, and hamstrings.

KNEE-UP • Lifting your knee so that your foot is raised 3–6 inches off the ground (short height), 6–12 inches (medium height), 12–24 inches (high height), or up to 36 inches (extra-high height, or knees-to-chest). The higher you lift your knee, the more you use your stomach muscles. (See pages 188–190, Abdominals Sets #3—Leg Raise Step—to #5—Crunches).

LEG CURL • A hamstring exercise. While standing, bend your knee and raise your lower leg up behind your body until your heel touches the back of your thigh (like a Biceps Curl). (See page 171, Thighs Set #3—Leg Curl.)

LEG EXTENSION STEP • A quadriceps exercise. Raise your knee in front of your body and straighten your leg out fully with each step. This is the opposite of the Leg Curl. (See page 172, Thighs Set #4—Leg Extensions Step—for more details.)

LEG LIFT • Generally, a walking-in-place step that works your quadriceps and hamstring muscles as you raise and lower your leg. You do it by lifting your knee straight up (as you would to march in place). Also called the Knee-Up Step, this movement uses your quadricep muscles to raise your upper leg. You can also bend your knee and bring your heel up to the back of your thigh, as you do with Leg Curls. (See page 171, Thighs Set #3—Leg Curl—for a detailed description.)

LEG PUSH-BACK STEP • Straighten out your back leg and push off with your rear foot. You will feel your thighs and buttocks/hips contracting. A hamstrings and buttocks/hips exercise. Before taking each step, straighten your back leg and raise it off the ground. (See also page 178, Buttocks/Hips Set #2—Leg Push-Back—for more details.)

LEG-RAISE STEP • These are like marching steps. (Also called Knee-Ups or Knee-Up Steps.) An exercise for abdominals and quadriceps. With each step, raise your knee up high to involve your abdominal muscles in the stepping motion. (See also Leg Lift, Knee-Up, and page 188, Abdominals Set #3—Leg-Raise Step—for more details.)

LUNGE STEP • With each step, you slowly sink into the knee with your forward leg. An upper-leg and buttocks/hips exercise. Each time you take a step forward, backward, or to the side, lower and raise your body on one leg. Take a Stride Stretch Step before you begin to lower your body (unlike the simultaneous step-and-lower motion of the Squat Step). Keep your back leg straightened and your forward leg bent, even after your heel strikes the ground; notice that for a Stride Stretch Step you would straighten the leg upon the heel's impact. In order to prevent overbending or straining your knee, be sure that your forward knee is directly over or behind your ankle. (See page 167, Thighs Set #1—Lunge Step.)

ONE-LEG HEEL RAISE • (See page 179, Calves and Shins Set #2—Heel-Raised Steps and page 208, Set #5—One-Leg Heel Raises.)

OUTER EDGE HEEL-TOE ROLL • After you strike the ground with your heel or forefoot, roll your foot forward or backward before taking the next step. This version of the Heel-Toe Roll is easier on your joints. Turn your ankle out slightly after your heel strikes the ground, and roll forward on the outer edge of your foot. This maintains the alignment of your lower and upper leg, resulting in less pressure on your knee joint. Execute the Forefoot-Heel Roll on the outer edge of your foot as well.

PIVOT STEP • Soldiers on parade and marching bands use this step. As soon as you step forward and execute a right heel strike, roll your foot forward to the ball and pivot turn your body counterclockwise 180 degrees by pivoting on the balls of your front foot and back foot. Keep your feet anchored to the ground. You are now facing in the opposite direction. (See Chapter 11, Choreography, page 219, for more details.)

SIDE STEP • Stepping to either side and back again turns walking in place into a dancelike routine. An exercise for the buttocks/hips and outer thighs. Step to the left or right by lifting your leg and extending it sideways, then landing on your forefoot first and rolling down to your heel. To initiate the next step, roll your body weight onto your forefoot again. This is done most comfortably while walking in place, but can be done on the move by turning the side of your body toward the direction of travel. Variations are the Cross-Over Step and Side Lunge Step. (See also pages 180–182, Buttocks/Hips Sets #3—Buttocks Squeeze—through #5—Side Lunge Step.)

SIDE-STEPPING • Like stepping forward, you can sequence Side Steps into a continuous movement as you do when you dance. In this exercise, you take a series of Side Steps in the same direction. For example, for Side-Stepping to the left, take a left Side Step then a right foot Side Step to the left, placing your right foot hip-width apart from your left foot again. Lunge Steps on the move involve Side-Stepping. (See page 167, Thighs Set #1—Lunge Step.)

SIDE-TO-SIDE CROSS-OVER STEP • By changing the angle of your steps to a diagonal, you work your inner thighs more. These are Cross-Over Steps taken alternately to the left side and back again, then to the right side and back again. For a left Side-to-Side Cross-Over Step, cross your left foot over in front of your right leg, plant your left forefoot, and roll down onto the heel. Shift your body weight to the left foot and lift your right foot slightly off the ground. Step down as you cross your left foot back over your right and return it to the hip-width position.

SIDE-TO-SIDE STEP • An in-place Side Step exercise. Step to the side and back again, first with your left foot and then with your right foot. In-place Lunge Steps are a variation of Side-to-Side Steps. (See page 167, Thigh Set #1—Lunge Step.)

STEP-DOWN • (See Step-Up.)

STEP-UP • An exercise for quadriceps, hamstrings, and buttocks/hips. Lift your leg and plant your foot on a higher surface, such as a stair step. Shift your body weight to the foot. Step onto it to lift your whole body up to the level of the raised surface. With a step-up bench, you can step up and down in different directions. Step-Ups are similar to Lunge Steps and Squat Steps, since they involve raising and lowering your body with each step you take.

STRIDE STRETCH STEP • A multipurpose exercise that works your leg, abdominal, and buttocks/hips muscles all at once. The forward step is 3–12 inches longer than a regular walking step. The longer your stride, the more you use your midriff muscles, hips, legs, abdominals, and buttocks/hips. Some Walkshapers can reach a stride that, measured from the back of the heel to the tip of the toes, is equal to their height.

THREE-COUNT STEP • (See Count Step.)

360-DEGREE TURN-AROUND WALK • This is a graceful way to walk out of a room or leave a friend by turning to say good-bye. Take a right Cross-Over Step, followed by left back Cross-Over Step. Continue around with another right Cross-Over Step and a final left back Cross-Over Step. You're now ready to walk away. (See Chapter 11, Choreography, page 219, for more details.)

TOE-OFF • When walking on the move, push off with your back foot, keeping your toe in contact with the ground until your leg is fully straightened. This allows you to work more of your hamstring muscles as you bring the foot forward during the Stride Stretch. The Toe-Off is also related to Buttocks/Hips Set #2—Leg Push-Back, on page 178.

TOEING-IN AND TOEING-OUT STEPS • (Also called Foot Turns or Ankle Flexing.) Generally, you should keep your feet parallel to one another and pointed in the direction of travel. By gently turning your forefoot inward or outward as you step, you will work a different part of your calf muscles. These steps allow you to step while exercising your inner (Toeing-In) and outer (Toeing-Out) calf muscles. They also help you develop greater flexibility in your ankles. (See page 206, Calves and Shins Set #4—Toeing-Out and -In.)

TWO-COUNT STEP • (See Count Step.)

Arm Moves

You may have already tried some of these on your own, moving your arms in different directions while you walk (perhaps imitating some gym exercises). You may have discovered that you can move your arms in different directions, bending and extending each arm as you take a step with your opposite leg. Regular walkers give their upper-back and arm muscles a light workout. Walkshaping strengthens and tones all the upper-back and arm muscles by hitting them from different angles.

Basic Arms

ARM PUMP • All of the other arm moves in Walkshaping are based on the muscle-controlled principle of the Arm Pump. Use this motion when Walkshaping. Instead of simply swinging your arms forward and back, pump them in a very controlled way. Choose a Bent Arm Pump (bent to 45 or 90 degrees) or a Straight Arm Pump with a slightly bent arm. While walking, pump your right arm forward and your left arm back as you take a left step, and your left arm forward and your right arm back as you take a right step. Instead of the ballistic actions of swinging, throwing, punching, and chopping, Walkshaping uses the muscle-controlled movements of pumping, pulling, pressing, raising, or squeezing. Arm Pumps distribute the work among several muscles, making it more of an aerobic than a body-shaping exercise.

ARM SWING • Basically, this is a shoulder- and back-limbering exercise. Swing your arms forward and back as you walk; you might notice that you already do this to maintain your balance while walking. Swing your right arm forward and your left arm back as you take a left step, and your left arm forward and your right arm back as you take a right step.

Even though you pump your arms instead of swinging them in Walkshaping, you'll still use Arm Swings to recuperate between sets of Arm Pumps and Upper-Body Workouts.

SINGLE ARM MOVE • A movement practiced with one arm at a time. Often, the arms alternate so that the same movement is performed first with one arm, then with the other, as in Single Arm Curls, for example.

DOUBLE ARM MOVE • A movement practiced with both arms simultaneously. When you do this, you increase the intensity or calorie-burn rate of the exercise. Move your arms in the same direction, as in Biceps Curls and Triceps Extensions; in opposite directions, as in Flys and Arm Raises; or to one side and then the other, as in Double Arm Cross-Overs from the side.

Super Arms

ARM CROSS-OVER PUMP • A chest-exercise variation of the Arm Pump. While walking, pump your right arm across your chest to the left side as you take a left step, then pump your left arm across your chest to the right side as you take a right step. This motion uses your chest muscles (i.e., inner and outer pectorals) and adds quickness to your movements. (See page 135, Chest Set #1—Cross-Over Arm Pump; page 141, Chest Set—Fist Turn and page 143, Chest Set #6—Pull-Over Pump.)

ARM CURL • An exercise for biceps and forearms. Using your bicep muscles, bend your arms at the elbows. Curl up your right arm as you take a left step and your left arm as you take a right step. For greater synchronization of your moves, curl down your right arm as you curl up your left, and curl down your left arm as you curl up your right; or curl both arms up and down simultaneously. Synchronize this movement with Three- or Five-Count Steps. For the Three-Count Step, take two steps as you curl up and one step as you curl down. For the Five-Count Step, take three steps as you curl up and two steps as you curl down. (See pages 127–134, Biceps Sets #1–5.)

ARM EXTENSION • (also known as Triceps Extension) An exercise for triceps, shoulders, and forearms. As you straighten your arms, you are using your triceps muscles. Notice that the Arm Extension mirrors the Arm Curl: both start from the bent-arm position, and the Curl brings the lower arm toward the upper arm just as the Extension moves the lower arm away. Depending on the position of your elbow (down, back, or out), you can extend your arm in various directions. Take a left step as you bend back your right arm and extend or straighten your left arm. Take a right step as you bend back your left arm and extend or straighten your right arm or, extend and bend both of your arms simultaneously. (See pages 145–149, Triceps Sets #1–5.)

ARM FLY • Named for its resemblance to a butterfly flapping its wings. Extend your arms shoulder-height in front of you and bend them at right angles to resemble a butterfly's wings. From this position, bring both arms together at the elbows and forearms.

ARM PRESS • This is a rowing motion in which your hands start at your chest, then you press them out and pull them back. It is a chest exercise that involves either pushing your arms away from your body or pressing them in front of you. Presses, like pumps, use a number of muscle groups, including your forearms, triceps, and chest (when arms are pressed from the chest level), or shoulders (when arms are pressed out or above the shoulders from shoulder level).

To synchronize arm and leg movements, move your right arm when you take a left step, and vice versa. Use a Three- or Five-Count Step to press out and bring back both arms. For the Three-Count Step, press out or up for two steps and bring back for one step. For the Five-Count Step, press out or up for three steps and bring back for two steps.

ARM PULL-OVER • A back exercise that duplicates the action of the Pullover weight-training machine. Pretend you're holding on to a bar at shoulder height, then push it over your head. Continue the motion while pushing your elbows downward as if pulling the bar behind your body. Raise the imaginary bar over your head, then back down to your sides to complete the exercise.

ARM RAISE • In this exercise, you raise your arms over your shoulders as if you were reaching for the top shelf of a cupboard. Also called the Lateral, this exercise works your shoulder and upper-back muscles. For maximum resistance, raise your arms while they're straightened out. However, you also do bent Arm Raises during exercises such as Shoulders Set #4—Clean and Press-Up—and Set #5—Upright Row and Shrug. Raising your arms to the front works your front shoulder muscles (e.g., front deltoids); to the sides, your middle-shoulder muscles (middle deltoids), to the back, your rear-shoulder muscles (rear deltoids). Alternate raising your arms to the chest, shoulder, head, and overhead levels to work harder and increase your range of motion. For the best balance and synchronization, raise your right arm as you take a left step and your left arm as you take a right step, and lower your left arm as you raise your right arm, and vice versa. Or raise and lower both arms simultaneously. (See pages 150–155, Shoulders Sets #1–5.)

ARM ROTATION • A shoulder exercise. Straighten your arms and rotate one or both around your shoulder joint(s). You will look like a windmill or weather-vane duck as you rotate your arms. A 360-degree arm rotation is called a Windmill Arm Pump. Variations include a 180-degree rotation. The greater the rotation arc, the more of your upper-body muscles you use. Rotate each arm backward by raising it above your head. Take a left step as you raise your right arm and begin to rotate it backward. Take a right step as you raise your left arm and begin to rotate it backward. (See also Windmill Arm Pumps in Chapter 8, page 112.)

ARM ROW • A back exercise that uses a number of muscles, including your triceps and shoulders. This movement imitates a sawing or rowing motion. Start by reaching out from your body (or down, for the Upright Modified Rows exercise) as if you were pressing your oars forward while rowing a boat. Then, pull straight back, using your back muscles as you bend your arms at the elbows and press your elbows back. When doing Double Arm Rows, squeeze your "wings" together for extra back-muscle contractions. Since the rowing motion also uses your shoulders and upper arms, the Double Arm Row will provide the maximum back work.

Rowing uses a pressing motion to work the front of your body, chest muscles, and front shoulders, but also a mirror-image pulling action to work the back of your body, back muscles, and back shoulders. The Handshake Pump, done with ski poles, uses a similar press-and-pull action.

While walking, take a left step as you extend forward and row with your right arm, and pull your left arm back. Take a right step as you extend forward and row with your left arm, and pull your right arm back. (See pages 158–161, Upper Back Sets #1–4, and page 155, Shoulders Set #5—Upright Row and Shrug.)

ARM SCISSOR • Your arms can be bent or extended when you move them across your chest, like scissor blades. A chest-exercise variation of the Arm Squeeze. Bring your arms together, crossing one over the other for the maximum squeeze of the muscles. Take two steps while crossing your right arm over your left arm, then bring your arms back to your sides. Take another two steps as you cross your left arm over your right arm, then bring your arms back to your sides. (See page 141, Chest Set #1—Double Arm Scissor.)

ARM SQUEEZE • (also called Fly Pumps; Elbow Squeeze) This multi-purpose exercise works your chest, shoulder, or back muscles, depending on the direction of movement. Bring your arms across your chest and hug yourself, squeezing the front-body muscles between them to contract your chest muscles. Extend your arms behind your body and squeeze them together to contract your back muscles. Since this is a double-arm move, do it with a Three- or Five-Count Step. For the Three-Count Step, take two steps while squeezing your arms together and one while pulling them apart. With the Five-Count Step, take three steps while squeezing your arms together and two while pulling them apart. Arm Squeezes are used in Double Arm Cross-Over Pumps, Fly Pumps, Scissor Pumps, and Elbow Squeezes.

BENT ARM PUMP • (See Arm Pump.)

BICEPS CURL • (See Arm Curl.)

CONCENTRATION CURL • Instead of just bending and extending your arm at the elbow joint, move it slowly, squeezing the muscle. To increase or decrease the range of motion of your arm curls, start each curl with your arm bent to a 90-degree or a 45-degree angle. A shorter range of motion allows you to do more repetitions of exercise for a fully pumped up or fatigued muscle. Practice Concentration Curls only after you've completed regular Arm Curl sets. (See Arm Curl.)

CROSS-OVER PUMP • (See Arm Cross-Over Pump.)

ELBOW SQUEEZE • This is like the Arm Fly except that you squeeze your elbows together and turn your wrists inward. A chest- and back-exercise variation of the Arm Squeeze. Bend and extend arms from the sides of your shoulders and elbows up. From this position, pull arms down and squeeze them against the chest. For a Three-Count Step, take two steps as you squeeze your elbows together and a third step as you bring them back to your sides. For the Five-Count Step, take three steps as you squeeze your elbows and two while bringing your arms back.

FIST TURN • This refers to the starting position of your fist when you use it during an exercise. Turning your fist during an exercise works more of your muscles. The direction in which you turn your fist is determined by whether your palm begins by facing up, out, down or inside. For Biceps Curls and Upright Rows, turn your fists outward by turning clockwise with the right fist and counterclockwise with the left fist. For Triceps or Arm Extensions, turn your fists out by turning the right fist counterclockwise and the left fist clockwise.

FORTY-FIVE (45)-DEGREE ARM PUMP • (See Arm Pump.)

NINETY (90)-DEGREE ARM PUMP • (See Arm Pump.)

PRESS-OUT • (See Arm Press.)

ROW BACK • (See Arm Row.)

STRAIGHT ARM PUMP • (See Arm Pump.)

TRICEPS EXTENSION • (See Arm Extension.)

WINDMILL PUMP • (See Arm Rotation.)

Torso Moves

Basic Torso

BASIC TORSO MOVE • Practice standing erect and tall, because you will hold your body erect and tall while standing as well as while walking. An imaginary line connecting your ear, shoulder joint, hip joint, knee joint, and ankle joint should run to the ground to form a right angle.

LOWER-BODY POSTURE • Keep your knees slightly bent unless you're specifically instructed to fully extend your legs (see page 74, Leg Extension step).

MIDDLE-BODY POSTURE • Correct overarching your lower back with the Pelvic Tilt Exercise (see page 113).

UPPER-BODY POSTURE • Correct a jutting chin or leaning too far forward with the Chin Tuck: tuck your chin straight back into your neck as you put your head and shoulders back. (See page 105, Chapter 8, Whole-Body Workout).

Super Torso

TORSO BEND-OVER • This movement does not occur often in everyday living. Most of us don't bend at the waist unless we are picking up something. Therefore, proceed with caution. This is a lower-back exercise. Slowly, bend over at the waist and straighten up again in degrees: for Level I, 5–10-degree range; for Level II, 10–15-degree range; for Level III, 15–30-degree range; for Level IV, 30–45-degree range; and for Level V, 45–90-degree range. (See pages 192–197, Lower Back Sets #2–4 for more details.)

If you have back problems, avoid Bend-Over exercises and substitute Alternate Lower Back Sets #2A–5A for the Bend-Over Sets.

TORSO TURN • This exercise is for the abdominals. Turn your torso toward the front at your hip line for abdominal work and to the back for lower-back work. When turning your torso, keep your upper body straight, your shoulders squared, and your arms extended at shoulder height.

TURN FORWARD • This is an abdominals exercise that involves turning your torso forward of your hip line by rotating your left shoulder behind you and your right shoulder across your body to the left, and vice versa. As you rotate right forward, take a left step. As you rotate left forward, take a right step. Keep arms and shoulders aligned and fixed, rotating them as one unit. Don't let your arms bend back or over-rotate away from your shoulders.

TURN BACK • In this lower-back exercise, you turn by rotating your body from your hip line backward. As you turn your left shoulder back, take a left step. As you turn your right shoulder back, take a right step. Keep your shoulders squared by keeping your arms raised to shoulder height and extended directly from the sides of your body. (See also Torso Turn, page 83, and Alternate Lower Back Set #5B—Turn Backs, page 201.)

ELBOW-TO-KNEE TRUNK TURN • An exercise for the lower and upper abdominals. Turn your torso and bend down to touch your elbow to your opposite knee. This combines the Knee Up with the Trunk Turn. (See Trunk Turn, page 186, Torso Turn, page 83, and Abs Set #4— Elbow-to-Knee Step, page 188.)

CRUNCH • An exercise for abdominals and the lower back. Here you assume the fetal position while standing and squeezing your stomach muscles. Bend your upper body over as you alternate lifting up your left and right knees to touch your chest. After they touch, lower your leg and straighten up your body. The exercise is a combination of the Knee Up and the Torso Bend Over. As each knee comes close to or touches your chest, squeeze your stomach muscles. Use a Double Arm Pump to help you maintain your balance. (See Knee-Up, page 74, Torso Bend-Over, page 83, Lower Back Set #2—Bent-Over Walk, page 194, and Abs Set #5—Crunch, page 190.)

TORSO TURN-FORWARD • (See Torso Turn.)

SIDE BEND • A strengthening and stretching exercise for the oblique muscles. Bend your torso to the side instead of front and back. Bend to the left side as you take a left step, and, to your right side as you take a right step. For more muscle work, turn your shoulder across the front of your body and bend down to the opposite side, rotating your upper body toward the side you are bending. In other words, rotate toward the left as you do a left Side Bend by pumping your right arm across your chest. Rotate toward the right as you do a right Side Bend by pumping your left arm across your chest. This turn-and-bend movement keeps your oblique muscles from becoming too thick.

PELVIC TILT • To avoid overarching your lower back, tuck your buttocks/hips under as you pull your stomach muscles in. This is an abdominals and lower-back exercise. Straighten your lower back by pulling in your stomach and tilting your pelvis forward. (See Lower Back Set #1, page 192.)

Now that you've learned the individual movements, let's start to put them together into body-sculpting walking routines.

PART THREE

The Walkshaping Program

CHAPTER 7

The Six-Week Walkshaping Workout

Walkshaping is based on body sculpting and aerobic walking. If you already work out with weights, you'll know many of the exercises for the upper-body portion of the workout. If you're an exercise walker or you do aerobics, you'll recognize many of the stepping movements. But Walkshaping is a unique system of exercise that allows you to isolate your ten major muscle groups and shape up while walking aerobically.

Minutes

If you're sedentary and out of shape, start with the 12- or 20-minute program. During the Six-Week Shape-Up Routine, I encourage you to walk daily, interspersing the Whole-Body and concentrated Body-Parts Routines. This allows you to build up your total weekly mileage and repetitions and, therefore, the total number of fat calories you burn by alternating your arm and leg work. If you're a busy person, the 12-minute Walkshaping Program is probably the best workout for you, because it will give you the most results in the least amount of time.

Sets

Practice 1–5 sets or series of repetitions of the same exercises each workout period. The more time you have, the shapelier and fitter you will become. Do 1–5 sets of exercises for each of ten body parts; depending on your level of strength and fitness (and the size of the muscle group you will be working), do 5–25 repetitions of that exercise.

Reps

Each mile you walk consists of 1,200 to 1,500 arm and leg repetitions, depending on how long your stride is. You'll practice walking with both arms and legs fully engaged for a total-body workout, and again for a concentrated-muscle-group workout, to tone your body and gain muscular endurance. Eventually, this format will allow you to do up to 5 sets of 5–25 repetitions each of 50 different exercises; that's 5 exercises per muscle group.

A 10-minute walk takes you one third of a mile to one mile, which translates to 500 to 1,500 steps and Arm Pumps, depending on the length of your stride and your walking speed. Even a 30-minute mile allows you to perform 20 sets of body-sculpting exercises with 25 repetitions per set (or 40 sets at 12 repetitions each). You'll be able to do at least one set, and up to two sets, of each of the 10 body-parts exercises, and still have 5 minutes left over for walking and arm pumping at an aerobic pace. Allowing 2 minutes for warm-up and stretching and 1 minute for a cool-down walk brings you within the 12-minute limit. If you increase your exercise period to 20 minutes, you'll be able to do 2 sets (or 1–3 miles of walking); with 30 minutes, you can do 3 sets, or 2–5 miles of walking; and so on. If you're out of shape, it will take at least three and up to five weeks to reach this level of maximum efficiency, so we double the time it will take while you get in shape.

Each of the arm, leg, and torso exercises you do while walking is composed of a precise series of muscle-controlled movements, including bending, extending, turning, squeezing, pushing, pulling, lifting, and lowering.

I have combined all of these into one exercise program to provide the most effective workout. Stretch your muscles fully by lengthening them, moving your limbs and torso through the greatest range of motion while keeping the resistance constant. Contract the muscle fully by squeezing it hard on the final part of the exercise. Also, use the maximum resistance possible without fatiguing the muscle too quickly or straining it from overuse. A variety of movements lets you work the muscle groups more intensely and from every angle.

Counts

Counts in an Upper-Body Routine are measured by the number of steps or arm movements you make, in a Lower-Body Routine they are measured by the number of arm movements.

A Two-Count Step means that you take a left and a right step. Notice that in Walkshaping, all of the exercise routines start on the left foot. Also, pump the right arm forward at the start of the exercise whenever you can. A Three-Count Step consists of a left-right-left step. We also use Four-Count and Five-Count Steps (e.g., left-right-left-right-left). The Two- or Four-Count Step methods are used when you do single- or alternate-arm pump movements.

The Three- or Five-Count Step methods are used when you do Double Arm Pump routines or multiple-part movement routines such as the Clean and Press-Up. These odd-numbered counts allow you to alternate the beginning of the exercise repetition, starting once with your left foot and the next time with your right foot.

Do the repetitions to a count of 1 (fast), 2 (moderate), or 3 (slow) seconds each. For stretching, the counts refer to the number of seconds you hold a stretch in one position without bouncing up and down. Repeat the stretch on each side of your body.

Each Repetition

Each step and arm repetition counts for a lot in Walkshaping, so be sure to concentrate from the beginning on learning the proper technique. Remember:

1. Move your arm, leg, or torso through the full range of motion.

2. Breathe in and out with each repetition. If you hold your breath, you'll deprive your muscles of the oxygen needed and reduce the number of calories you burn. In addition, holding your breath prevents muscles from fully releasing, cuts off circulation, and pinches nerves.

3. If you catch yourself jerking, swinging, or throwing out the movement, drop your pace until you can take control of your muscles again. Give the muscle an extra squeeze at the peak of each bend/extend movement.

Breaths

Breathe in and out through your mouth rhythmically when doing all the Walkshaping routines. Inhale on the easy part of the exercise, and exhale on the difficult part.

Avoid the temptation to hold your breath when increasing your walking speed or when you strain to lift, push, or pull a resistance device. This is a natural tendency: by holding your breath, you contract your torso muscles so that they will assist with the action. To counteract this tendency, synchronize your breathing with your exercise counts. Inhale on the easiest part of the exercise, since this is when your muscles are doing their least work or are about to do their most work. Breathe in when you start, then breathe out as you flex or work your muscles. Breathe in when stretching out the muscle; breathe out when you're contracting, flexing, or squeezing your muscles.

When doing low-intensity exercises (such as stretching), which don't raise your heart rate significantly, practice inhaling through your nose and exhaling through your mouth. For all other exercises, inhale and exhale through your mouth. This mouth-only breathing method allows the most air to enter your lungs and, therefore, the most oxygen to reach your working muscles. Incidentally, it will also maximize the number of calories you burn while exercising.

Steps

In Walkshaping you'll be taking a variety of short to long (or high) steps in many different directions. The basic step used in any Walkshaping routine starts on your left foot and with your right arm. The Leg Lift is a step taken while walking in place. Measure a Leg Lift from the ground up to the bottom of your foot: low (foot is 6 inches off the ground), medium (6–12 inches), high (knee is waist-high), or extra high (knee to chest). The Stride is a step taken while walking on the move. Stride length is measured from the heel of your back foot to the toes of your forward one: short (6–12 inches), medium (1–3 feet) or long (3–6 feet). By stretching your Strides or raising your Leg Lifts, you make walking a more dynamic exercise, which particularly shapes your thighs, buttocks/hips and legs.

For balance and rhythm, move your left leg with your right arm and your right leg with your left arm. Also, turn your torso from your right shoulder to your left leg side and from your left shoulder to your right leg side.

The Routines

Each workout consists of five basic routines:

Warm-Up 1–5 minutes

Stretching 1–5 minutes

Whole-Body Walk 3–15 minutes

Body-Parts Routines 6–30 minutes

Cool-Down Walk 1–5 minutes

FIVE WALKSHAPING WORKOUTS					
	12 min. (1 set)	20 min. (2 sets)	30 min. (3 sets)	45 min. (4 sets)	60 min (5 sets)
1. Warm-Up Walk	1 min.	2 min.	3 min.	4 min.	5 min.
2. Stretching	1 min.	2 min.	3 min.	4 min.	5 min.
3. Whole-Body Walk	3 min.	4 min.	6 min.	9 min.	15 min.
4. Body-Parts Routines	6 min.	10 min.	15 min.	24 min.	30 min.
5. Cool-Down Walk (stretching)	1 min.	2 min.	3 min.	4 min.	5 min.
TOTAL	12	20	30	45	60
Number of Reps	5–8	9–15	16–20	21–25	25+
Exercise Time	10	20	30	40	50

The Warm-Up Walk (1–5 minutes)

The purpose of the Warm-Up Walk is to get the blood circulating to all of your major muscle groups and to prepare your heart and muscles for more vigorous exercise. When you break a sweat, you know that you're warmed up. As the weeks pass, you can vary your warm-up with different upper- and lower-body combination routines, as long as you do each at a moderate pace.

Start by working your whole body at a slow to moderate pace. Walk slowly in place or on the move using Super Steps—Stride Stretch Steps—or 6- to 24-inch-high Leg Lifts, with chin-height to head-height Arm Pumps. (Later, add a variety of slow-paced Arm Pumps and Super Steps from your Body-Parts Routines.) Maintain large movements through the full range of motion, along with a slow to moderate pace and a steady, consistent rhythm.

The Stretching Routines (1–5 minutes)

Always do a Warm-Up Walk before doing the stretching exercises. Then do at least the Four Basic Stretches (see page 118) without bouncing, and hold each stretch for 5–30 seconds, depending on your fitness level. Remember, stretching is necessary for avoiding injury and increasing flexibility. If you have time, you might also want to stretch before and after the Body-Parts Routines.

The Whole-Body Walk (1–5 minutes)

The Whole-Body Shaping Routines involve moving all of your body in an even and balanced way. The effort you put forth will be distributed evenly over most of your muscle groups, with larger groups like your shoulders and thighs doing more of the work. By not singling out any one muscle for extra work, you can practice the exercises on consecutive workout days.

This is a more vigorous version of the Warm-Up Walk; you do a series of balanced upper- and lower-body steps and Arm Pumps. Whole-body Walkshapers tone all of the major muscle groups and burn calories at a very high rate. Since you don't single out or isolate any muscles, you can do the whole-body exercises for miles and miles of walking, through thousands of repetitions. In between sets of the Body-Parts Routine, return to the Whole-Body Walk instead of resting.

The Body-Parts Routines (6–30 minutes)

These routines are the heart of the Walkshaping Program, the exercises used to develop and define specific muscles and muscle groups.

The Body Parts concentration exercises are ranked from 1 to 5, according to their degree of difficulty. Less-fit beginners can start by doing just the first set in each individual Body Part Routine. Those in fair condition do two sets; in good condition (intermediate) three sets; in very good condition four sets; and in excellent condition, five sets. The first set in each Body-Part Routine hits the muscles broadly;

each additional set works the particular muscles more specifically. This technique trains the muscles efficiently without overworking them with repeated exercise.

You'll be doing an Upper Body and a Lower Body Workout on alternate workout days, to allow your fatigued muscles to rest and recuperate between workouts.

Day One: The Upper-Body Workout

The Basic Workout

Remember: do your Whole-Body Routines (Warm-Up Walk, Stretching, Whole-Body Walk, and Cool-Down Walk) on the day before and after you do your Upper Body Workout.

Depending on the length of the workout you're doing—12, 20, 30, 45, or 60 minutes—do 1–5 sets of each of the five Upper-Body Routines.

The following exercises take you from large to small muscle groups (the way a bodybuilder would train). For variety, I've interspersed biceps and triceps sets. Do the workout as follows:

Biceps and Forearm Routines

1. Hammer Curl
2. Palm-Up Curl
3. Palm-Down Curl
4. Palm-Out Curl
5. A. Double Arm Curl
   B. Raised Arms Curl
   C. Concentration Curl

Chest Routines

1. A. Bent Arm Cross-Over
   B. Straight Arm Cross-Over
   C. Double Arm Cross-Over
2. Fly Pump with Twist
3. Press-Out (double arm)
4. Elbow Squeeze
5. Fist Turn
6. Pull-Over Pump (double arm)

Triceps Routines

1. Elbow-Down Extension
2. Elbow-Back-of-Hip Joint Extension
3. Fists Behind Hipline Arm Extension
4. Side-Cross Extension
5. Elbow-Up Extension

Shoulders Routines

1. Front Lateral
2. Side Lateral
3. Back Lateral
4. Clean and Press-Up
5. Upright Row and Shrug

Upper Back Routines

1. Row Back
2. Modified Upright Row
3. Row-Out
4. Back Row-Up
5. Pull-Down/Pull-Over

All of the upper-body exercises are detailed with photographs in Chapter 9.

Step Accompaniments

Steps and Leg Lifts accompany the Body-Parts Routines. When beginning, start by using short, quick steps and low Leg Lifts, but as you practice the lower body workout exercise, lengthen your stride or raise your leg higher and use the Stride Stretch Steps and Knee Ups as a step accompaniment. Of course, the longer or higher your step, the more you will exert yourself, although this will also slow down the pace of your walk. As a rule, practice easy steps with harder arm movements and easy arms with harder leg movements.

Day Two: The Lower-Body Workout

Do the Lower-Body Workout on alternate workout days to give your upper-body muscles a day of rest. Again, depending on the length of your exercise period and your fitness level, choose 1–5 exercises from among the following lower-body-exercise sets. Work your way in the order presented, from easiest to most difficult. Exercise your largest muscle groups first, and end with the smallest. (Lower-back exercises that require the slowest pace make a nice transition to the Cool-Down Walk.)

Thighs Routines

1. The Lunge Step
2. Cross-Over Step
3. Leg Curl
4. Leg Extension Step
5. Squat

Buttocks/Hips Routines

1. Heel Dig
2. Leg Push-Back
3. Buttocks/Hips Squeeze
4. Side Leg Lift
5. Side Lunge Step

Abdominals Routines

1. Belly Breathing
2. Trunk Turn
3. Leg-Raise Step
4. Elbow-to-Knee Step
5. Crunch

Lower Back Routines   OR   Back Savers Routines

Lower Back Routines	Back Savers Routines
1. Pelvic Tilt	1. Pelvic Tilt
2. Bent-Over Walk	2A. Leg Push-Back
3. Bent-Over Row Back	2B. Look-Back Walk
4. Bent-Over Row-Up	3A. Back Step
5. Bent-Over Arm Raises	4A. Back Cross-Over Step
	5A. Trunk Turn
	5B. Turn-Back

Calves and Shins Routines

1. The Toes-Raised Walk
2. Heel-Raised Walk

3. Heel-Toe Rock
4. Toeing-Out and -In
5. One-Leg Heel Raises

All of the lower-body exercises are detailed with photographs in Chapter 10.

Arm Accompaniments

Do Single and Double Arm Pumps, Presses, Pulls, and Curls as an accompaniment to the Lower-Body Routine. Work your arms in opposition to your leg movements, and do Torso Turns for better balance and rhythm. Do medium- to long-arc pumps at chest to head height when working only one leg, and low to medium (at chest to chin height) Arm Pumps when doing Double Leg Bends or other harder routines, such as the lower-back sets.

Beginners should stick to the basic Bent Arm Pump at chest to chin height. Advanced walkers can add a greater variety of arm moves (see page 78). Do them with your arms bent, or straightened with the elbows slightly bent.

The Program

Use the following chart as a guide to tailor your program to your needs and abilities. For the best results, I recommend that you walk daily to meet your basic weekly mileage goals: 12–15 miles per week if you weigh less than 150 lbs. or 15–21 miles per week if you weigh more or want to lose more than ten lbs.

Practice the basic Pump 'N Walk for 10–40 minutes a day and do 1–5 sets of the body-shaping routines, alternating days of upper- and lower-body routines. Level I's practice 5–12 repetitions of each exercise in slow motion; Level V's practice 25 or more repetitions at a brisk pace.

Beginners should start at Level I or II and work their way to Level III over a six-to-eight-week period as they shape up and become stronger. Intermediate and advanced walkers start at Level III or IV and work up from there. Remember to work at your own level and rest or slow down if you feel that you are overexerting yourself.

If you're just starting to exercise after a long period of inactivity, be sure to consult a physician and show him or her your Walkshaping Program before you start.

PROGRESSIVE LEVELS CHART					
Fitness Levels		**Practice Levels—Pump 'N Stride**		**Walkshaping/Stretching Routines**	
	Workout (minutes)	**Miles (day/wk)**	**Speed* (minute miles)**	**Reps or Seconds Held Per Set**	**Sets (per session)**
I (Poor)	12	up to 1 / 7	60–30	5–12	1
BEGINNER					
II (Fair)	20	2 / 14	30	12–15	2
III (Good)	30	3 / 21	20–17	15–18	3
INTERMEDIATE					
IV (Very Good)	45	4 / 28	17–15	20–25	4
V (Excellent)	60 +	5 / 35	15–11	25+	5
ADVANCED					

*A 60-minute mile means you walk 1 mile per hour; in a 30-minute mile, you walk 2 miles per hour; etc.

Adding Weights

After you've practiced the routines freehanded for at least one week, you are ready to move to adding weight, in increments of ½ pound if you're under 150 pounds and of 1 pound if you weigh over 150 pounds. The under-150-pounds group can build up to 3 pounds per hand weight; the over-150-pounds group can build to 5 pounds per hand weight.

If you're practicing Walkshaping in place, you can use a different amount of weight for different sets of exercises. The under-150-pounds group can use 3-, 5-, and 8-pound weights. The over-150-pounds group can use 5-, 10-, 15-, and 20-pound weights. Heavier weights can be used for chest, biceps, and upper-body exercises, while lighter weights must be used for the generally weaker lower back, shoulders, and triceps. For leg work that involves knee-bending, such as squats, lunges, and leg lifts, lighter weight should be used, because these body parts are already bearing enough weight.

If You Haven't Done Any Weight Training Before

To determine whether you are ready to use weights, do the routines for one week without resistance devices. If you are able to keep your arms pumping and legs lifting for five minutes without resting, you can add weight to Set #2. If you can keep it going for 10 minutes, you can add to Set #3; 15 minutes, add to Set #4; 20 minutes, add to Set #5.

Adding Resistance

A little bit of trial and error will be needed to find the height, distance, or thickness needed to duplicate the weight-loading effort of various resistance devices. Page 65 contains a rough equivalency chart to guide you.

It's valuable to alternate between weight and resistance devices. Resistance devices work your muscles by varying their function. A 6-inch step bench increases the workload on your thighs without using weights or restricting movement. Walking sticks and stretch cords work your muscles by pulling rather than lifting. By pulling, you are less likely to use jerking or ballistic (throwing) motions, and this resistance stretches your muscles as it strengthens them. In the workout section that follows, I've provided you with sets of routines that let you use at least three different resistance devices in your daily Walkshaping workout.

Here is a suggested schedule for incorporating weights and devices into your workout:

FIRST WEEK • Do the Walkshaping routines without resistance devices.

SECOND WEEK • Introduce one light-weight resistance device, such as ski poles or stretch cords.

If you are doing a walking-in-place routine, you can add secondary devices like ankle weights and the step-up bench.

THIRD WEEK • Add a second resistance device. Weights are preferable, since they are more versatile than stretch cords. Begin doing the whole routine, using one device on one day and another device the next.

FOURTH WEEK • Add a third resistance device, the stretch cord or ski poles. Use a different device on each of the three days you work out using resistance. When doing your workout routine in place, divide it into thirds, using a different device during each period.

FIFTH WEEK • Add secondary resistance devices like ankle weights and weight vests to the on-the-move routines for extra muscle shaping and calorie burning.

SIXTH WEEK • Continue with your Week-Five program.

If You Don't Like to Use Weights and Resistance Devices

Many walkers don't like to use special equipment. With Walkshaping, you can continue to do all of the routines freehanded, using the weight of your own body parts as a resistance device. Keep in mind that you will still be trading speed for a greater range of motion. Your pace will decrease as your level of work increases.

If You Do Too Much Too Soon

When you can pump your arms and legs for fifteen minutes continuously while walking, begin adding weights.

Of course, some of you may want to cheat and add weights right away. If you do, try doing only the first set with weights for the first week and all other sets without weights.

You Know When You've Gone Too Far

When muscle soreness lasts more than two days, you know you went too far on a particular exercise. You may even have pulled a muscle. This is most likely to happen if you haven't done any weight training and are not used to exercising all of your muscle groups. Please try to avoid this situation. Progress gradually at your own pace. If you overdo it, to ease the soreness, give that part of your body a rest until the pain subsides. If possible, continue training your other body parts, working around the sore muscle. Try to do your Whole-Body Walks for overall toning and calorie burning, maintaining a daily and weekly average of walking miles.

Where to Start: Your 12-Minute-a-Day Walkshaping Program

If you've never done bodybuilding or calisthenic exercises, the 12-Minute Walkshaping Program can serve as your starter program. It will get you in shape as you learn the basic Walkshaping techniques. If you already walk for exercise, incorporate the 12-Minute Program into your daily walk session. If you're shy about trying new exercises outdoors, practice the 12-Minute Program in place. If you're not comfortable doing even the 12-Minute Walkshaping Program, practice the individual upper- and lower-body sets one at a time during your regular walking session. If you cannot do all 12 repetitions of a particular exercise, do as many as you can—even if it's only one. Continue walking the way you normally do, and when you've gained strength and confidence, do the additional repetitions for that set.

You can also build up gradually by phasing each body-parts set into your regular walking session. Once you've mastered a set, add it to the other Body-Parts Routines you already know. If a particular body-parts set gives you difficulty, substitute another. Once you're doing more than one set for a specific body part, you can also practice your favorite set, up to four sets.

Walkshaping is simple, because it combines walking with everyday movements—pulling with or raising your arms, bending over, and dipping down. One way to prepare yourself to do the Upper- and Lower-Body Routines is to rehearse. Do 1 or 2 repetitions of each new way to walk first at your seat, then in place, and finally during your regular walk. Spend your first two weeks gradually building up your repetitions for each body set from one to twelve by practicing each body-parts set separately. As you progress, test your strength and endurance by doing the sets in the order prescribed and reducing the amount of Pump 'N Walk time or repetitions between each set.

Making Progress

Most of you take six weeks to complete and move through each of the five levels of the Walkshaping program. Your minimum goal should be to reach Level III—i.e., 3 sets of body-shaping exercises, 30 minutes a session, 3–5 times a week. If you find any level too easy and your fitness levels are higher than that level, you can accelerate your program by moving to the next level after one to three weeks of practice at that level. If you can't easily do the prescribed 12 to 25 repetitions of any exercise (even without weights), you fall into Level I and should start with fewer than the prescribed number of repetitions. Don't start adding weight or resistance for any exercise until you can do at least 12 repetitions without muscular strain. Once again, your goal should be to reach Level III, a 30-minute-a-day Walkshaping routine.

Extra Shaping Routines

If you are not satisfied with your progress in a particular body area, do extra routines for that area, up to three extra sets. Women may want to do extra thigh and buttocks/hips sets, such as Lunge Steps, Leg Push-Backs, and Buttocks Squeezes. Men, on the other hand, may be interested in extra sets for the arms, chest, shoulders, and stomach, such as Biceps and Triceps Curls, Fly Pumps with Upright Rows, and Press-Ups.

CHAPTER 8

The Whole-Body Workout

The Whole-Body Workout consists of the Warm-Up Walk, the Stretching Routine, the Whole-Body Walk, and the Cool-Down Walk. These are walking exercises that stretch, strengthen, and tone all or most of your muscle groups.

Whole Body walking routines start and finish every Walkshaping workout. These routines are easier to do than the Body-Parts Routines, because they distribute the workload over all your muscle groups. In the beginning, you may need to rest or revert to the Step and Swing Style every one or two minutes. I will give you both the in-place and on-the-move version of each routine. The in-place version is easier to practice because you can do it right next to your chair as you read this book. It will also help you break down exercises into parts by practicing in slow motion, allowing you to concentrate your attention on specific parts of each movement.

Even if you don't perform the focus routines, you should try to walk every day. Walking is great for your circulation, and it raises your metabolism so you'll burn more calories during the rest of the day. It stretches and strengthens your muscles, making minimum-mileage goals easier to reach. It relaxes you by releasing the muscle tension created by daily stresses. Even if you miss your regular workout, walking keeps you physically active. Practice the Whole Body routines whenever you walk, whether on a stroll in the park or in your neighborhood.

Warm-Up Walk (1–5 minutes) (Fig. 8–1)

This exercise lubricates your joints and gets the blood flowing to all of your major muscle groups to prepare you for stretching, aerobic walking, concentrated shaping exercises, and practicing your walking techniques. The Warm-Up Walk is a slow-motion walk done in place or on the move; use it to practice combinations of full-range Arm Pumps, Bends, Extension Steps, and Lifts. *Never skip the Warm-Up Walk* as limbering up helps prevent muscle strain, joint damage, or other serious injury. The Warm-Up Walk is the best time to introduce yourself to the Bent Arm Pump, the Leg Lift, and the Stride Stretch Technique.

Bent Arm Pump

The Bent Arm Pump (arms, shoulders, and upper back) is an upper-body exercise that replaces the standard arm swing. Since you're lifting and lowering your arms with continuous muscle control and tension, you get a better workout than if you were just swinging your arms. First, bend your arm at the elbow and maintain this position throughout the movement. Pump your arms forward and back along the sides of your body. Use a loosely clenched fist so that your arms don't tire from extra muscle tension. You can pump your bent arm with five levels of exertion, the first requiring the least work. With a loosely clenched fist, rotate your arm forward around your shoulder joint so that the fist is either 1) at chest height, 2) at chin height, 3) at head height, 4) overhead, or 5) behind your head. Do these with one or both arms. (See Figs. 8–2 to 8–6 for illustrations of the various types of Arm Pumps.)

Fig. 8–1 • Before practicing the walking techniques, do the Warm-Up Walk In Place (Gary Yanker demonstrates)

Fig. 8–2 • Cindy demonstrates Bent Arm Pump, fist at chest-height

Fig. 8–3 • Bent Arm Pump, fist at chin height

Fig. 8–4 • Bent Arm Pump, fist at head height

Fig. 8–5 • Bent Arm Pump, fist overhead

Fig. 8–6 • Bent Arm Pump, fist behind the head

Single and Double Arm Pumps accompany many of the exercise routines, because the Bent Arm Pump allows you to do thousands of repetitions before becoming fatigued. You'll also use the Bent Arm Pump with weights and resistance aids, since it's easier to hold, carry, push, and pull these items when your arm is bent at a 90-degree angle than when your arm is straight.

The Stride Stretch Step (legs, hips, buttocks/hips, stomach) (Figs. 8-7, 8, 9)

This is the basic Walkshaping step for use on the move: it's 3 to 12 inches longer than a regular walking step, or 3 to 6 feet in total length if measured from front-foot toe to rear-foot heel. Lengthening your stride in this way stretches the muscles in your legs, hips, and buttocks and engages your stomach muscles more than regular walking. The Stride Stretch Step makes your muscles work harder and contract more fully. This increase in stride length will, in time, increase your walking pace, your stability, and your heart rate.

Many of the Body-Parts Routines are done with the Stride Stretch Step, because the longer step allows you to execute Arm Pumps and arm extensions with a greater arc of movement. The Stride Stretch Step has several variations: one simple modification is the Lunge Step, which requires more exertion, because you lower your body as you step, lengthening your stride while also adding more weight or resistance. You will still use the "quick, short step" (a fast-paced version of your normal walking step of 1–3 feet) in Walkshaping, but will do so less often than you would in standard aerobic and speed-walking programs.

The Leg Lift is an in-place equivalent of the Stride Stretch Step. Like the Stride Stretch Step, the Leg Lift also requires more effort and exertion than the standard walk step. The Leg Lift Step is done by raising the leg up rather than forward. Variations include Low Leg

Fig. 8–7 • Short Stride length

Fig. 8–8 • Medium Stride length

Fig. 8–9 • Stride Stretch length

Lifts, Side Knee-Ups, Cross-Over Knee-Ups, and Step-Ups. The Knee-Up Leg Lift involves raising the knee first as you bend the leg using the front of the thigh or the quadriceps, or the upper leg muscles (Figs. 8–10 through 8–13).

Pump 'N Stride Walk

The Bent Arm Pump and the Stride Stretch Steps are called Pump 'N Walk when used together. This combination creates the basic movement from which all Walkshaping routines proceed. Practice the Pump 'N Walk with head-height 90-degree Bent Arm Pumps until you feel comfortable with the motion.

Warm-Up Walk In Place (Figs. 8–14, 15)

START • Stand with your feet hip- to shoulder-width apart. Hang your arms loosely by your sides (Straight Arm Pump), or bend them, elbows at right angles tucked into your waist (Bent Arm Pumps). Keep your fists loosely clenched.

MOVE • With knee bent, lift your left leg 1 to 2 feet off the ground. Flex your foot so it's parallel to the floor (beginners may point their toes). As you lift your leg, pump your bent (right) arm, raising it until your fist is level with the top of your head.

Fig. 8–10 • Low Leg Lift, Beginner (forefoot down)

Fig. 8–11 • Medium Leg Lift, Beginner (forefoot down)

Fig. 8–12 • Medium Leg Lift, Advanced (forefoot up)

Fig. 8–13 • Knee-Up Leg Lift

Fig. 8–14 • Correct Posture: Full Body—standing, feet hip-width apart, chin tucked in

Fig. 8–15 • Warm-Up Walk In Place

Next, lower your arm and leg simultaneously, landing on your toes. Then roll your foot back to your heel for a full-foot plant. As you lower your bent arm and pass your fist alongside your body, continue pushing your arm back until your fist reaches behind the line of your hip joint. Your upper arm should now be extended back and, again, should be almost parallel to the ground. Now, repeat the movement with your right leg and your left arm. Once you've mastered the basic opposite arm/leg movement while walking in place, synchronize your left and right side movements by doing them simultaneously and rhythmically.

As you pump your right fist overhead, pump your left fist back behind your hip-joint line, and vice versa. As you lift your right leg, pump forward your left arm and pump back the right arm, and vice versa.

To get the most from your workout, be *conscious* of your form. Don't swing or throw your arm back and forth. Instead, guide it as you rotate it around your shoulder joint, using your shoulder muscles to raise and lower your arm. Use your biceps muscle to keep your arm bent at a 90-degree angle and squeeze the biceps and deltoid muscles as the arm passes over your head. As you lower your arm, use your triceps muscle to push it around your shoulder and behind the line of your hip joint. At this point, give your triceps muscles a squeeze as you push your arm straight back. Also, make sure that you don't kick up your legs. Lift and lower them by using your calf and thigh muscles.

Use your shin muscles (tibialis anterior) to raise your forefoot, and your forefoot to move your foot parallel to the floor. Squeeze your buttocks/hips muscles when your heel returns to press against the ground, remembering not to lock back into the knees. Once you've been doing the workouts for a while, good form will become second nature.

COUNT • Each set of Warm-Up Walks in place takes 1 minute, at a pace of 30–60 steps per minute.

VARIATIONS • Substitute the Double Arm Pumps for the Single Arm Pumps as you get fitter. For better results, do the Warm-Up Walk with any arm movement that employs a wider range of motion around your shoulder joints.

Warm-Up Walk On the Move (Fig. 8–16)

Fig. 8–16 • Warm-Up Walk On the Move, from the side

START • With your feet hip-width apart, take a left Stride Stretch Step forward as you pump your right arm overhead. At the same time, pump your left arm back so that the fist is behind the line of your hip joint. As you step forward, step straight ahead so that you don't narrow your foot placement, since this will make it difficult for you to maintain the parallel foot placement used in the Stride Stretch Step position.

MOVE • Raise the heel of your back right foot while rolling on the outer edge of your foot all the way up onto your toes. Your back leg should now be straightened fully. Before lifting it, slide it forward about 1 to 2 inches above the ground. As you do so, sink down on your forward knee. As your right foot passes your left leg, straighten your left leg and extend your right foot forward. Next, pull your right forefoot up so that the heel of the right leg strikes the ground first; your foot should form a 45-degree angle with the ground upon impact. While your right foot is moving forward from the back position, your left arm will be pumping from behind the line of your left hip forward and up to the height of the top of your head. It will pass along the left side of your body as your right foot passes your left leg and your left knee begins to bend. Your left fist should reach the height of the top of your head at the same time that your right heel strikes the ground.

VARIATIONS • You can accompany the Stride Stretch Step with a variety of Double Arm Pumps. For the on-the-move Warm-Up Walk, it's important that the arms be pumped in a full range of motion that utilizes the major muscle groups in the upper body; use the Windmill Arm Pump, Front Arm Circle Pump, or Torso Turn, described in Chapter 6. After a few weeks, you'll be able to do a medley of Arm Pump exercises while doing the Warm-Up Walk.

PRACTICE • Do 1–5 minutes of Warm-Up Walk routines at a pace of 2–3 ½ miles per hour, or 60–90 steps per minute, depending on your fitness level.

DEVICES • After the first week, practice your Warm-Up Walk with weights and resistance devices. Be sure to start with the lowest weight or resistance level and to maintain a slow to moderate pace.

Later, you can make your Warm-Up Walk more interesting by adding other arm moves, such as Rows (you do this motion already if you use ski poles). Be sure that you warm up with full-range arm movements rather than short-range ones (e.g., Biceps or Triceps Curls). Full-range moves bring more blood to all of the muscle groups. Long or high steps, rather than Leg Curls and Extensions, warm up more of your leg muscles.

Posture-Shaping Routine In Place
(5 seconds to 1 minute)

No single Walkshaping exercise provides more dramatic improvement than this one. It's also the best prescription against back pain, Americans' number-one medical concern. It's useful to practice the posture-shaping exercises in front of a full-length mirror, as you did for your photo poses. If your posture is aligned with the pressure points, you'll be able to feel and see that you're doing these exercises correctly. Eventually, posture shaping will become a corrective movement that you'll do whenever you catch yourself out of proper body alignment while sitting, standing, or walking.

START • With your toes pointed forward, place your feet hip-width to shoulder-width apart.

MOVE • Bend your knees slightly, hold in your stomach, and tilt your pelvic girdle under your body. Now pull your stomach in more, and

Fig. 8–17 • Head Centering, chin right

Fig. 8–18 • Chin-Down to neck

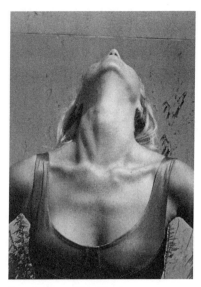

Fig. 8–19 • Head Back

sink down a little more. Put your shoulders and head back as you let your arms hang loosely by your sides. Next, tuck your chin straight under into your neck, as a marine might do when coming to attention. Make sure your head is centered directly over your shoulders and parallel to the ground (Fig. 8–14). Do not tilt your head back so that your chin is in the air or drop your head down so that your chin dips toward your chest.

HEAD CENTERING • Turn your head slowly to the right until your chin line is parallel to your shoulder (Fig. 8–17). Hold for four counts. Turn your head slowly to the left so that the line is now parallel to your shoulder. Hold for another four counts. Now bring your head back to the center. Imagine a line running from the ground through your belly button and up through the center of your chin, splitting your nose, and running up between your eyes. Bend your head forward and try to touch your chin to your neck (Fig. 8–18). Hold the position four counts, then bring your head back to the center. Now slowly bend your head back while jutting your chin into the air (Fig. 8–19). Hold the position for four counts, then slowly return your head to center.

Pelvic Tilting (Figs. 8-20 through 8-23)

START • Hold the Proper Posture position.

MOVE • With your knees slightly bent, stretch your arms forward to form a giant hollow in your chest and stomach, making a C with your body. Then suck in your chest and stomach as much as you can, and slowly straighten up through the spine. Tuck your pelvic girdle under your torso and sink into your knees again, feeling how this movement flattens your back.

REPEAT • Do 5–12 repetitions of the exercise while standing in place.

Belly Breathing (Figs. 8–24, 25)

This exercise will help you breathe more deeply when doing all of the exercise routines in the Walkshaping Program.

START • Hold the proper-posture position.

MOVE • Inhale slowly, feeling your stomach (not your chest) fill with air. Allow your stomach muscles to expand, creating a "potbelly." Hold for two counts. Exhale slowly for four counts, contracting your rib cage first and then your stomach. Pull in your stomach muscles until you've pushed out all of the air. Repeat 5–12 times.

Posture-Shaping Routine On the Move

The purpose of this exercise is to correct your posture while you walk. Eventually, you'll also use this movement whenever you catch your-

Fig. 8–20 • Pelvic Tilt, hollowed in

Fig. 8–21 • Pelvic Tilt, flat back

Fig. 8–22 • Pelvic Tilt, rolling up

self walking with poor posture. Apply the same principles to walking on the move as you do to walking in place. Practice the exercise as you move along, but learn it while walking in slow motion, freeze-framing each part of the movement.

Stretching Your Step (Fig. 8–26, 27)

START • Hold either the hip-width standing position or the Stride Stretch Step with the left foot forward, striking with your heel first.

MOVE • From the Stride Stretch position, turn your ankle out slightly, and roll forward on the outer edge of your front foot all the way to the toes. Then roll back again to the heel-strike position. From the standing position, take a short step straight forward with your left foot and strike with your heel. Without stepping back, lift your front foot and slide it forward another 3 to 12 inches. Hold this position. Your left foot should remain parallel to your right foot and at the same hip-width distance from it as it was when your feet were side by side. Extend your arms out for balance.

If you've stepped too far, you may lose your balance. Check your alignment. If you need to adjust, slide your front foot back a little. Squeeze your buttocks/hips muscles as you tilt your pelvic girdle under, and hold in your stomach. At the same time, adjust your shoulders and head by tucking in your chin and pulling back your shoulders. Straighten out the position of your back foot if it's turned

Fig. 8–23 • Pelvic Tilt, final position

Fig. 8–24 • Belly Breathing: belly out

Fig. 8–25 • Belly Breathing: belly pulled in

outward or inward. Your feet should stay hip-width apart and on a parallel line with each other. If they are not, step back and adjust to the hip-width stride before stepping forward again.

Raising Your Step (Figs. 8-28, 29)

START • With your right foot forward, hold the Stride Stretch Step position.

MOVE • Raise your back heel; at the same time, raise your front right forefoot. As you are doing this, pump your left bent arm forward to head height and your right bent arm backward to elbow or shoulder height. Hold this position for two counts, then lower yourself back to the ground. Do six counts of this exercise with your right foot forward and another six counts with your left foot forward.

Heel-Toe Rock (Figs. 8-30, 31, 32, 33)

START • Hold the Stride Stretch position with your right foot forward.

MOVE • Bend your left arm at a right angle so that your fist is level with your chin. Push your right arm back so that the fist is behind your hip

Fig. 8–26 • Posture Shaping On the Move: stretching your step, lifting foot then placing it forward again 3–12 inches—from short step

Fig. 8–27 • Posture Shaping . . . —to Stride Step

Fig. 8–28 • Raising Front Forefoot and Back Foot Heel at the same time: Flat-Footed

line. Raise your right forefoot and your left heel at the same time. Now slowly roll forward with both feet on the outer edge of each foot. As you do, slowly reverse the direction of your arms, pumping the left arm back and the right arm forward. Keep your feet parallel.

REPEAT • Do this Heel-Toe Rock exercise six times. Then place your left foot forward and your right foot back and repeat six times.

Breathing Routines

Deep, full breaths help your posture. Likewise, the other Posture-Shaping exercises in this chapter will help you by strengthening the muscles you'll need to breathe more deeply, opening up your chest and abdominal cavity to allow an increased airflow.

The idea behind this exercise is to help you synchronize your arm pumping and breathing as you walk in place. Make the same number of arm and leg movements when you breathe in as when you breathe out. For example, if you breathe in for a left and right step, breathe out for the next left-right step series. Train yourself to breathe in and out during every repetition of the Walkshaping exercises, since holding your breath restricts your movements and slows the rate at which you burn off calories. Incorporate these exercises into your Warm-Up Walk.

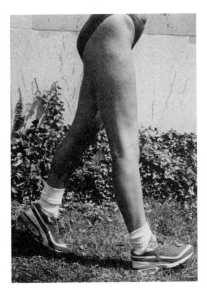

Fig. 8–29 • Raising Front . . . Raised

Fig. 8–30 • Heel-Toe Rock from Stride Stretch position On the Move: Toes-Raised

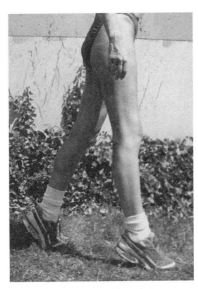

Fig. 8–31 • Heel-Toe Rock from Stride Stretch position On the Move: Heels-Raised

Fig. 8–32 • Practice easier in-place version of the Heel-Toe Rock with feet hip-width apart and side by side: Toes-Raised, pump both arms forward for a better balance (Katia demonstrates)

Fig. 8–33 • In Place Heels-Raised, pump both arms back for better balance

Fig. 8–34 • Elisabeth demonstrates Calf and Achilles Tendon Stretch

Four Basic Stretches

Do these stretches after your warm-up and cool-down routines. Hold each stretch at least for 5, but preferably for 30–60, seconds on each side, depending on your fitness level (I–V). Do not bounce.

Stretch #1: Calf and Achilles Heel Stretch (Fig. 8–34)

The Calf and Achilles Heel Stretch lengthens the muscles you use most. If the calf muscles get tight from a lot of walking, they can overpower your shins, resulting in painful shin splints. To prevent this, do this stretch often.

Take a Lunge Step forward. Now push down the heel of your back foot until you feel the stretch in your calf. Be sure to keep your front and back feet parallel. Hold each stretch for 5–30 seconds. You can sink deeper into the stretch as you get better, but remember not to bounce.

Fig. 8–35 • Quadriceps and Ankle Stretch

Fig. 8–36 • Lunge Stretch

Fig. 8–37 • Hamstring Stretch

Stretch #2: Quadriceps and Ankle Stretch (Fig. 8–35)

If you have difficulty balancing, you may want to stand near a wall or tree for this stretch. Grip your right foot with your right hand and gently pull your heel toward your buttocks/hips. Feel the stretch on the front of your thigh, shin, and ankle. Repeat the stretch, standing on the other leg. Remember to keep your standing leg slightly bent, your stomach pulled in, and your pelvis gently tucked so as to prevent the arching of your lower back.

Stretch #3: Lunge Stretch (Fig. 8–36)

Take a Lunge Step forward, then sink straight down by bending your forward knee. Feel the stretch in your groin and thigh. Remember to hold the front knee directly above your ankle. Do not let it drift over your toes.

Stretch #4: Hamstring Stretch (Fig. 8-37)

Take a left Lunge Step forward. Next, lean back on your right foot, bending the right knee and straightening your forward leg as you flex your foot. Balance yourself on your front heel. Push your forward right hip back.

Hold the position for 6–30 counts and repeat the stretch with your right foot forward. Gently rest your hands on your thighs. As you become more flexible, sink back more into the hips and lower the torso. (See page 219, Choreography for Upper Back, Upper Arm, Shoulder, Neck, and Chest Stretches.)

Basic Walkshaping Techniques

Before you begin Day One, your Upper-Body Workout day, let's review the basic techniques. All of the arm and leg movements are essentially the same whether walking with or without weights or resistance devices.

Basic Body-Stance Do's and Don'ts (while standing and walking)

Do keep your feet hip-width to shoulder-width apart. Do keep your feet parallel—some people have a tendency to turn in or out. Do keep your body in proper alignment, with your head centered over your shoulders. Don't look ahead any closer than fifteen feet away or you'll bend your head down and throw out your posture. Don't lock out your elbows and knees. Do keep your eye and chin line parallel to the ground. When you catch yourself jutting your chin forward tuck it straight back into your neck. Do hold your stomach in and tuck your pelvis under so that your lower back is flat and not arched. Do keep your elbows and knees bent (even if it's only slightly) throughout the Walkshaping exercises. Don't rock your body or bob your head. Do keep all of your movements smooth and controlled by your muscles.

Basic Arm Pump

Do keep your arms bent at right angles. Don't swing them; do pump them straight forward and straight back with your elbows close to your sides. Avoid ballistic or throwing actions like swinging and punching. Pumping controls the arm movement with your muscles and burns 40 percent more calories than arm swinging does. Keep your arms locked at right angles. Don't bend and extend your arms unless the specific body-shaping exercise calls for it, as in Biceps Curls, Press-Ups, or Triceps Extensions.

Loose Fist

Use a loosely clenched fist when you pump, curl, press, and extend your arm. To do this, touch your thumb to your middle finger and curl your other fingers around it. This enables you to perform twice the number of arm repetitions that you could with a tightly clenched fist.

Turning Your Fist

The direction you turn your fist in as you move your arms affects how much you shape and tone your muscles. It also makes it easier to synchronize your arm and leg movements. Do start, execute, and complete each of your arm movements with your palms facing in the specified direction, with palms-up, -down, -out (facing away from your sides), -front, or -back (facing behind your body). The direction in which your palms face also changes when you hold certain weights and resistance devices.

Steps

In Walkshaping we take a variety of short to long (or high) steps in many different directions. To make walking a more dynamic exercise, we stretch our Strides and raise our Leg Lifts. This particularly shapes our thighs, buttocks/hips, and legs.

Opposite Arm/Opposite Leg

Synchronize your arms and legs and Torso Turns. For balance and rhythm, move your left leg with your right arm, and your right leg with your left arm (called opposite arm/opposite leg). Turn your torso from your right shoulder to your left leg side, and from your left shoulder to your right leg side.

Breathing

Breathe in and out through your mouth rhythmically when doing all the Walkshaping routines. Holding your breath saps your strength, slowing you down and burning fewer calories, while unnecessarily raising your blood pressure. Inhale on the easy part of the exercise, and exhale on the difficult part.

Counts

The Walkshaping exercises are done by counting out equal numbers of arm, leg, and torso movements performed with synchronized breathing.

EVEN COUNTS • Two- and Four-Count Steps are used with most single-arm exercises. Two- and Four-Count Steps involve two alternate steps and two arm movements: left step with right arm, and right step with left arm. Use this for exercises that move one arm and one leg at a time. Breathe in and out for the same number of arm/leg movements. For example, breathe in slowly as you take two (or four) steps and Arm Pumps, then breathe out as you take another two (or four) steps and Arm Pumps.

ODD COUNTS • Use Three- and Five-Count Steps with most double-arm exercises or combination exercises or when you do a long-range arm movement. The odd number of counts lets you begin each repetition on a different foot, making your exercise feel more balanced and rhythmic. Take a left, right, then another left step as you do an Upper Body Routine involving simultaneous movement. Use two steps for the most strenuous part of the arm movement and the third step for the easiest part. Breathe in on the easy part (one count) and breathe out slowly (two counts) on the strenuous part.

FIVE-COUNT STEP • Take three steps on the hard part and two steps on the easy part. Or, if you're doing a combination exercise (e.g., the Clean and Press-Up in Shoulders Set #1), three steps for one combination and two steps for the Press-Up. For example, step left, right, and left as you raise your arms to your shoulders, then left and right as you raise and lower your arms over your shoulders, then left as you put your arms back again to the starting position.

In Place/On the Move

Practice the whole program in place at least once to familiarize yourself with the routines. Then take some or all of the exercises out for a walk. This versatility also allows you to split up your routine, doing some sets indoors and some outdoors. If you find exercising in public to be embarrassing or if some of the exercises seem too outrageous, save them for your in-place indoor routine.

Adding Weights

If you're practicing Walkshaping in place, you can use different amounts of added weights for different sets of exercises. The under-150-pounds group can use up to 3-, 5- and 8-pound weights; the over-150-pounds group can use 5-, 10-, 15-, and 20-pound weights. Use heavier weights for chest, biceps, and upper-body exercises, and lighter weights for the generally weaker lower back, shoulders, and triceps. For leg work, use lighter weights for exercises like Lunge Steps and Leg Lifts, which involve knee-bending, because these body parts already bear enough weight, relative to the points that are used to move them.

Rules for Adding Weight

Use your level of muscle strength to determine the range of weight you can add safely and comfortably to various parts of your body. Walking with weights, or against resistance measures, requires both muscular strength and cardiovascular endurance.

Walking with Resistance

It's valuable to alternate between weight and resistance devices. Resistance devices work your muscles by varying their function. Stepping up on a 6-inch step-up bench increases the workload on your thighs without adding weight to them or restricting their movement. Walking sticks and stretch cords make your muscles perform a pulling rather than a lifting action, which stretches your muscles as it strengthens them.

Taking a Bigger Step (Legs, Back, Abdominals)

Take Super Steps to get the maximum muscle-shaping and fat-burning effects from each exercise. Increased step height and length shapes your leg and midriff muscles more than regular walking. Combine your Super Steps with Arm Pumps to work your upper leg, lower back, and abdominal muscles—this is as effective as doing Buttocks/Hips Lifts, Back Extensions, and Stomach Curls at your local gym.

Posture Shaping (Whole-Body)

Walkshaping helps your posture, which is the key to muscle balance and proportion. Always hold proper posture throughout the exercises, and correct yourself immediately when you notice that your posture is out of alignment.

CHAPTER 9

The Upper-Body Workout

Now that you've warmed up your muscles and aligned your joints, you are ready to concentrate on shaping and strengthening specific muscle groups.

Practice the upper-body exercises in this chapter and the lower-body work in Chapter 10 on alternate days. For each body part, do: Set #1 if you're Level I (for the 12-minute-a-day program), Sets #1 and #2 if you're Level II (20-minute-a-day program), and Sets #1–5 for Level V (60-minute-a-day program).

Practice the walking-in-place version first, right next to your open book. As you learn the exercises, you'll also be memorizing them; then you can walk outdoors without your book.

The upper-body exercises in this chapter are broken down into five sets, each ranked according to its degree of difficulty. The first set is the easiest; it works the entire muscle group. The subsequent sets require greater skill; they also work specific muscles within the group. Completing four sets of each exercise will allow you to target your muscles from all angles, thus producing the "overload" effect, which signals your body to develop muscle.

While bodybuilders do their exercises in descending order (from the largest to the smallest muscle group), Walkshapers vary their routines. As long as you reach your quota of miles and repetitions, you can work your body parts in any order, and can even split up routines if you wish. For example, you needn't do all of the Set #1 exercises for all body parts before you move on and do all of the Set #2 exercises, and so forth.

The beginner profile for walking and body sculpting will serve you well for your six-week goals. It orders the muscle groups as biceps (easy), chest (hard), triceps (easy), shoulders (hard), and upper back (hard).

May I Change the Order?

Absolutely. I want you to create an exercise routine that works for you so you'll be motivated to do it. If you're more comfortable working your chest first, then by all means do so. It's important, however, not combine your lower-body routines with upper-body ones, since this would make some of your muscles work two days in a row without allowing them time to rest and recuperate. Also, mixing routines makes it difficult to keep track of your exercises.

If you can't complete a set of repetitions, don't give up; just postpone. Resume your basic Pump 'N Walk until you regain your composure. Then as soon as you're ready, make the transition back to the Body-Parts Routine by counting out 1, 2, 3, ready, set, start. Use the same "transition walk" between the sets of routines; as you finish each set, practice the Pump 'N Walk routine before continuing to the next set. If you need more recuperation time, continue with the Pump 'N Walk until you've regained your strength, then go on to the next set.

Of course, if you begin to suffer any physical distress, nausea, dizziness, or severe breathlessness while exercising, bring yourself down to a slow walk, then rest completely. Consult a physician.

Biceps and Forearms

Fig. 9–1 • Gary demonstrates First Position Upright Row

As its name suggests, the biceps is a two-headed muscle. Its basic function is to lift and curl the arm and turn the wrist upward. Another muscle group, the triceps, straightens the arm and turns the wrist downward.

When you're Walkshaping, your biceps bend and hold your arms at a 90-degree angle; when you're just walking and swinging your arms, your biceps don't do nearly as much work. But for the biceps to be a powerful and shapely muscle, it requires a curling exercise as well. The Biceps Curl, a rhythmic arm motion, complements the leg action used in walking. (Advanced walkers should substitute it for the basic Arm Pump.)

Forearms consist of two major muscles: the flexors, which curl the palm toward your wrist, and the extensors, which curl the knuckles up and back. The forearms are exercised indirectly through the rest of the arm exercises.

Practice Levels

Level I should do 5–12 repetitions with each arm (or 10–24 total); Level II: 12–15; Level III: 15–20; Level IV: 21–25; and Level V: 25–30.

Biceps Set #1: Hammer Curl (single or double arm) (Figs. 9–2, 3)

This exercise strengthens and shapes the entire biceps muscle as well as the sides of your forearm muscles. The movement is the same whether you're walking in place or on the move.

START • Turn your loosely clenched fists to the palms-in (facing each other) position, as if you were holding a hammer in each hand. Hang your arms straight down by your sides.

MOVE • *Single Arm:* Keep your elbows tucked in by your sides, and curl your left fist up toward your shoulder. At the top of the arc, flex or squeeze your biceps muscle. Now lower your forearm until it is back by your side. Stretch out your biceps muscle fully at the end of the curl-down, being careful not to lock your elbow. When you are midway through the left curl-down, start the right-arm curl. *Double Arm:* Curl up both arms as you take two steps. Then curl down both arms on the next step.

STEP ACCOMPANIMENTS • With Single Arm Biceps Curls, practice either Two- or Three-Count Steps. With Double Arm Biceps Curls, practice Three-Count Steps. *Two-Count:* Take a left step as you curl up your

Fig. 9–2 • Carlo demonstrates Biceps Set #1—Hammer Curl In Place

Fig. 9–3 • Biceps Set #1—Hammer Curl On the Move

Fig. 9–4 • Biceps Set #2—Palm-Up Curl

Fig. 9–5 • Biceps Set #2—Palm-Up Curl, with weights

right arm, then a right step as you curl up your left arm. *Three-Count:* Take a left and a right step as you curl up your right arm, then a left step as you curl it down. Take a right and a left step as you curl up your left arm, and a right step as you curl it down.

REMEMBER • Tighten your stomach muscles by holding them in. Keep your elbows pressed to your waist to prevent your body from rocking back and forth as you curl and walk. If you can't, you're using too heavy a weight or resistance load; take it down a notch or two before continuing. As you alternate Arm Curls and Strides or Leg Lifts, work rhythmically to synchronize your arm and leg movements with your breathing and counting.

DEVICES • *Cords:* Anchor the cord at your waist or behind your back, and wrap it around your elbow. Be sure to lower your weights slowly, taking advantage of the "negative resistance." Stretching out the cord creates "positive resistance." *Poles:* Do not plant the poles on the ground. Instead, pump them like hand weights, and shorten the sticks if necessary.

TRANSITION • Between this set and the next, do a set of 12–25 Bent Arm Pump 'N Walk steps. Now go on to Set #2 of Biceps, or to Set #1 of the Chest Routines.

Biceps Set #2: Palm-Up Curl (single or double arm) (Fig. 9-4)

This is another exercise to shape the entire biceps muscle and forearm.

START • Hang your arms by your sides with elbows slightly bent and fists clenched loosely in the palms-up position.

MOVE • Curl up your right arm until your fist reaches shoulder height. Turn your fist outward for extra biceps work. Be sure to raise and lower your arm with full muscle control. Lower your left arm to the starting position and begin your right. As your arm curls down, stretch the biceps muscle fully, but without locking your elbow joint.

STEP ACCOMPANIMENTS • Do Leg Lifts, Stride Stretch Steps, or Quick Steps. Practice Two- or Three-Count Steps as you did in Biceps Set #1.

DEVICES • *Walking Sticks or Poles:* Beginners: Shorten poles or do Double Arm Curls with both sticks held horizontally. *Weights/Cords:* Hold weights and stretch cords loosely in your fists and pump from waist to shoulder level. (Fig. 9–5)

TRANSITION • Do 25 reps of Bent Arm Pump 'N Walk steps. Next, go either to Biceps Set #3 or Sets #1–2 of the Chest Routines.

Biceps Set #3: Palm-Down Curl (single or double arm) (Fig. 9–6)

Fig. 9–6 • Biceps Set #3—Palm-Down Curl

This exercise strengthens and shapes the entire biceps muscle and provides an excellent forearm workout.

START • Hold your arms by your sides with the elbows slightly bent and your fists turned to the palms-down position.

MOVE • Curl your left arm up until your fist is at shoulder height and your palm is forward. Flex your left biceps muscle at the peak of the movement. Curl your left arm down, stretching your biceps muscle without locking your elbow. As you do so, begin curling up your right arm. Hold your elbows into your body lightly as you alternate curling your right and left arms.

STEP ACCOMPANIMENTS • Use Leg Lifts, Stride Stretch Steps, and Quick Steps with the Two- or Three-Count Step. *Single Arm:* Take a left step while curling up your right arm, then a right step while curling up your left arm. *Double Arm:* Take a left and right step curling up and a left step curling down. Start the next repetition with a right step.

DEVICES • *Poles:* Use shortened walking sticks, or do Double Arm Curls with horizontal sticks. Grip the sticks with your thumbs over fingers and your fists facing palms down.

TRANSITION • Do 25 repetitions of the Pump 'N Walk, then proceed either to Biceps Set #4 or to Sets #1–3 of the Chest Routines.

Biceps Set #4: Palm-Out Curl (single arm) (Figs. 9-7 through 9-10)

Fig. 9–7 • Biceps Set #4—Palm-Out Curl: First Position, Palms Out

This exercise strengthens and adds definition to the biceps and forearm. It takes advantage of a full wrist turn to train the biceps muscle.

START • Hold your fists by your sides, palms-down and facing away from your body.

MOVE • Rotate your forearm to curl your right arm, and as you do, start to turn your fist clockwise: starting from the palm-away position, turn palm-down, continue palm-in, and finish in the palm-up position. Reverse this movement on the downward motion, turning your fist counterclockwise until it returns to the original palm-away position. Before completing the arc, begin curling up your left arm. Keep your wrist aligned with your forearm (as opposed to "breaking the line" by bending at the wrist).

STEP ACCOMPANIMENTS • Because the arm movement in this exercise is more complex, do a Three-Count, rather than a Two-Count, Step.

Fig. 9–8 • Biceps Set #4—Palm-Out Curl: Second Position, Palms Down

Fig. 9–9 • Biceps Set #4—Palm-Out Curl: Third Position, Palms Up

Fig. 9–10 • Biceps Set #4—Palm-Out Curl: Final Position, Palms Out

Start with your feet side by side and hip-width apart, or from the Stride Stretch Step with your right foot forward. *Step #1:* Take a left step as you turn your right fist clockwise and curl up to the palm-in position. *Step #2:* Take a right step as you turn your right fist counter-clockwise to curl down to the palm-away position. *Step #3:* Take a left step as you curl down your right arm and begin to curl up your left arm.

DEVICES • *Poles:* Do the Biceps Curl with doubled-up poles that are either collapsed or extended.

TRANSITION • Do 25 repetitions of the Pump 'N Walk. Then go to Biceps Set #5 or to Chest Sets #1–4.

Biceps Set #5: Arm Curl (Fig. 9–11)

A. Double Arm Curl

Fig. 9–11 • Biceps Set #5—Double Arm Curls, Palms Up

This exercise lets you strengthen and shape your biceps and forearms by curling more slowly and with more weight or resistance. Involve the muscles of your shoulders and upper back by raising your arms to shoulder height before curling them.

START • With your feet hip-width apart (or closer, to shoulder-width apart, if you're pumping a heavy weight) and your arms by your sides, bend your elbows slightly, turn your fists palms-up, and loosely clench your fists.

MOVE • Curl up both arms simultaneously, taking Three-Count Steps to complete each curl-up and curl-down. *Count 1:* Take a left step and begin to curl. *Count 2:* Right step as fists reach shoulder height, then curl down again. *Count 3:* Left step as arms reach the starting position. Repeat the movement, this time beginning with a right step. You'll start the third repetition on the left foot.

REMEMBER • With Three-Count-Step cycle, alternate the starting feet as you begin each repetition. This will allow you to curl more slowly and to concentrate on flexing and stretching your biceps. Also, by curling up both arms together it exerts your upper body more, increasing your calorie burn.

STEP ACCOMPANIMENTS • Do either the Three- or Five-Count Steps with high and low Leg Lifts, Quick Steps, or Stride Stretch Steps.

Fig. 9–12 • Biceps Set #5—Double Arm Curls, with poles gripped together

Alternatively, the Lunge Step allows you to slow down the pace of the Double Arm Biceps Curl even more.

The Five-Count-Step Double Biceps Curl goes as follows: start your first cycle on your left foot. Take a left, a right, and then another left step as you curl up your arms to your chest, then a right and a left step as you control them down. Repeat the cycle starting on your right foot, then again beginning on your left step.

DEVICES • *Poles:* Poles work well for this and most other Double Arm Pump Routines. Use a narrow or wide grip to hold them horizontally (Fig. 9–12). *Weights:* Dumbbells can be pushed together to simulate long bar pumps. *Cords:* Wrap cords once around the hips and below the buttocks.

TRANSITION • Do 25 repetitions of the Pump 'N Walk, then go to either Biceps Set #5B, if you choose more biceps work, or Sets #1–5 of the Chest Routines.

B. Raised Arm Curl

This exercise allows you to add resistance to your Double Arm Curls by curling the weight further from your body. It also strengthens your shoulder muscles.

START • With your arms bent and elbows at at chest height, extend your arms and turn your fists to palms-up.

MOVE • Keep elbows at chest height as you curl your arms up to shoulder height. Turn your fists out at the top and squeeze your biceps before lowering your arms again.

STEP ACCOMPANIMENT • Use Three-Count Steps with low Leg Lifts and Quick Steps. This is the first example of the arms high, legs low principle: the more your arms are working against gravity, the more you should reduce the workload from your legs. Use low and short steps. This will help prevent exhaustion.

TRANSITION • Do 25 repetitions of the Pump 'N Walk, then go to either Biceps Set #5C or to Chest Sets #1–5.

C. Concentration Curl
Lower-Range Curls (Fig. 9–13)

START • Hang your arms by your sides with your elbows tucked in and your fists palms-up.

MOVE • Curl your arms up 45 degrees until your fist is at chest height. Squeeze your biceps, then curl your arms back down. Do 25–100 repetitions of the Lower-Range Curls.

Upper-Range Curls (Fig. 9–14)

START • Bend your arms to 90 degrees, and tuck in your elbows by your sides.

MOVE • Curl your arms up 45 degrees to shoulder height. Squeeze your biceps. Curl your arms back down again. Do 25–100 repetitions of the Upper-Range Curls.

If you feel energetic during your final sets, try to pump up your biceps fully with a short-range Concentration Curl. This is a curl of 10–45 degrees, done for 50–100 repetitions. It is designed to work on the peak, or highest point, of your biceps. The shorter range allows you to pump up your biceps without lifting your arm through a full range of motion. Start the curl by bending your arm at a 45-degree angle instead of a 90-degree angle, and then returning to a 45-degree angle when you curl down. Save these curls for the end of the Biceps Routine.

TRANSITION • While walking, you can make the transition smoothly from the faster gait of your concentrated Biceps Routine by resuming the Single Bent Elbow-High Arm Pump and low Leg Lift. Do 25 repetitions of the Bent Arm Pump 'N Walk, then go to Sets #1–5 of the Chest Routine.

Chest Routines

Ordinarily, training the chest is difficult when you're standing (most bodybuilders do their chest work while lying on their backs), but my routines compensate for this by having you do more repetitions with lighter weights. These routines also work your chest muscles through a greater range of motion, and graduate you from single- to double-arm work as soon as you are strong enough.

Fig. 9–13 • Biceps Set #5C—Lower-Range Concentration Curls, both arms shown at a short (10–45 degree) range of motion

Fig. 9–14 • Biceps Set #5C—Upper Range Concentration Curls

Fig. 9–15 • Chest Set #1A—Bent Arm Cross-Over Pumps, left to right side

Practice Levels

Level I should do 5–12 repetitions for each arm (or 10–24 total); Level II: 12–15; Level III: 15–20; Level IV: 21–25; and Level V: 25–30.

Chest Set #1: Cross-Over Arm Pump

The three versions of this exercise work the whole chest.

A. Bent Arm Cross-Over (Fig. 9–15)

START • Bend both arms at a 90-degree angle, with your elbows at your sides and your fists palms-up.

MOVE • Pump your right arm diagonally across your chest until your fist reaches the top of the left side of your head, behind your left ear. Turn your right fist counterclockwise as you pump across so that the palm is facing away from your body at the top of the movement. As you pump your right arm back down, pump your left arm across to your right ear. Turn your left fist clockwise. Take a left step as you pump your right arm across and a right step as you pump your left arm across.

STEP ACCOMPANIMENTS • Use the Two-Count-Step method with low to medium-high Leg Lifts and medium- to long-length Strides. Take a left step as you pump your right arm across your chest to your left ear, then a right step as you pump your left arm across your chest to your right ear.

DEVICES • *Poles:* Beginners: shorten your poles. *Cords:* Stretch cords from the waist or the feet.

TRANSITION • Do 12–25 repetitions of the Pump 'N Walk. Then go to either the Straight Arm Cross-Overs or to Chest Set #2 or Set #1 of the Triceps Routine.

B. Straight Arm Cross-Over (Fig. 9-16)

This exercise works the pectoral muscles. You can also do the same Cross-Over Pumps with each arm bent slightly at the elbow. This will add more resistance to your exercise because your arm is being moved away from your chest in a greater arc.

START • Hang your arms by your sides with elbows slightly bent and fists palms-in.

MOVE • Keeping your arm straight, pump your right arm diagonally across your chest to the height of your left ear, turning your fist counterclockwise so your palm faces out. As you pump your right arm back down to the starting position, begin pumping your left arm diagonally across to your right ear.

STEP ACCOMPANIMENTS • Use the Two-Count-Step method with low to medium-high Leg Lifts and medium- to long-length Strides. Take a left step as you pump your right arm across your chest to your left ear, then a right step as you pump your left arm across your chest to your right ear.

DEVICES • *Poles:* Beginners: shorten your poles. *Cords:* Stretch cords from the waist or the feet.

Fig. 9–16 • Chest Set #1B—Straight Arm Cross-Over Pumps

Fig. 9–17 • Chest Set #1C—Double Arm Cross-Over Pumps: First Position, fists stacked by side

TRANSITION • Do 12–25 repetitions of the Pump 'N Walk. Then go to either the Double Arm Cross-Overs or to Chest Set #2, or to Set #1 of the Triceps Routine.

C. Double Arm Cross-Over (Figs. 9–17, 18)

This version is for advanced walkers who need more resistance work. It resembles a golfer's swing.

START • Cross your left arm over your body, placing your left fist by your right hip. Both of your fists should now be at your right side, palms-in. Stack your right fist on top of your left thumbs-side-up. To keep them moving together, you can interlace the left pinkie and right index finger, or place them side by side, with their knuckles facing each other and pressed together.

MOVE • Hold your fists together and pump them diagonally from your right hip up across your body until they reach behind your left ear. Then pump them down again to your right side. As you reach this position, press your arms back until they're behind the line of your hip—this gives an extra squeeze to your pectoral muscles. Be sure to lift the elbow on your pumping side to head height; you'll feel the work shifting from your shoulders to your chest muscles. Repeat 12–25 times. Then move your arms to your left side and stack your right fist over your left. Pump your arms from your left hip diagonally up to your right ear. Repeat 12–25 times.

STEP ACCOMPANIMENTS • *In Place:* Use Two-Count Steps with low Leg Lifts and Quick Steps. *On the Move:* Use medium to long Strides. Take a left step as you raise your arms from your right hip to your left ear, then a right step as you lower them back down from the left ear to the right hip. Reverse the movements for the left side.

Fig. 9–18 • Chest Set #1C— Double Arm Cross-Over Pumps: Second Position, fists between shoulder and ear

DEVICES • *Poles:* Advanced walkers: hold your pole grips side by side. *Cords:* Double up and pump cords from either side of your waist. *Weights:* Hold weights side by side, and pump together.

TRANSITION • Do 12–25 repetitions of the Pump 'N Walk. Then go to Chest Set #2, or to Triceps Set #1.

Chest Set #2: Fly Pump with Twist

This exercise works the lower pectorals.

START • Bend your arms and raise them in front of you. Bring your elbows and wrists together, palms-back and in line with your chin (Fig. 9–19).

MOVE • Keeping both arms bent at a 90-degree angle, move them outward so that they extend away from your shoulders and your fists are in line with your ears on either side of your head, palms-out (Fig. 9–20). Your arms form two V's on either side of your body. Pump your arms back down across your chest until your elbows and wrists meet with your fists palms-in. As you turn your fists to face your chest (palms-back), squeeze your pectoral muscles.

STEP ACCOMPANIMENTS • Do low Leg Lifts and medium Strides. Use a Three-Count Step, alternating the left or right foot to begin each three-count cycle. The first cycle begins with a left step: as your fists come together, exhale and take a left step as your arms extend up and out. Then take a right and a left step as your fists come together. Start the next repetition on the right foot, stepping as your fists move to the V position.

Fig. 9–19 • Chest Set #2—Fly Pump with Twist: First Position; fists chin-to head-height, palms-in, and elbows together

Fig. 9–20 • Chest Set #2—Fly Pump with Twist: Second Position, arms back

Fig. 9–21 • Chest Set #2—Fly Pump with Scissor Pumps: fists cross over instead of going to chin, with weights

DEVICES • Weights, poles, and cords all go well with this exercise. *Cords:* Pull cords from a waist or foot anchor. *Poles:* Grip poles, one in each hand.

VARIATION • *Fly with Scissor Pumps:* For advanced walkers: For maximum pectoral contraction, let your fists meet, pass each other, and cross over in a scissors motion. Feel the extra flex in your chest muscles. Reverse this sweeping arc motion and return your arms to the original position (Fig. 9–21).

TRANSITION • Do 25 repetitions of the Pump 'N Walk, then go either to Chest Set #3 or to Triceps Sets #1–2.

Chest Set #3: Press-Out (double arm)

This exercise works the entire chest area. It's the walking version of bench presses.

START • Bend your arms and bring both fists to your chest with fists bent back palms-front. Your elbows should point out from your chest (Fig. 9–22).

MOVE • Press your fists and arms straight forward until they are extended away from your chest, the elbows slightly bent. When your arms are extended in front of your chest, turn your fists inward to palms-up if you are not using poles (Fig. 9–23).

STEP ACCOMPANIMENTS • Use Three-Count medium-length Strides or low to medium-high Leg Lifts. Take a left and a right step as you push out your arms from your chest. Take a left step when you bring your arms back to your chest. Start the three-step cycle again, this time on the right foot.

DEVICES • *Cords:* Wrap or anchor the cords to your waist or around your back. *Poles:* Double up your poles and turn them horizontally.

VARIATIONS • Concentrate on upper and lower pectoral muscles by starting the movement with your fists at a higher or lower chest position. *Advanced walker:* press up (instead of out) at a 45-degree angle (Fig. 9–24) to add greater work to your upper pectorals. This movement most closely simulates the work of an incline press.

Fig. 9–22 • Chest Set #3—Double Arm Press-Out: First Position; fists to chest, palms-out, knuckles up

Fig. 9–23 • Chest Set #3—Double Arm Press-Out: Second Position; arms extended, elbows slightly bent, fists extended parallel in front of your chest, palms-down

Fig. 9–24 • Britt demonstrates Chest Set #3—Press-Up at an angle

TRANSITION • Do 25 repetitions of the Pump 'N Walk, then go either to Chest Set #4 or to Triceps Sets #1–3.

Chest Set #4: Elbow Squeeze (double arm)

This exercise works the inner pectoral muscles. It also works your shoulders.

START • Start with your wrists and elbows touching in front of your chest. Your fists are at chin level, with the palms facing toward you.

MOVE • Raise your elbows so that they are pointing out at ear level and your arms are parallel to the ground (Fig. 9–25). Your fists should be palms-down and pulled apart 3–5 inches, with the knuckles facing each other. Push your arms down. Squeeze your pectoral muscles as you press your elbows together, and turn your fists inward so they are touching again, with the palms facing toward you (Fig. 9–26).

REMEMBER • Keep your fists at chin level throughout this entire routine.

STEP ACCOMPANIMENTS • Use a medium to long Stride or a low to medium Leg Lift with Three- and Five-Count Steps. Take a left step

Fig. 9–25 • Alexa demonstrates Chest Set #4—Elbow Squeeze: First Position; arms open, fists to top of head, elbows and shoulders high, palms facing forward

Fig. 9–26 • Chest Set #4—Elbow Squeeze: Second Position; elbows and fists together in front of chest, pectorals squeezed, palms facing back

Fig. 9–27 • Close-up of upper torso: stacking your fists one on top of the other. Left fist at chest height; right fist above it, at chin height.

as you raise your elbows to ear height, then a right and a left step as you lower your arms and squeeze your elbows together. Take a right step to begin the next repetition cycle.

DEVICES • *Poles:* Use single-arm grip. Punctuate the beginning and end of the routine with a double pole plant, then raise your grips, fists together palms-back. Use a Five-Count Step.

TRANSITION • Do 25 repetitions of the Pump 'N Walk, then go either to Chest Set #5 or to Triceps Sets #1–4.

Chest Set #5: Fist Turn (or Double Arm Scissor)

This exercise develops the whole chest area but places special emphasis on the outer and inner areas of the pectoral muscles.

START • Extend your arms in front of you and stack your fists, right atop left. Raise your elbows and extend them outward. Rotate both fists to the right. Raise your fists 6 inches higher, so the right one is in line with your chin and the left one is in line with your chest (Fig. 9–27).

MOVE • Keep your fists apart, one above the other, as you rotate both your right and left arms in a clockwise motion, as if you were holding a pole with both hands and turning it. Rotate only to the point where your left fist is directly over your right fist (Fig. 9–28). Both palms should be facing left and should be the same distance apart as they were when you started. Now rotate your arms counterclockwise to reverse the movement, turning your fists back again through your starting palms-down position, and continuing until your right fist is above your left fist. Both palms should be facing the right side of your body.

STEP ACCOMPANIMENTS • Use a Two- or Three-Count Step with medium Leg Lifts and Strides. Take the left step as you twist your fists clockwise toward your left side to palms facing left. Take your right step as you twist your fists counterclockwise to palms facing right.

DEVICES • *Poles:* Walking poles are particularly useful in performing this exercise. Because you can hold on to them and keep your arms equidistant, they help you to execute the twisting motion by creating resistance for your arm and chest muscles (Fig. 9–29). *Cords:* You'll have to change to a scissors movement when using the cords. Raise your fists to chest height with palms down, but do not stack them. Take a left step and cross the right fist over the left until it's even with

Fig. 9–28 • Closer in on fists themselves after rotation, left fist over right fist

Fig. 9–29 • Katia demonstrates Chest Set #5—Fist Turns, with ski poles

Fig. 9–30 • Chest Set #5—Fist Turns, with cords: use Special Scissors Action arm movement when using the stretch cords. SHOWN: Right fist passing over left fist.

your left shoulder. At the same time, move your right fist in a parallel movement to your right shoulder. Take a right step as you raise and cross your left fist over your right one (Fig. 9–30).

TRANSITION • Do 25 repetitions of the Pump 'N Walk. Then go either to Chest Set #6 or to Triceps Sets #1–5.

Chest Set #6: Pull-Over Pump (double arm)

This bonus set of exercises is designed to develop your chest muscles and to expand your rib cage. The chest-muscles group is so large that you can do extra sets of exercise without tiring.

START • With arms bent and elbows out, lay your fists against your stomach, touching your belly button.

MOVE • Holding your fists together, pump your arms up in an arc over your head until your fists are behind your head and turned palms-inward (Fig. 9–31). Breathe in as you move them up, to expand your rib cage. As you pump, extend and straighten your arms. Make sure that your elbows never lock: keep them bent at 120-degree angles. Now pump your arms back down to your waist, tracing the same sweeping arc with your fists, which turn outward as they pass the hip joint (Fig. 9–32). Squeeze down on your upper chest as you breathe out.

REMEMBER • Keep your arms close to your body and resist the urge to let your back arch as you raise your arms.

STEP ACCOMPANIMENTS • Low Leg Lifts and medium to long Strides work best with this exercise. Do a Two- or Five-Count Step, taking a left (or a left-right-left) step as you pump up, then a right (or a right and a left) step as you pump down. You're ready to begin the next repetition on the right step.

DEVICES • *Weights/Cords:* Weights offer the best resistance for this movement, but cords, anchored to your waist or to the ground, will also work. While your palms face each other when you're freehanded or using weights, if you're using poles or cords they should face down instead.

TRANSITION • Do 25 repetitions of the Pump 'N Walk. Then go to Sets #1–5 of the Triceps Routines.

Fig. 9–31 • Chest Set #6—Pull-Over Pump: First Position; fists side by side, palms facing one another, elbows extending outward

Fig. 9–32 • Chest Set #6—Pull-Over Pump: Second position; Raise your arms overhead, bring fists together, and turn them inward. SHOWN: Mouth opening for inhale.

Fig. 9–33 • Gary demonstrates Triceps Set #2—Elbow-Back-of-Hip Extension

Triceps Routines (Fig. 9-33)

Alternate these sets with the biceps routines—e.g., first biceps set, first triceps set, second biceps set, second triceps set, etc. Or intersperse them with the more vigorous shoulder, chest, and upper-back routines.

As the name implies, the triceps muscle is a three-headed muscle group, which is larger than the biceps. Both the triceps and the biceps are used when you straighten your arm. The muscle you train depends on which elbow position and forearm angle you use in your arm movements. To work the triceps, focus on the straightening movement of your arm as opposed to the bending movement. Therefore, to shape your triceps, choose an exercise such as the Elbow-Back-of-Hip Extension or the Elbow-Up Extension, where the elbow joint is higher than your forearm at the beginning of the movement. For balance, make sure that you work the triceps at least as much as, if not more than, the biceps muscles.

Practice Levels

Level I should do 5–12 repetitions with each arm (or 10–24 total); Level II: 12–15; Level III: 15–20; Level IV: 21–25; and Level V: 25–30.

Triceps Set #1: Elbow-Down Extension (or Elbow-Down Triceps Press)

START • Place your arms by your sides and bend them at a 90-degree angle. Keep your elbows tucked in to your sides and your fists facing your body.

MOVE • Straighten your left arm down and backward, keeping it in line with your body. As you do, turn your left wrist clockwise until the arm is fully extended and your elbow is straight but not locked. Feel your left triceps muscles flexing as you turn your left fist out to the palm-away position (Fig. 9–34). Bend your left arm back up to its starting position as you begin to straighten your right arm back. Feel your right triceps flex as you turn your right fist counterclockwise to the palms-away position.

STEP ACCOMPANIMENT • Use medium to high Strides and Leg Lifts in a Two-Count Step. Take a left step as you straighten your left arm back and bend your right arm up, then a right step as you straighten your right arm back and bend your left arm up.

REMEMBER • Keep your elbows close to your body throughout the movement.

VARIATIONS • Once single-arm Extensions become too easy for you, proceed to double-arm Extensions. Extend both arms back simultaneously as you straighten them. Turn both fists and arms away from your body to further work your triceps.

DEVICES • *Cords:* Wrap cords around the back of your neck. *Poles:* Do single-arm pole pumps. It is difficult to double up your walking poles for this and other double-arm triceps exercises, except those that are done at head level.

TRANSITION • Do 12–25 repetitions of the Pump 'N Walk, then go either to Triceps Set #2 or Shoulders Routines Set #1.

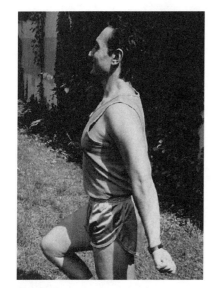

Fig. 9–34 • Carlo demonstrates Triceps Set #1—Elbow-Down Extension: Second Position; 90-degree bend, left arm extended, elbows by hip joints

Triceps Set #2: Elbow-Back-of-Hip Joint Extension (or Triceps Push-Back) (single arm)

START • Bend both arms at a 90-degree angle with your fists palms-down (palms-in if using walking poles) and your elbows tucked into your body (Fig. 9–35).

MOVE • Alternately push each arm back until the elbow is behind the line of your hip. Turn your left fist clockwise so that your palm faces away from your body. Feel the flex of your left triceps muscle. Bend your left arm forward again to its front starting position. As you do, extend your right arm back and straighten it out. Turn your right fist counterclockwise as you flex your triceps muscles.

REMEMBER • Keep your arms close to the sides of your body, with the elbows tucked in. Want a sure-fire way to know which Arm Pumps go with which steps? Just remember this simple rule: Single Arm Pumps done below the shoulder can be accompanied by higher Leg Lifts and longer Strides. If you're doing Double Arm Pumps and Pumps above the shoulder, use medium to high Lifts and shorter Strides.

STEP ACCOMPANIMENTS • Use medium to long Stride Stretch Steps and medium to high Leg Lifts. Practice Two- or Four-Count Steps. Take a

Fig. 9–35 • Britt demonstrates Triceps Set #2—Elbow-Back-of-Hip Joint Extension. First Position: left arm bent to 90 degrees. Second Position: right arm extension.

Fig. 9–36 • Triceps Set #2—Elbow-Back-of-Hip Joint Extension: elbows behind, fists in line with back of buttocks/hips, with devices

Fig. 9–37 • Triceps Set #3—Fists Behind Hipline Arm Extension: First Position

left step, and extend your left arm back as you bring your right arm forward. Then take a right step, and extend your right arm back as you bring your left arm forward (Fig. 9–36).

VARIATIONS • Once single-arm sets become too easy, practice this as a double-arm set and use a Two- or Three-Count Step.

TRANSITION • Do 12–25 Pump 'N Walk steps and then go either to Triceps Set #3 or to Shoulders Sets #1–2.

Triceps Sets #3: Fists Behind Hipline Arm Extension

Because you are working against gravity, this exercise places more of a workload on the triceps muscle.

START • Bend both arms at a 90-degree angle and push them back until your fists are just behind the lines of your hips and your elbow joints are behind the line of your body. Turn your fists to the palms-down or palms-in position (Fig. 9–37).

MOVE • Extend your left arm back while turning your left fist clockwise to palm-out. Feel your left triceps muscle flex. Reverse the movement and return left arm to starting position. As you do so, extend and straighten your right arm back, turning your wrist counterclockwise to palm-out. Flex your right triceps muscle, and reverse the movement to return your right arm to the starting position.

STEP ACCOMPANIMENT • Use a Two-Count (or Four-Count) Step with medium to long Strides or Leg Lifts. *Two-Count Step:* Take a left and then a right step as you extend and straighten your left arm back out and bend your right arm forward. Take a left and then a right step as you extend and straighten your right arm out and bend your left arm forward.

Five-Count Step: Take a left, a right, and a left step as you extend your left arm back, then a right and a left step as you bend your left arm forward. Take a right, a left, and a right step as you extend your right arm back, then a left and right step as you bend your right arm forward. Begin the next Five-Count-Step cycle with the right foot.

REMEMBER • Keep your elbows as close to your body as you can.

DEVICES • *Cords:* If you have trouble attaching your cords to your waist or to the floor, hold one end of the cord by your waist using your left hand. With your right hand, pull and hold the other end of the cord down by your right side as you bend and extend your right arm, doing the whole set of repetitions on your right side. Change sides.

TRANSITION • Do 25 reps of the Pump 'N Walk and then go either to Triceps Set #4 or to Shoulders Sets #1–3.

Triceps Set #4: Side Cross Extension

Fig. 9–38 • Avis demonstrates Triceps Set #4—Side Cross Extension: right arm extended out with right step

This exercise shapes and strengthens the inner head of the triceps muscle.

START • Bend both arms to a 90-degree angle with palms-down, then cross them in front of your body so your right fist is over your left fist (Fig. 9–38).

MOVE • Extend and straighten your left arm down to your left side and away from your body. Continue pressing the arm back as you turn your fist clockwise to palm-back-and-away, flexing your left triceps. As you bend your left arm back into place, begin to extend and straighten your right arm. Repeat, using your right arm.

REMEMBER • Don't lean over. Keep your torso erect while performing the exercise.

STEP ACCOMPANIMENT • Use the Two-Count (or Five-Count) Step with medium to long Strides and low to medium Leg Lifts.

Two-Count Steps: Take a left step as you extend your left arm down and bend your right arm forward. Take a right step as you extend your right arm down and bend your left arm forward.

Five-Count Steps: Take a left, a right, and a left step as you extend your left arm down. Take a right and a left step as you bend your left arm forward. Take a right, a left, and a right step as you extend your right arm down and a left and right step as you bend your right arm forward. Begin the next Five-Count-Step cycle with the right foot.

DEVICES • *Cords:* Double-wrap the cords around your waist and pull them away, alternating between the left and right sides of your body. *Poles:* Grip poles with palms-in.

TRANSITION • Do 25 reps of the Pump 'N Walk. Then go either to Triceps Set #5 or to Shoulders Sets #1–4.

Triceps Set #5: Elbows-Up Extension (single or double arm)

START • Bend both arms at a 90-degree angle and raise your elbows to shoulder-height (Position 1: Easier Fig. 9–39) or overhead (Position 2: More Difficult Fig. 9–40). Turn fists to palms-back.

MOVE • Extend and straighten one or both arms from Position 1—or from Position 2—straight up over your head. As you extend your arm, turn your fist out; the right fist will turn counterclockwise, and the left fist will turn clockwise. As you bend your right arm back into place, begin to extend and straighten your left arm straight out (Position 1) or straight up (Position 2). Flex your triceps in the final extended position. This exercise can also be done as a double-arm move.

STEP ACCOMPANIMENT • Use low to medium Leg Lifts and short to medium Strides in a Two- or Three-Count Step.

Two-Count (single-arm): Take a left step as you extend your right arm out (or up). Take a right step as you extend your left arm up (or out).

Three-Count: Take a left and a right step as you extend both your arms and turn out your fists. Take a left step, and bend your arms back. Repeat the exercise starting with a right step.

Fig. 9–39 • Triceps Set #5—Elbows-Up Extension: First Position (Easier); elbows raised shoulder-high and arms extended out

Fig. 9–40 • Triceps Set #5—Elbows-Up Extension: Second Position (More Difficult); elbows raised to head-height and arms extended overhead

DEVICES • *Cords:* From waist level, stretch your cords until your fists are at head height or your wrists are bent. *Poles:* Use individual poles for the single-arm moves and doubled-up poles for the double arm.

TRANSITION • Do 25 reps of the Pump 'N Walk, then go to Shoulders Routines Set #5.

Shoulders Routines

Whenever you raise your arms, you use your shoulder muscles. The exercises in this section use the Double-Arm Pump, because this movement provides the additional resistance needed to train the shoulders' large muscle group: the deltoids and trapezius. The deltoids (or delts), like the triceps, are a three-headed muscle group. The trapezius (or traps) are part of the shoulders, although they also belong to the upper back as well. You will exercise your traps every time you shrug your shoulders. Your traps assist your deltoids when you raise your arms (especially when you raise both arms together from below your shoulders). The action of shrugging helps you to disengage the delts, thereby shifting the workload onto the traps.

When you raise your arms above your shoulders in a press, you use your delts more than your traps. But when using Walkshaping's basic Bent Arm Pumps, you train the shoulders, the triceps, and the chest and upper back muscles since you are moving your arms horizontally as well as up and down.

The following routines will isolate your shoulder muscles. By straightening your arms and raising them up and down, you're working against gravity more than you would if you were doing the same exercise with arms bent. A straightened arm offers more weight or resistance, because the further the weight is from the working joint or muscle, the heavier it feels and the greater the distance you have to move it.

Shoulders Set #1: Front Lateral (single and double arm) (Fig. 9–41)

This exercise develops and shapes the shoulders, especially the anterior (front) deltoids. Do it with Single Arm Pumps at the beginning, and Double Arm Pumps later.

Fig. 9–41 • Shoulders Set #1—Front Lateral (single or double arm): palms-down, left arm held by side, right arm raised

START • Hold your arms out, with your fists turned so that your palms face down.

MOVE • *Single-Arm Lateral:* Alternate right and left Arm Raises. Start to raise your right arm as your left is being lowered, and your left arm as your right is being lowered. *Double-Arm Lateral:* With your elbows slightly bent, raise your arms to shoulder height, keeping them parallel to the ground. You should look like you're sleepwalking. Feel the flex in your delts before slowly lowering your arms, controlling the weight all the way down.

REMEMBER • Exhale when you raise your arms and inhale when you lower them. Keep your palms facing down and your shoulders pressed down.

STEP ACCOMPANIMENTS • Use low to medium-height Leg Lifts and medium-length Strides. Use a Two-Count with Single Arm Raises and a Three-Count with Double Arm Raises.

   Two-Count Step: Take a left step as you raise your right arm and a right step as you raise your left arm.

   Three-Count Step: Take a left and a right step as you raise both arms, then another left step as you lower them. Start the next repetition with a right step.

DEVICES • *Cords:* Anchor cords under your step-bench or to your waist.

TRANSITION • Do 12–25 reps of the Pump 'N Walk. Then go either to Shoulders Set #2 or to Upper Back Set #1.

Shoulders Set #2: Side Lateral (single or double arm)

This exercise shapes all three heads of the deltoid, especially the middle one. Start with Single Arm Side Laterals and advance to Double Arm Side Laterals. This exercise is most comfortable when done with double arms and the Three-Count Step. You look like a bird flapping its wings in slow motion.

START • Hold your arms in front of your body slightly, with fists palms-in and side by side.

MOVE • Pump up by raising your arm(s) up and out until your fist(s) are shoulder to ear height (Fig. 9–42). As you reach the top, turn your fist(s) out and your elbow(s) up to give your delts an extra squeeze (Fig. 9–43). Now gradually lower your arms to the starting position.

REMEMBER • Control your arm movements as you raise them up and down. Pump, do not swing, your arms. As you get tired, avoid the tendency to rock your body with the movement of your arms.

STEP ACCOMPANIMENTS • Do short to medium-length Strides and low Leg Lifts. Practice the Two-Count Step with single alternating arm raises, and the Three-Count Step with double arms.

Two-Count: Take a left step as you raise your right arm. Take a right step as you raise your left arm and lower your right.

Three-Count: Take a left and a right step as you raise both arms up, then a left step as you lower them. Start the next repetition with a right step.

DEVICES • *Poles:* Hold each pole separately for the Single and the Double Arm Raises, keeping them parallel to the ground. Grip poles with palms-in, keeping them in a horizontal position, parallel to the ground.

TRANSITION • Do 12–25 reps of the Pump 'N Walk. Then go either to Shoulders Set #3 or to Upper Back Sets #1–2.

Shoulders Set #3: Back Lateral (double arms)

This exercise builds and shapes the rear and side deltoids.

START • Stretch out your arms behind your body, with your elbows bent moderately at about 120 degrees. Put your fists behind your buttocks/hips, palms-away (Fig. 9–44).

MOVE • Raise both arms outward, extending them away from your body until your fists reach ear level and are at arm's length from your head (Fig. 9–45). Your fists should turn out from your body to palms facing front and away. Lower your arms together to the starting position.

STEP ACCOMPANIMENTS • Use short to medium-length Strides and low to medium-high Leg Lifts with a Five-Count Step: take a left, a right, and a left step as you raise your arms, then a right and a left step as you lower them slowly. Start the next repetition with a right step.

DEVICES • *Cords:* Anchor the cord below your feet and at the front of your waist. *Poles:* Grip walking poles with your fists turned palms-in so that they face each other (Fig. 9–45).

TRANSITION • Do 25 repetitions of the Pump 'N Walk, then go either to Shoulders Set #4 or to Upper Back Sets #1–3.

Fig. 9–42 • Shoulders Set #2—Side Lateral: single arm raised

Fig. 9–43 • Shoulders Set #2—Side Lateral: arms raised with weights and cords, fists palms-away behind buttocks/hips

Fig. 9–44 • Shoulders Set #3—Back Lateral: arms stretched behind body

Fig. 9–45 • Shoulders Set #3—Back Lateral: arms raised with fists at shoulder to ear height

Shoulders Set #4: Clean and Press-Up

This two-part exercise shapes your entire deltoid muscle group. Start with Single Arm Press-Ups before graduating to Double Arms.

START • With your arm(s) bent at 90-degree angle by your side(s), turn your fist(s) to palms-down or palms-in (when using poles) (Fig. 9–46).

MOVE • *Part One: The Clean.* Turn your fist(s) palms-front as you raise your arm(s), bringing your forearm(s) back until your fist(s) are at shoulder-height with palms-up (Fig. 9–47).

    Part Two: The Press-Up. Press your arm(s) up overhead until they are extended, with the elbow(s) slightly bent. Your arm(s) should form a straight line that is perpendicular to the ground and aligned with your ears (Fig. 9–48).

STEP ACCOMPANIMENTS • Use short to medium-length Strides and low Leg Lifts with the five-count-stepping method:

Count One: Take a left step as you bring your fist(s) slightly forward.
Count Two: Take a right step as you raise your arm(s) and curl your fist(s) back to your shoulder(s).

Fig. 9–46 • Shoulders Set #4—Clean and Press-Up: First Position

Fig. 9–47 • Shoulders Set #4—Clean: fists raised to shoulders

Fig. 9–48 • Shoulders Set #4—Press-Up: along ear line

Count Three: Take a left step as you press your arm(s) overhead.

Count Four: Take a right step as you bring your fist(s) back down to your shoulder(s).

Count Five: Take a left step as you lower your forearm(s) back to the extended-out position.

DEVICES • *Poles:* Double-plant poles on counts one and five to start and end each repetition. *Cords:* Cords can be attached under your step bench or at your waist belt.

VARIATIONS • To vary this exercise, press up from behind your head. To do this, place your fists up behind your ears with the palms facing up. Now press your arms straight up behind your head and in line with the back of your head.

TRANSITION • Do 25 reps of the Pump 'N Walk. Then go either to Shoulders Set #5 or to Upper Back Sets #1–4.

Shoulders Set #5: Upright Row and Shrug (double arm)

This two-part exercise shapes the traps and the front delts. To perform this exercise properly, you must use Double Arm Pumps.

START • Place your arms by your sides, with your fists slightly in front of your body and palms-back (Fig. 9–49).

MOVE • *Part One.* Raise your arms up as you bend your elbows out. Turn your fists palms-down, and trace a path straight up along your body until they reach right under your chin. Your forearms should be perpendicular to your body now, making a straight line across your chest, with an elbow pointing out to either side. Shrug your shoulders as you squeeze your trapezius muscles. Your elbows should be raised up (higher than your fists) so they are in line with your ears. Be sure to keep your fists anchored under your chin while you do the exercise (Fig. 9–50).

Part Two. First "unshrug" your shoulders, letting the trapezius muscles relax. Then, using a rowing motion, lower your arms downward slowly along the same path they were raised, to the starting position.

Fig. 9–49 • Shoulders Set #5—
Upright Row and Shrug: fists in front
of body

Fig. 9–50 • Shoulders Set #5—
Upright Row and Shrug: fists under
chin, elbows at shoulder height

STEP ACCOMPANIMENT • Use low Leg Lifts or short to medium-length Strides with a Five-Count Step:

Count One: Take a left step as you move your fists, from the side of your body with palms-in to slightly in front of your body with palms-down.

Count Two: Take a right step as you row your fists up along the front of your body to your chin.

Count Three: Take a left step as you shrug your shoulders and lift up your elbows.

Count Four: Take a right step as you relax your shrug.

Count Five: Take a left step as you row down your arms with your fists in front of your body.

Count One: Take a left step as you begin to row up your arms again.

DEVICES • *Cords:* Anchor the cords under a step-up bench or at the waist. You can get more of a stretch from your waist cords by turning your fists to palms-up when you row up and shrug. Also, press your fists up to ear level and your elbows to head level. *Poles:* Double-plant with individual poles on count 1. Also, poles can be doubled up and gripped like a barbell.

TRANSITION • Do 12–25 repetitions of the Pump 'N Walk, then go to Set #1 of the Upper Back Routines.

Upper-Back Routine

Because we tend to move in a forward direction most of the time, the muscles on the front of our bodies are naturally stronger than the muscles on the back (the hamstrings, back, and triceps). This muscle imbalance can lead to postural misalignments, such as sunken shoulders, and to long-term medical problems like pinched nerves, torn muscles, and damaged joints. To avoid these problems, do the upper-back routines that follow.

Unlike many body-shaping programs, Walkshaping divides the back area into two parts: upper and lower. You will train the lower back as part of your lower-body workout. You've already trained the upper part of your traps as part of the Shoulders Routine; now you will train the middle and lower portions. As you recall, the traps are muscles that are used to move the shoulder girdle up, to the back, or to the front. They form a flat, triangular muscle, extending out and down from your neck and between your shoulder blades.

The latissimus dorsi (lats) is the largest muscle of the upper body. With some help from the rhomboids, the lats pull your shoulders downward and to the back. For example, if you find yourself hunching forward, pulling your shoulders back and downward will strengthen your lats. The lats are worked with a rowing motion, and also with pulling or chin-up motions. It's important to isolate the back muscles: to do so, try to shift your movement until you feel the work effort coming from your back muscles rather than your arms and shoulders.

The distance between your fists or grips when you do double-arm exercises determines whether you work the upper, middle, or lower part of your lats. The closer the grip, the closer to your spine you work (i.e., rhomboids), and the higher up you'll work your lats. If you work with your fists close together, you'll develop the outer back; a wide grip works the inner and upper back.

It is difficult to isolate the lats or the traps completely, so each upper-back exercise will also strengthen smaller back muscles, like the teres major, infraspinatus, and rhomboid. This is also the case with exercises that work the middle and lower traps.

While the back muscles are not multiheaded like the biceps, triceps, and quadriceps, you can still train them by doing the arm and torso exercises from different angles.

As for the shoulders, upper-back work generally requires both arms working together. Double Arm work should be accompanied by short to medium-length Strides or low to medium-height Leg Lifts. To build up to this stage you should start with the Single Arm Pumps first, and do the Double Arm Pumps when you're stronger.

Practice Levels

Level I: Do 5–12 for each arm (or 10–24 total); Level II: 12–15; Level III: 15–20; Level IV: 21–25; and Level V: 25–30.

Upper Back Set #1: Row Back

This exercise strengthens the entire back, focusing on the lats and traps. You should look like you are sawing wood with both arms simultaneously.

START • Bend your arm(s) completely, with the elbow(s) out by your side(s). Place your fist(s) on (either) side of your body at chest level with palm(s) down, about 3–6 inches in from your side(s) (Fig. 9–51). This exercise can be done with one or both arms, although double-arm work will provide the greater resistance that this large muscle group needs to be exercised effectively.

MOVE • Push your arms straight out until they are extended fully in front of your body. Before pulling them back, grasp at imaginary oars by opening and closing your fists. Now visualize pulling the oars as you row them back in an even motion along the line perpendicular to your chest. As your fists reach your chest, pull your elbows back and flex your lat muscles to pull your shoulders down and back (Fig. 9–52).

STEP ACCOMPANIMENTS • Practice the Row Back with medium to long Strides and medium to high Leg Lifts. Use a Two-Count for Single Arm and Three-Count for Double Arm Row Backs. Take a left (or a left and a right) step as you push your arms straight out and a right (or left) step as you pull your arms back.

DEVICES • *Cords:* Attach cords to a door or some other anchor 3 feet from your body. Or substitute Upright Rows or Bent-Over Rows for Row Backs (see Lower-Back Routines, page 97). *Poles:* Keep your

Fig. 9–51 • Eileen demonstrates Upper Back Set #1—Row Back: First Position, fists by chest

Fig. 9–52 • Upper Back Set #1— Row Back: arms extended and fingers grasping

Fig. 9–53 • Upper Back Set #2— Modified Upright Row: arms rowed up, lats flexed (front view)

palms in so that you can plant and pull your poles straight back. Start your plant with a handshake-like motion, then pull straight back as if you were sawing. Do not let your fist and forearm drop down; keep them parallel to the ground.

TRANSITION • Do 12–25 repetitions of the Pump 'N Walk and then go either to Upper Back Set #2 or to the Cool-Down Walk.

Upper Back Set #2: Modified Upright Row

This exercise strengthens the traps and upper lats.

START • With both arms extended down, bend elbows slightly and place fists 5 inches apart, palms-back, in front of your body. Bend slightly (5–10 degrees) at the waist.

MOVE • Bend your arms with elbows outward as you raise your fists up toward your shoulders. Press your elbows back as you flex your lats (Fig. 9–53). Lower your arms again.

The difference between this exercise and the Upright Row is that here, your fists end up at shoulder height rather than at your chin.

STEPS ACCOMPANIMENTS • Practice short to medium Strides and low to medium Leg Lifts using a Two-Count (or Three-Count) Step. Take a left (or a left and right) step as you row up. Take a right (or a left) step as you lower your arms to the starting position.

VARIATION • Use a Five-Count Step. Take three steps while rowing up and two while rowing down.

DEVICES • *Weights:* Using a wide grip, hold weights parallel and evenly throughout the action (as you would hold a barbell). *Poles:* Double up poles, using a wide grip to simulate the action of rowing up with a barbell. *Cords:* Pull up cords from under a step-bench or grip waist-anchored cords with palms-up.

TRANSITION • Do 12–25 repetitions of the Pump 'N Walk, then go either to Upper Back Set #3, or to the Cool-Down Walk.

Upper Back Set #3: Row-Out

This exercise shapes and strengthens your middle lats as well as your rhomboids and teres major.

START • Hold your fists away from you at chest height, palms-down. Bend your arms at the elbows until they form a closed loop, as if you were hugging someone (Fig. 9–54). Knuckles should be facing each other, with your forearms parallel to the ground.

MOVE • Slowly pull your arms apart and raise them until your elbows are at shoulder level behind your body. Your fists should be at chin level on either side of your head. Press your elbows back until you feel your traps and lats flexing (Fig. 9–55). Now return to the starting position by closing your arms slowly.

STEP ACCOMPANIMENTS • Use short to medium-long Strides and low to medium-high Leg Lifts using a Two-Count (or Three-Count) Step. Take a left (or a left and a right) step as you pump your arms out, then a right (or a left) step as you pump them back to the starting position.

DEVICES • *Cords:* Let the cord straps run from your waist or feet over the outside of the upper arms and across your elbow joints to the outside of the forearms. Grip cords palms-down. *Poles:* Hold fists palms-in and lift the poles together, holding them perpendicular to the ground.

TRANSITION • Do 12–25 repetitions of the Pump 'N Walk, then go either to Upper Back Set #4, or to the Cool-Down Walk.

Fig. 9–54 • Michael demonstrates Upper Back Set #3—Row-Out: First Position; palms-down and knuckles together, with arms forming a downward closed looplike hug

Fig. 9–55 • Upper Back Set #3—Row-Out: arms out, fists at chin height, palms-out, elbows at shoulder height behind body

Upper Back Set #4: Back Row-Up

This exercise shapes the traps and the upper-lats area.

START • With your arms hanging by your sides, place your fists palms-back just behind your body (Fig. 9–56).

MOVE • Pull your fists straight up along the front of your body, bending your arms so that your elbows point away from your body. Pull your fists as high as they will go from under your chin up to the top of your head, until your shoulders feel flexed. When you reach the top, give your traps and lats an extra squeeze by shrugging and also by turning your fists to palms-front and pushing as high as your elbows will go. Then turn your fists to palms-back again and lower them down your body, returning to the starting position (Fig. 9–57).

STEPS ACCOMPANIMENT • Do medium to long Strides and Leg Lifts using the Two-Count or Three-Count Step. Take a left (or a left and a right) step as you pull up your arms, then a right (or left) step as you lower your arms down to the starting position. Use the Three-Count Step and alternate your feet at the beginning of each repetition.

DEVICES • *Poles:* With your fists turned palms-in, hold poles horizontally. *Cords:* Grip cords palms-down and let cord straps run from waist

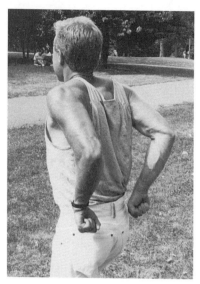 

Fig. 9–56 • Gary Croxton demonstrates Upper Back Set #4—Back Row-Up: palms back behind line of body

Fig. 9–57 • Upper Back Set #4—Back Row-Up: returning to starting position.

or feet over the outside of the upper arms and across the elbow joints along the outside of the forearms.

TRANSITION • Do 25 repetitions of the Pump 'N Walk, then go either to Upper Back Set #5 or to the Cool-Down Walk.

Upper Back Set #5: Pull-Down/Pull-Over

This two-part exercise simulates the actions of both pull-over and pull-down weight-training machines, shaping and strengthening your lower and middle lats.

START • Bend both arms, at your sides, to a 90-degree angle. Push your fists back behind the line of your hips or buttocks (Fig. 9–58).

MOVE • First, breathe in slowly and continuously as you pump your arms over your head on either side. Bend your forearms back behind your head and over the more flexible region behind your shoulders. Throughout the exercise, keep your arms bent at a 90-degree angle and your fists turned palms-up.

Then, loosen and tighten your grip as you raise your arms over your head and back behind your body in an 180–320 degree rotation of your shoulder joints. Push back with your elbows to flex your lats, still inhaling slowly. Flex your upper lats five times, pushing your arms back and out with the elbows bent and pointing away from your body. Lower your arms lightly and quickly back over your head (Fig. 9–59). Straighten your arms down in front of your chest on either side of your body until your fists reach your thighs. Return to the bent-arm starting position and begin the rotation cycle anew.

STEPS ACCOMPANIMENT • Use short to medium Strides and low Leg Lifts with a Five-Count Step. Take a left (or a right and a left) step as you raise your arms up over your head, then a right and a left step as you pull down your arms, pushing your elbows back and flexing your upper lats. Begin the movement again with a right step.

REMEMBER • Keep your chin tucked in and your elbows bent at a 90-degree angle throughout the entire arm-shoulder rotation.

DEVICES • *Cords:* Anchor the cords at the back of your waist or under steps and run them up your back and over your shoulders. *Poles:* Turn the poles upside-down and grab the pole grips with your fists palms-in. Or, double up your poles and grip them together diagonally.

TRANSITION • Do 12–25 repetitions of the Pump 'N Walk, then go to the Cool-Down Walk.

Fig. 9–58 • Upper Back Set #5— Pull-Down/Pull-Over: First and Final Positions; fists behind hip joint, elbows 90 degrees behind body (push back with elbows)

Fig. 9–59 • Upper Back Set #5— Pull-Down/Pull-Over: move, forearms overhead, fists behind head

Cool-Down Walk (1–5 minutes)

Continue walking at a slow to moderate pace (2–3½ miles per hour on the move, 30–60 steps per minute while walking in place). Practice the chest- to chin-Height Arm Pumps with medium Strides or low to medium Leg Lifts. After completing the Cool-Down Walk, do the Four Basic Stretches in Chapter 8, page 118.

Bent-Over Versions

You can also do the whole series of upper-back exercises by bending over and straightening up your upper body, but only after you strengthen your lower back sufficiently for it to take repeated movement. Move now to the Lower-Body Workout. Practice the lower-back routines every other day for at least three weeks before attempting the bent-over version of the upper-back routines.

CHAPTER 10

The Lower-Body Workout

Start these routines after you've completed the Warm-Up Walk (1–5 minutes), Stretching (1–5 minutes), and the Whole-Body Walk (3–15 minutes). (If you prefer, you can save the Whole-Body Walk for after you do this routine.) The Lower-Body Routines give you a good aerobic workout, since you do them while moving. Use the Pump 'N Walk as a transition between sets of the Lower-Body Routines.

Do the Lower-Body Workout on alternate workout days, to give your lower body a day of rest. On "off" days, you can do either the Upper-Body Workout or just go for a stroll. Be sure to do at least two Upper- and two Lower-Body Workouts per week. As with the Upper-Body Workout, select the number of sets you will do based on your level of fitness and the amount of time that you've allotted to your Walkshaping workout (i.e., Levels I–V, or 12–60 minutes per workout day).

Order of Exercise

Since walking is, by itself, already a light lower-body workout, it's even more important to isolate and concentrate on the particular muscles that you want to tone. I've arranged the exercise routines here so you work from large to small or weak muscles (thighs/buttocks/ hips to calves/lower back). The long abdominals muscle is the exception: I saved it for second to last because: a) you have to slow down your walking pace to do Torso Turns properly; and b) you don't want to wear yourself out at the beginning of your Upper-Body Routine by expending the concentrated energy needed for abdominal work. The abdominals are also a nice warm-up for the lower-back set that follows. Your lower back is exercised last because, at this point, you want to slow down the pace of your exercise in preparation for the Cool-Down Walk, which ends the routine.

In arranging the Lower-Body Routines, I've tried to provide an equal number of exercises that stretch and strengthen the same muscles. For example, the Whole-Body Walk and the Stride Stretch Step not only shape your leg muscles; they stretch them out each time you strike with your heel, elongate your step, and straighten your leg. The Biceps Curls stretch out your triceps, and the Triceps Extensions stretch out your biceps. At the end of this chapter, I'll give you a series of stretching exercises that correspond to the muscles that you've worked.

CAUTION: *Walkers with knee or hip problems should consult their doctors before doing any of the deep-knee-bend exercises.*

Thighs Routines (Fig. 10–1)

Your thigh muscles are the largest and most powerful muscles in your body. They consist of the quadriceps, the hamstrings, and the adductors. The quadriceps is a four-headed muscle on the front of the upper leg that is used to straighten out the leg, just like the triceps is used to straighten out the arm. The hamstring, or biceps femoris, is the muscle at the back of the upper leg that is used to bend back your leg.

Regular walking works the thigh muscles, but only slightly. Climbing works the thighs and buttocks/hips harder because the legs have to bend and straighten more radically on inclines and declines. The Walkshaping leg routines make you bend your knees more by having you sink your body lower when using your legs; they also involve higher Leg Lifts and up-and-down steps. All of this extra work shapes and defines your thigh muscles more than regular walking does.

Practice Levels

Level I should do 5–12 repetitions with each leg (or 10–24 total); Level II: 12–15; Level III: 15–20; Level IV: 21–25; and Level V: 25–30.

Thighs Set #1: Lunge Step

This exercise shapes and strengthens the whole thigh, especially the inside and the top.

START • Place your feet side by side, at hip-width to shoulder-width apart. Maintain this stance throughout the routine.

MOVE • *Part One: In Place/On the Move.* Take a giant step forward with your left foot. Strike heel first, then roll down onto the rest of your foot until it's flat on the ground. Bend your left knee forward until it's directly over your ankle. Your lower leg should be perpendicular to the ground: do not let your knee go farther forward than your ankle. Let your body sink straight down as you bend your back knee and raise your back heel off of the ground. *Beginners:* Aim for higher lunges (don't bend your knees as much) until you are comfortable with sinking lower. *Advanced walkers:* You may find that your back knee touches the ground (Fig. 10–1, 2, 3).

Part Two: In Place. Get ready to take a right Lunge Step forward. Do this by raising the toes of your left foot and pressing down on your heel, stepping back to the starting position. *On the Move:* Lift your back (right) foot off of the ground and take a right Lunge Step forward. *In Place/On the Move:* As your right foot passes forward under your body, press into your left heel and straighten your left leg until

Fig. 10–1 • Gary demonstrates Thigh Set #1—Lunge Step (Easy): don't sink down as far

Fig. 10–2 • Thighs Set #1—Lunge Step (More Difficult): take a left Lunge Step forward. SHOWN: left knee over left ankle

Fig. 10–3 • Thighs Set #1—Lunge Step, with poles. Poles give you better balance to sink lower. Place feet parallel to one another.

the knee is only slightly bent. Finish extending your right leg forward, striking the ground with your heel. Continue alternating right and left Lunge Steps. Repeat 12–25 left and right Lunge Steps as part of this set.

ARM ACCOMPANIMENTS • Practice chest- to chin-high Bent Arm Pumps with your Lunge Steps, using the two-count Arm Pump method. Beginners, pump your fists to chest height; advanced walkers, pump your fists to chin height. As you take a left Lunge Step, pump your right arm forward and your left arm back. As you take a right Lunge Step, pump your left arm forward and your right arm back. Use a loosely clenched fist, and pump your arms straight forward and straight back. On the backward move, be sure that your fist is even with or behind the line of your hip joint. *Advanced walkers:* pump your arm back further, so your fist is behind the outer edge of your buttocks/hips.

REMEMBER • Keep your knee bent forward at a 90-degree angle above your heel with every step. You'll stress your knee joint if you lunge further. Also, keep your feet hip-width apart. Slow down your walking speed substantially until you've mastered the Lunge Step technique. If you find yourself swinging or kicking your legs forward, you're going too fast.

Fig. 10–4 • Series of pole-bounding Lunge Steps

VARIATIONS • If at first it is difficult to take repeated left and right Lunge Steps, then intersperse one to three Lunge Steps with one to three Pump 'N Walk steps. *In Place:* Advanced walkers: practice your Lunge Steps using a 6-inch-high step-bench, rolling through the foot and pressing off with the heel. *On the Move:* Advanced walkers: sink deeper, touching your back knee to the ground.

BACKWARD LUNGE STEP   Step back with your right foot and sink down. Bring your right foot forward again, next to the left foot, and step forward with the right, sinking onto your knee as you lunge. Each time you bring your feet down side by side, execute a double pole plant on the side of each foot. When stepping back with your foot, execute a pole plant backward with the opposite hand and a pole plant forward with the same-side hand.

BACK-AND-FORTH LUNGE STEP   To add variety to your walking-in-place routines, alternate left and right Lunge Steps backward and forward. Take a front-left Lunge Step. Step back with your left foot to a back-left Lunge Step. Repeat with a right Lunge Step forward. Then step back with your right foot to a back-right Lunge Step.

SIDE LUNGE STEP—IN PLACE   Take Side Lunge Steps. These are executed in the same way as front and back steps, but add greater variety to a walking in place routine.

DEVICES • *Poles:* Poles are very useful for the Lunge Step and for all deep-knee-bend exercises. They allow you to support yourself while practicing, gradually shifting the weight to your muscles. *Beginners:* do a double pole plant with each Lunge Step to reduce the stress on the forward knee and to sink down lower. *Beginners:* do not use any weight or resistance devices other than poles. *Advanced walkers:* use light arm weights, stretch cords, and walking poles with your Lunge Steps.

POLE BOUNDING   This is a more rapid version of the Lunge Step, for advanced walkers only. It uses the power poles to connect each Lunge Step to the next one, causing you to bound forward (Fig. 10–4).

TRANSITION • Do 12–25 repetitions of the Pump 'N Walk. Then go either to Thighs Set #2 or to Set #1 of the Buttocks/Hips Routines.

Thighs Set #2: Cross-Over Step (front and side-to-side)

This exercise strengthens and shapes your inner and outer thighs and your obliques.

Fig. 10–5 • Thighs Set #2—Cross-Over Step, with Cradle Pump

START • Place your feet parallel and hip-width to shoulder-width apart.

MOVE • *In Place:* Take a left Cross-Over Step by lifting your left foot straight up 6–12 inches and crossing it over sideways in front of your right leg. Bend your knees so that you can step further to the right. Place your left foot 6–12 inches beyond your right foot and directly parallel to it. Strike with the outer edge of your left foot and roll the foot down sideways to flatten it (Fig. 10–5). Now reverse the movement, bringing your left foot back until it returns to its starting position. Repeat the exercise on the right, continuing to alternate left and right Cross-Over Steps.

On the Move: Raising your left foot up 6 inches, step forward and beyond your right foot. Lower your left foot, making sure that your heel strikes first, then roll down through the foot to a firm flat plant. Your left foot should be aligned with the outside edge of your right foot. Try not to cross over more than 2 feet, so you can maintain parallel foot placement. Before taking your right Cross-Over Step, shift your weight to your left (forward) foot. Then lift your right (back) foot 6 inches off the ground and cross it in front of your forward leg. Complete the exercise on the right side.

VARIATION • Travel forward by turning sideways so your right side faces front. Do 12–25 left side Cross-Over Steps. Then turn so your left side faces front, and do 12–25 right-side Cross-Over Steps.

ARM ACCOMPANIMENTS • Use a chin-height to head-height Arm Pump. *In Place:* When taking a left Cross-Over Step sideways, pump your right arm forward. When taking a right Cross-Over Step sideways, pump your left arm forward. During the transition step, either do no Arm Pumps or two quick ones, in order to synchronize your leg and arm movements. *On the Move:* Pump your left arm forward as you take right Cross-Over Steps and your right arm forward as you take left Cross-Over Steps. You can also use Double Arm Cradle Pumps: Stack your fists by your left hip. As you take a right Cross-Over Step, pump your fists together from your left to your right side; vice versa with left Cross-Over Steps.

REMEMBER • The further sideways that you step, the more you'll stretch and flex your inner thighs. Also, be sure to flatten your foot fully before taking the next step.

DEVICES • *Legs—In Place:* Advanced walkers can use ankle weights or can practice Cross-Over Steps on and off a step-bench. *Cords:*

Anchor the cords at your feet or waist. Pump forward or up at shoulder-to-head height. *Weights:* Pump no higher than your chin. *Poles:* Plant both poles in front and on either side of the foot that has just crossed.

TRANSITION • Do 12–25 repetitions of the Pump 'N Walk, then go either to to Thighs Set #3 or to Buttocks/Hips Sets #1–2.

Thighs Set #3: Leg Curl

Fig. 10–6 • Thighs Set #3—Leg Curl, On the Move: right pump, left leg curl

Like a Biceps Curl for your leg, this exercise strengthens and shapes the hamstring muscles, in the back of your thighs.

START • Place your feet side by side, hip-width apart.

MOVE • *In Place:* Without lifting your upper leg, curl your left heel toward your buttocks. Flex your hamstring. Lower your foot and repeat with the right leg.

On the Move: Step forward with your left foot, keeping your feet hip-width apart. Curl your right heel toward your buttocks/hips and hold for one count as you squeeze your hamstring and buttocks muscles. Lower your right leg, bringing it in front of your body until your right heel strikes the ground. Now curl your left hamstring (Fig. 10–6).

ARM ACCOMPANIMENTS • Practice chin- to head-high Arm Pumps.

In Place/On the Move: Pump your right arm forward as you curl up your right leg. Reverse arms for the left side. Also do Double Arm Pumps for best balance.

DEVICES • *Ankle and Leg Weights:* The in-place Leg Curl adapts well to ankle weights. (We have yet to determine whether the on-the-move Leg Curl can be done with ankle weights.) *Arms:* Use Arm Raises instead of Arm Pumps. *Cords:* Stretch up your left cord as you curl your right leg, then your right cord as you curl up your left leg. *Poles:* Plant your right pole as you strike with your left heel and curl up your right leg, then your left pole as you strike with your right heel and curl up your left leg.

TRANSITION • Do 12–25 repetitions of the Pump 'N Walk, then go either to Thighs Set #4 or to Sets #1–3 of Buttocks/Hips Routines.

Thighs Set #4: Leg Extension Step

This exercise shapes and strengthens the quadriceps. It is a combination of a march and the Stride Stretch Step. The higher you raise your leg with each step, the more you work your thighs.

START • Keep your feet side by side, hip-width apart. Bend your arms at right angles and place them by your sides.

MOVE • *In Place:* Shift your weight to your right foot. Lift your left leg, and pull in your abdominals to balance yourself on your right leg. Raise your left knee so your foot is 6 inches off the ground. Straighten your left leg, keeping your heel 6–12 inches off the ground. After you have fully straightened your leg (Fig. 10–7), return your foot to its starting position. You are now ready to do a right Leg Extension.

On the Move: Extend your left leg as if taking a step forward, raising your knee higher than you would normally, so that your left foot is at least 6 inches off the ground. Use your quadriceps muscles to lift up your lower leg. Straighten out your leg, lifting your heel forward and raising it until it is 12 inches off the ground. As you step forward, keep your heel 12 inches off the ground until your leg is fully straightened, but not locked. Flex your quadriceps hard and gently lower your leg down for the heel strike. Bend your back (right) leg and squeeze your thigh muscles. This will help you lower your leg gradually and allow

Fig. 10–7 • Thighs Set #4—Leg Extension Step, In Place: leg straightened out before left heel-strike

Fig. 10–8 • Thighs Set #4—Leg Extension Step: arm extended toward the opposite extending leg

Fig. 10–9 • Thighs Set #4—Leg Extension Step, In Place: with ankle bands

your front heel to strike the ground with less impact. At the same time, toe off with your back (right) foot to move your body forward, rolling up to your toes on your right foot as your left heel strikes the ground. Shift your weight onto your forward foot, and extend your right leg.

ARM ACCOMPANIMENTS • Practice forward Arm Pumps (Fig. 10–8) at chest-to-chin height, alternating right Arm Pumps and left Leg Extensions with left Arm Pumps and right Leg Extensions.

DEVICES • *Poles:* Plant both poles simultaneously. Press down and use the poles to lower your body, pushing it forward for a smoother heel strike. *Cords:* Anchor the cords to ankle straps rather than wrapping them around your ankles. This will keep them from sliding up your leg (Fig. 10–9). *Weights:* For increased stability, practice 90-degree Arm Pumps, or pump and straighten your right arm parallel to the left leg as you are extending it forward. The movement is like a downward punch. As you extend your left leg out, extend your right arm out parallel to it, turning your fist palm-down in a counterclockwise direction. When your left heel strikes, begin to pull your arm back.

TRANSITION • Do 25 repetitions of the Pump 'N Walk, then go either to Thighs Set #5 or Buttocks/Hips Sets #1–4.

NOTE: The Leg Push-Back Routine (see page 178) makes a nice transition to the routines that come next because it involves the buttocks/hips as well as the hamstrings.

Thighs Set #5: Squat

This exercise strengthens and shapes your front thighs and buttocks/hips.

START • Begin with your feet hip-width apart.

MOVE • *Beginners: In Place:* Place your hands on top of your thighs, pushing onto them as you sink down (Fig. 10–10). Lower your buttocks/hips as if sitting on a chair, and then squeeze the gluteals as you return to a standing position, keeping your knees slightly bent. From this position, raise up onto your toes slightly while bending your knees into the squatting position, sinking down slowly. *On the Move:* Hold your arms out by your sides or in front of you for balance until you're strong enough to pump them as indicated, and bend your knees no more than 45 degrees (Fig. 10–11).

Advanced walkers: Bend your knees as much as 90 degrees. Raise arms up to chest height as you lower yourself (Fig. 10–12). As you straighten your legs and return to the starting position, roll back on your heels until your feet are flat. *In Place:* Step back with your right foot and then your left before starting your next Squat Step. After the squat, take a right and then a left step forward, bringing your feet side by side. *On the Move:* Once you are fully upright, step forward with your right foot and bring up your left foot. As soon as both feet are firmly planted side by side, sink down into the squat position as you shift your weight back to your heels. Once you reach the knee-bend position, straighten your legs again.

REMEMBER • Keep your back straight and your chin tucked in throughout this movement. Try to keep your chest lifted and to maintain a smooth, steady motion as you go down and up. Don't extend your knee past your ankle.

ARM ACCOMPANIMENTS • After mastering your Squat Steps with the Single Bent Arm Pump technique, practice the chest- to chin-high pumps using a Four-Count Step method. Pump your right arm forward and your left arm back as you take a left step forward and bring your right foot forward and place it parallel to your left. Then pump your left arm forward and your right arm back as you lower into the squat

Fig. 10–10 • Thighs Set #5—Front Squat (Beginners): hands braced on top of your knees

Fig. 10–11 • Thighs Set #5—Front Squat: knees bent to a 45-degree angle, with hands held out for balance

Fig. 10–12 • Thighs Set #6—Squat, with devices: sitting back on heels, knees bent to a 90-degree angle

position. Pump your right arm forward and your left arm back again as you rise. You're now ready to take a right step forward, accompanied by a left Arm Pump. Alternate arm pumping will help you to do Squat Steps with a balanced and fluid motion.

VARIATIONS • In between each Squat Step, take two or more Stride Stretch Steps to steady yourself and to stretch out your leg muscles.

DEVICES • *Poles:* Power poles help you balance and take weight off your knees. *Cords/Weights:* Pump light cords and weights with alternate arms. Anchor the stretch cords under a step, then do your Squats against the pulling resistance of the cord. *Step Bench:* Keep one foot on the step at all times when using cords.

TRANSITION • Do 25 repetitions of the Pump 'N Walk, then go to Sets #1–5 of the Buttocks/Hips Routine.

Buttocks/Hips Routines

The hip muscles include the buttocks muscles, the groin muscles, and the hip flexors and extensors. The buttocks consist of inner muscles: the gluteus maximus (large), gluteus medius (intermediate), and gluteus minimus (small), known collectively as glutes.

The glutes help stabilize your body when you walk. When you are balancing on just one leg, the glutes keep you from falling to the opposite side. The medius and minimus glutes are worked when you lift your leg to the side and to the front. The large glute is used to lift your leg backward and keeps your knee straightened; this is why straight-legged back-lift exercises work this muscle so effectively.

The large glute helps propel you up inclines, and the medium and small glutes help guide you back down. Therefore, for a great glute workout, a step bench is terrific. Although the glutes get strengthened from regular walking, they can be shaped even more by adding resistance to each leg as you move it.

The groin, or adductor muscle group, is used to swing your free leg forward and inward when you run, walk, or skate. These muscles are easily pulled when you go through the repeated and stressful actions of running and sprinting. Although there is little point in shaping the groin muscle, it can be strengthened and made more flexible with walking exercises.

The hip flexor muscles consist of the haunch muscle (iliacus) and its great lumbar muscle (psoas major), which are known together as the iliopsoas. These muscles are used to move your trunk forward when you're finishing a sit-up or to pull your knees up to your chest when you're hanging from a bar. Notice that in both cases your hips are flexed. The hip flexors are powerful muscles and are often stronger than the abdominal muscles they work with. They need to be kept relaxed so that the abs can be trained and shaped further. The best way to prevent your hip flexors from fully engaging during an exercise is to keep your knees bent or to bend at the hip.

While there is still no proof that body fat can be burned off selectively by targeting specific body areas (i.e., spot reduction), you can make trouble spots appear slimmer by toning and tightening the muscle around them. Since these buttocks- and hips-training exercises require strong foot and leg control, they can generally be done with ankle weights, even when you're walking on the move. With the thighs and buttocks/hips routines, you can also do your Walkshaping exercises with stretch cords wrapped around your ankles.

Practice Levels

Level I should do 5–12 repetitions with each leg (or 10–24 total); Level II: 12–15; Level III: 15–20; Level IV: 21–25; and Level V: 25–30.

Buttocks/Hips Set #1: Heel Dig

This exercise strengthens the buttocks muscles and shins and stretches out the calf muscles.

START • *In Place:* Stand with feet hip-width apart. *On the Move:* Use short- to medium-length Quick Steps.

MOVE • Take a left step forward. As your left heel strikes the ground, pull up your forefoot so that it forms a 45–90-degree angle with the ground. Instead of rolling forward on to your toes immediately, stay longer in the heel-strike position. Tightly squeeze your left buttocks muscles. Hold the squeeze as your foot rolls forward and your right foot initiates its step from behind.

Fig. 10–13 • Buttocks/Hips Set #1— Heel Dig, In Place

Fig. 10–14 • Buttocks/Hips Set #1— Heel Dig, On the Move

Release the buttocks-muscle squeeze when your right foot leaves the ground to take its forward step. Repeat on the right, concentrating on involving only the buttocks and shins.

In Place: Alternate legs. Dig, roll forward, and step back with your left heel, then do the same with your right heel (Fig. 10–13). *On the Move:* Take a Left Heel Dig forward, followed by a Right Heel Dig forward (Fig. 10–14).

Eventually, this Heel Dig exercise will improve your heel strike on your regular striding routine. You'll find yourself automatically contracting your buttocks during every step. You'll be performing hundreds of buttocks squeezes, which will dramatically tone and shape your derriere.

In the beginning, Heel Digs work better with short (12-inch long) Quick Steps. As you become more skilled, you'll be able to lengthen your stride while still using your buttocks muscles. If you stay with Quick Steps, you will keep up your walking pace and increase the number of your Heel Dig steps from 1,500 to 3,000 steps per mile.

ARM ACCOMPANIMENTS • Alternate chest- to chin-high right and left Arm Pumps with opposite left and right Heel Digs.

REMEMBER • Raise your forefoot up at no less than a 45-degree angle from the ground and hold the position for as long as you can.

DEVICES • *Legs:* Use ankle weights. Don't swing your leg when stepping. Guide them by using more muscle control. Or side-step onto a step-up bench, raising your lower leg out to the side for more height and resistance.

TRANSITION • Do 12–25 repetitions of the Pump 'N Walk. Then go either to Buttocks/Hips Set #2 or to Set #1 of the Abdominals Routines.

Buttocks/Hips Set #2: Leg Push-Back

This exercise shapes and strengthens the buttocks muscles. The leg movement resembles the "kick back" used by cross-country skiers.

START • Take a left Stride Stretch Step forward, keeping your feet in a hip-width stance. Raise your right (back) heel until you're on your toes.

MOVE • *In Place:* Roll forward onto your left foot as you transfer your body weight. At the same time, roll up to the toe on your back (right) foot. Push off your back foot and straighten out your back leg, lifting it 6 inches above the ground (Fig. 10–15). Flex your hamstring and buttocks muscles. Lower your right leg to the ground. Step back with

Fig. 10–15 • Buttocks/Hips Set #2—Leg Push-Back: back leg is straightened and pushed back as it leaves the ground

Fig. 10–16 • Buttocks/Hips Set #2—Leg Push-Back, On the Move, with devices

your left foot to bring it back in line with your right foot. Your feet should be side by side and hip-width apart. Now take a Lunge or Stride Stretch Step forward with your right foot, continuing the exercise on the right. Strike down with your heel and roll down your foot. At the same time, roll up to the toe on your back (left) foot. Raise your foot. Straighten out your leg fully. Lift up your leg about 6 inches as you push it back.

On the Move: Raise your back (right) heel as you bend your front (left) knee and flex your buttocks and hamstring muscles. Roll up your right foot, pushing your right leg straight back until your foot is 6 inches off the ground. At the same time, straighten your left leg and feel the hamstring flex, being careful not to push back into your knees. Beginning walkers, bend your back leg slightly in order to lift it higher; advanced walkers, keep your leg straightened (but knee slightly bent) as you push it back.

ARM ACCOMPANIMENTS • *In Place:* Hold your arms still or do a Double Arm Pump as you step back. Pump your left arm forward when you take your right Stride Stretch Step forward. At the same time, pump your right arm back as you toe off and raise your left leg back.

On the Move: Alternate right and left chest- to chin-high Arm Pumps. Pump your right arm forward as you take your left step forward. At the same time, pump your left arm back as you toe off, push back, and lift your fully straightened right leg off the ground (Fig. 10–16).

REMEMBER • In this exercise, it's the straightening and the bending of your legs that shapes the hamstring muscles. Be sure to roll all the way onto the toes of your back foot before you push your leg back. Also, take long strides to engage your thigh muscles.

DEVICES • *Cords:* Pump from a waist or foot anchor, raising and lowering your arms together as you lower your back leg. *Poles:* Alternately plant the right pole forward with the left heel and push back on the left pole as you push back and raise your right leg. This action makes you feel as if you're cross-country skiing, encouraging you to lengthen your stride and to push back further. *Weights:* Use hand weights, synchronizing the highest part of your Pump with the highest part of your back-leg lift.

TRANSITION • Do 12–25 repetitions of the Pump 'N Walk. Then, go either to Buttocks/Hips Set #3 or to Sets #1–2 of the Abdominals Routines.

Buttocks/Hips Set #3: Buttocks/Hips Squeeze

Fig. 10–17 • Buttocks/Hips Set #3— Buttocks/Hips Squeeze, In Place: pelvis tilted

This exercise, a more concentrated version of the Heel Dig, shapes the entire buttocks area. It consists of a series of pelvic tilts with simultaneous contractions of both buttocks muscles. The Buttocks Squeeze differs from the Heel Dig walk in that you squeeze both buttocks simultaneously as you begin each step and tilt your pelvic girdle under your body. It is also unlike the Posture Correction move, since that exercise doesn't emphasize tucking your pelvis.

START • With your feet in a hip-width stance, prepare to step forward on your left foot. Bend your arms at a 90-degree angle and raise them forward, with your elbows pointed down to your sides and away from your body.

MOVE • Before taking the step, squeeze both of your buttocks/hips muscles so your pelvis goes into a tucked position. Take a left step forward. Continue to hold and intensify your squeeze until executing your left-heel strike. Release, and prepare to reinitiate the squeeze.

In Place: Step back with your left foot to the hip-width stance, and get ready for a right step by tilting your pelvis forward and raising your right heel.

On the Move: Begin with your right step to continue forward, toeing up with your right (back) foot and bringing it up and under your body. At the same time, begin your Double Buttocks/Hips Squeeze and Pelvic Tilt (Fig. 10–17). As you complete the right step, contract your muscles until your right heel strikes. Repeat the left and right Double Buttocks Squeeze step.

ARM ACCOMPANIMENTS • Practice Single or Double Arm Pumps or Row Backs, at chin to head height. Loosely clench your fists as you pull or pump each arm back. Time the backward motion of your arms to coincide with the forward push of your buttocks. As you squeeze your buttocks harder, push your step forward.

DEVICES • *Poles:* Use double-pole plants. Pull back evenly, pressing down on the poles to balance yourself. *Cords:* Anchor cords behind the waist or under a step bench. Pull them up and over the shoulders from behind, then down across the chest on either side. Grip the outstretched cords to chest height, pulling down and back with both arms against the tension. *Weights:* Pump back weight as if you were doing Double Arm Pumps or Row Backs.

TRANSITION • Do 25 repetitions of the Pump 'N Walk. Then go either to Buttocks/Hips Set #4 or Sets #1–3 of the Abdominals Routines.

Buttocks/Hips Set #4: Side Leg Lift

Fig. 10–18 • Buttocks/Hips Set #4— Side Leg Lift, On the Move: left leg forward, right leg back

This exercise shapes your outer hips (Fig. 10–18).

START • *In Place:* Stand with you feet side by side and hip-width apart. *On the Move:* From the hip-width stance, place your right foot forward and your left foot back. Instead of extending the forward leg out to the side, you can extend the back leg out.

MOVE •

VARIATION A   *In Place:* Shift your weight to your right foot. Extend your left leg out to the side 45 degrees and pause there as you contract your adductors. Return your left leg to the starting position. Extend your right leg.

On the Move: Step forward onto your left foot. Next, raise your back (right) leg off the ground. Straighten it as you extend it out at a 45-degree angle to the right side. Then bring it back again to your side and then move it forward. After your right heel strikes the ground, shift your weight to your right (forward) leg. Do a side Leg Lift with your back (left) leg.

VARIATION B   Lift your left knee until your foot is about 6 inches off the ground. Straighten your left leg out to the side at a 45-degree angle. Squeeze your thigh muscles as you straighten your leg.

In Place: Bring your left leg back to the starting position, heel first. Shift your weight to your left leg and lift the right knee.

On the Move: Extend your left foot forward for a left-heel strike. Bring your right leg underneath you and into a knee lift until your foot is about 6 inches above the ground. Extend your right leg out to the side at a 45-degree angle. Straighten it while squeezing your thigh muscles. Keep your thighs tight as you bring your straightened right leg back to your side. Extend the right foot forward for a right-heel strike. Bring your left (back) foot forward to begin again.

ARM ACCOMPANIMENTS •

VARIATION A   *In Place:* Pump your left arm forward as you extend your left leg back and lift it to the side. Pump your right arm forward as you extend your right leg back and lift it to the side.

On the Move: Pump your right arm forward as you step left and extend your right leg to the side. Pump your left arm forward as you step right and lift your left leg to the side.

VARIATION B   Use forward and sideways Arm Pumps. Alternate the left-side Pump and left Leg Lift with the right-forward Pump and left-heel strike. To do a sideways Arm Pump, raise your bent arm away from your body until it's at shoulder height, then lower it again. As you lift your left leg out to the side, raise your left arm out to the side as well, keeping your right arm back. As you extend your left leg forward, pump your right arm forward. Repeat this complementary right-left arm movement as you do a right-side Leg Lift.

DEVICES • *Cords:* Wrap a cord loop around both ankles and keep it taut with your hip-width stance. *Poles:* Double-plant poles in front of you as you raise your leg to the side. Then plant the right pole with the left-heel strike and the left pole with the right-heel strike. *Weights:* Pump weights forward at chin to head height, raising them sideways to shoulder height. Ankle weights also work well with this exercise.

TRANSITION • Do 12–25 repetitions of the Pump 'N Walk. Then go either to Buttocks/Hips Set #5 or Abdominals Sets #1–5.

Buttocks/Hips Set #5: Side Lunge Step

This exercise shapes the buttocks, side hips, and inner thighs.

START • Stand with your feet hip-width apart.

MOVE • *In Place:* Take a left Lunge Step sideways, keeping your left foot parallel to and in line with your right foot. Raise your left leg to the side with your foot 6–12 inches off the ground and your leg bent at a 90-degree angle. As your left foot lands toe-ball-heel, sink down, bending your left knee and straightening your right leg. Feel your hips flex (Fig. 10–19). Squeeze your buttocks as you raise your body up and bring your left foot back to parallel and in line with your right foot. Take a right Side Lunge Step. Alternate sides (Fig. 10–20). Your torso should move from side to side with the leg that is stepping.

On the Move: Turn 90 degrees to the left, so that your right side faces the "front." Take a Right Lunge Step, but continue the movement. Straighten your right leg (which is now bearing most of your weight). Lift your right heel as you lift your left leg and pivot 180 degrees to the right. Take a Left Lunge Step. Alternate Left and Right Lunge Steps.

ALTERNATIVES • You can repeat all the Side Lunge Steps on the left side (6–12 reps) before doing an equal number on the right side. If performed on the move, this exercise will require a transitional step, either a Cross-Over Step or a Catch-Up Step. *Cross-Over Step:* After completing your left side Lunge Step, shift your weight to your left foot and cross your right foot over in front of your body. Bring your left foot behind the right foot and place it hip-width from the right foot (Fig. 10–21). *Catch-Up Step:* Shift your weight to your left foot and slide your right foot across until you can plant it hip-width from the left.

ARM ACCOMPANIMENTS • Alternate chin- to chest-height opposite Arm Pumps: right Arm Pumps forward with left-side Lunge Steps, and left Arm Pumps forward with right-side Lunge Steps.

REMEMBER • When changing direction on the move, lift your heel so that your entire leg can pivot without twisting the knee. You're primarily working the buttocks muscles on the side of your stepping leg, but the other side gets some work as well, particularly when you squeeze to raise yourself up and when you bring up or cross over your leg.

DEVICES • *Cords:* Use stretch cords or rubber bands around ankles or anchor them to your waist. *Bench:* Take a Lunge Step by stepping

Fig. 10–19 • Buttocks/Hips Set #5—Side Lunge Step, In Place (Side-to-Side): left side

Fig. 10–20 • Buttocks/Hips Set #5—Side Lunge Step, On the Move: alternate sides

Fig. 10–21 • Buttocks/Hips Set #5—Catch-Up Cross-Over Step

onto the bench. *Poles:* Double-plant walking poles away from your body on either side of your feet while doing Cross-Over or Catch-Up Steps, then double plant your sticks again closer together on either side of your feet.

TRANSITION • Do 25 repetitions of the Pump 'N Walk. Then go to Sets #1–5 of the Abdominals Routines.

Abdominals Routines

The abdominals are the core muscles of your body. When tightened, they enhance your overall torso shape. When doing exercises that strengthen your abdomen, you are also working to protect your back, because strong abdominals take the workload off of your lumbar region. So the same turning, bending, and leg-extending motions work both the abdominals and the upper and lower back.

The abdominal muscles (or abs) consist of the rectus abdominis, the obliques, and the intercostals. Although another muscle, the serratus, technically belongs to the chest area, it too is shaped by exercises (such as crunches) that train the muscles of the abdomen.

The rectus abdominus is composed of vertical muscles that run from the pubic bone to the ribs. You use this muscle when you bend your upper body toward your pelvis or back, and it also allows you to flex the spinal column. The obliques run on either side of your torso, connecting your ribs to your pelvis. The intercostals, located between each of your ribs, help to draw the ribs together and lift them up.

Not only do the abdominals support the body when it is bending forward, backward, or to the side, they also act as shock absorbers, mitigating stress to the torso and lower back caused by jumping, jerking, or twisting motions.

Walking alone helps to strengthen the abdominal muscles. The action of repeated Leg Lifts helps you maintain an erect body posture. You work these muscles by turning your torso as you change direction or in response to a change in road surface. In addition, you use your abs for balance with each step you take. Also, as you take deeper breaths while working out or walking, you use your abdominal muscles to expand and contract the chest and stomach. Finally, walking enhances the tone and definition of the abs, since fat is burned off, exposing the muscles underneath.

Of course, you'll never have a "washboard" stomach simply by walking, since it doesn't provide the abdominal muscles with a wide range of motion or the work effort that sit-ups and stomach curls do. Walkshaping's abdominal exercises are the closest you can get to doing sit-ups or stomach curls while standing up.

Dramatically toning and shaping the waist area aids your fat-burning program in a number of ways. By pulling in the abdominal muscles on the front and sides of your body, you'll gain a thinner waistline even before you've lost any fat. Tightened abs give you a "full" feeling, due to the inward pressure that is placed on your stomach, which in turn suppresses your appetite and makes you eat less in between meals. When you are strong in the middle, you feel strong, confident, and motivated to continue exercising the other parts of your body.

You may have realized that the Walkshaping exercises for the thighs and buttocks/hips have already worked your abdomen by making you raise your legs higher off of the ground. However, you can also work your lower abdomen by stretching your stride. This makes use of your oblique muscles to turn your torso sideways. Upper-body exercises assist abs work as well. By pumping your arms forward and backward in the opposite direction of your legs and torso, you add extra resistance for your abdominal muscles. In general, your abs get a bigger workout whenever your body is called upon to do greater and heavier amounts of work as it is with Walkshaping.

Practice Levels

Level I: Do 5–12 repetitions for torso (or 10–24 total); Level II: 12–15; Level III: 15–20; Level IV: 21–25; and Level V: 25–30.

Abs Set #1: Belly Breathing (Stomach Tuck or Diaphragmatic Breathing)

This exercise strengthens your abdominal muscles while improving your lung capacity and breathing rhythm.

START • Hip-width stance, 90-degree Bent Arm Pump.

MOVE • Use all varieties of Strides and Leg Lifts. Take a left step forward while pumping your right arm forward. Take a deep breath, allowing your stomach to expand as you fill it with air. Continue to

Fig. 10–22 • Abs Set #1: Belly Breathing (Stomach Tucks): breathe in as you push out stomach. Do not expand chest.

inhale air slowly as you take a right step. Take another left step, and then a right one. Continue to let your stomach expand (Fig. 10–22). Begin to pull in your stomach muscles as you breathe out and take a left, right, left and right step as you pull in your stomach completely and expel all of the air (Fig. 10–23). Now repeat the process.

In Place: Step up and down, alternately lifting each foot about 6 inches off the ground with opposite Arm Pumps. This continuous leg and arm action complements your Belly Breathing exercise.

ARM ACCOMPANIMENTS • Use alternate chin- to chest-level Bent Arm Pumps. In a Four-Count movement, pump your left arm forward as you step with your right foot, and so on as you inhale, filling your abdomen with air. Perform another Four-Count as you exhale and contract your abdominal muscles.

DEVICES • *Poles:* Use single pole-plants. *Cords:* Use single cord-stretches. *Weights:* Use weight-pumps.

TRANSITION • Do 12–25 repetitions of the Pump 'N Walk, then go to either Abs Set #2 or Lower Back Set #1.

Abs Set #2: Trunk Turn

Fig. 10–23 • Abs Set #1: Belly Breathing: expel air, as you pull in stomach

This exercise shapes and tones your oblique muscles. It is best done with walking poles, doubled up and placed across your shoulders.

START • Raise your arms over your shoulders and bend them at a 90-degree angle until both elbows point away from the sides of your body. Take a hip- to shoulder-width stance.

STEPS • Use short-to-medium-length Strides and low to medium-height Leg Lifts.

MOVE • Take a left step, holding your arms and elbows extended from your chest and hips squared to the front. Rotate your torso to the left, turning your shoulders until your right shoulder and elbow are pointed in the direction of travel, and your left shoulder and elbow are pointed behind you (Fig. 10–24). Your right elbow should point straight ahead as your left heel strikes the ground. Keep your biceps parallel to the ground and in line with your shoulders. Don't let your arms drop. Try not to slouch, bend forward, or let your arms rotate around your shoulders. Feel the flex in your oblique muscles and the stretch along your right side. Now reverse the direction, taking a right

Fig. 10–24 • Abs Set #2: Trunk Turn, In Place: freehanded, left foot, right elbow

Fig. 10–25 • Renee demonstrates Abs Set #2: Trunk Turn, On the Move, with poles: behind your neck, over your shoulders, right foot/left elbow

step and rotating your left elbow and shoulder to the right side until it is pointed in the direction of travel.

In Place: Alternately lift your right or left foot 6 inches off the ground as you rotate the opposite elbow. To add more lower-body resistance, do Torso Turns: alternately take a left then a right step forward, and step back in between reps.

REMEMBER • Hold your shoulders square and erect. Extend your arms out from your shoulders. Turn your shoulders sideways against your oblique muscles rather than bending down or pointing your shoulders down when turning your torso. Control your torso as you twist by pulling in your abdominals. Keep a wide stance during this exercise; the wider the stance, the more your lower body (e.g., pelvis) turns in the opposite direction to resist your upper body. Advanced walkers, practice the Trunk Turns with a Stride Stretch Step to add even more resistance.

DEVICES • *Weights:* Hold your weights over your shoulders with fists palms-up. You can also use ankle weights if you keep the pace. *Poles:* Double up your poles and hold them over your shoulders behind your neck (Fig. 10–25). If you have back problems, hold them in front of your body across your chest or abdomen. *Cords:* Criss-cross cords across your back and anchor them under your step-up bench. Do the exercise on top of your bench, stepping front and back lengthwise.

You can also anchor the cord to the back of your waist belt, or stretch it across your back and grip it with your raised fists to anchor it. *Bench:* Do the Torso Turn while standing on the step-up bench or with the forward leg stepping on and off of the bench.

TRANSITION • Do 12–25 repetitions of the Pump 'N Walk. Then go either to Abs Set #3 or to Lower Back Set #1–2.

Abs Set #3: Leg-Raise Step, or Knee-Up

Fig. 10–26 • Abs Set #3: Leg-Raise Step or Knee-Up, In Place

This exercise shapes and strengthens the lower abdominals.

START • Place your feet in the hip- to shoulder-width stance. Bend your arms at a 90-degree angle, with your elbows at your sides.

MOVE • Use short- to medium-length Strides and low- to medium-height Leg Lifts. Do a left-knee lift until your knee is at waist height. (*Beginner walkers:* lift your knee only as high as is comfortable until you're stronger—see Fig. 10–26.) Your foot should be flexed and parallel to the ground. Once you raise your knee up, extend your leg forward and execute a Heel Strike. As you plant your left foot, raise your right knee waist-high and repeat the Knee-Up exercise with this leg.

In Place: Lower your legs back down to the starting position. As your endurance increases, raise your knee to chest height. *Advanced walkers:* Bend your knee at a 120-degree angle, raise it, and bring your foot further forward. This will make it harder to lift your knee, since it adds more resistance work for your lower abdominals.

ARM ACCOMPANIMENTS • Use chest- to chin-height Arm Pumps for in-place and on-the-move routines. Pump your right arm forward and your left arm back while lifting your left knee.

DEVICES • *Cords:* Use ankle cords for extra resistance on the in-place version of the Leg Raise steps.

TRANSITION • Do 25 repetitions of the Pump 'N Walk, then go either to Abs Set #4 or to Lower Back Sets #1–3.

Abs Set #4: Elbow-to-Knee Step

This exercise strengthens all of the abdominal muscles, especially the obliques.

Fig. 10–27 • Abs Set #4: Elbow-to-Knee, In Place: left leg, right elbow

START • Keep your feet hip-width to shoulder-width apart. Bend your arms at right angles, and keep your elbows tucked in by your sides.

MOVE • As you exhale, squeeze your abdominals and raise your left knee straight up to chest height. Turn your torso toward the left, crossing your right arm in front of your body and touching your right elbow to your left knee. Your right arm should pump forward until the fist reaches chin height.

Beginners: If lifting to chest height is too difficult, lift as high as you are able. Don't try to touch your elbow to your knee, however, if this will cause you to bend down. Instead, just bring your elbow across so that it is directly over your knee.

On the Move: Step forward, extending your left leg, and do a Heel Strike. At the same time, pump back with your right arm and pump forward with your left arm. Pull in the abdominals and lift your right knee (Fig. 10–27).

In Place: Step straight down with your left leg to return to your original position. Do a forefoot plant and roll your left foot down to your heel. Repeat the exercise with your right leg and a left-to-right Torso Turn.

ARM ACCOMPANIMENTS • Keep your arms fixed or anchored throughout the exercise, since they are being used as levers to add balance and resistance to the Lower-Body Routine. Use the Two-Count Step method. Alternate arm/Torso Turns, pointing with your elbow in the direction of the upward moving leg.

REMEMBER • Hold your abdominal muscles in as you turn your torso. When your elbow is pointed and your knee raised, you should feel the muscles contract fully.

DEVICES •

ARMS *Poles:* Double up the walking poles and hold them with palms-out across your shoulders behind your neck. They should be at shoulder height for beginners and over the head for advanced walkers. *Cords:* Criss-cross your cords behind your back and anchor them to your waist or under your feet. With palms-out, grip the handles and hold them with your arms at shoulder-height and bent at 90-degree angles. *Weights:* Hold your weights palms-out or palms-up with your arms at shoulder-height.

LEGS *Weights:* Use ankle weights. *Bench:* Use a step-up bench, alternately placing your stationary leg on top of the bench and raising your exercising leg from the ground. The bench allows you to raise and lower your leg through a wide range of motions.

TRANSITION • Do 25 repetitions of the Pump 'N Walk. Then go either to Abs Set #5 or Lower Back Sets #1–5.

Abs Set #5: Crunch

Fig. 10–28 • Abs Set #5: Crunch: right leg, double arm crunch

This exercise shapes and strengthens all of your abdominal muscles.

START • Place feet in a hip- to shoulder-width stance. Extend arms forward at shoulder height and bend them at a 90-degree angle, with fists, palms-in, raised to head height.

MOVE • Contract your abdominals as you pull down both of your arms to your sides and lift up your left leg, bringing your knee to your chest. Keep your abdominals contracted, holding for at least one whole count.

On the Move: Return your arms to shoulder height. Extend your left leg forward, raising your forefoot for a left Heel Strike. As your left heel strikes, begin to pull your arms down again, and raise your right knee to your chest. Your knee should touch your chest as your fists reach your hip joints. Give your abdominal muscles a full flex, and extend your right leg forward for the Heel Strike (Fig. 10–28). Repeat the exercise, alternating your right and left legs.

In Place: Raise your arms to shoulder height as you lower your left leg straight down onto your forefoot. As you roll down to your left heel, raise your right heel. Pulling your arms down, lift up your right knee to your chest. As your fists reach the line of your hip joint, your knees should touch your chest. Give your abdominal muscles a full squeeze, and lower your right leg to the ground. Repeat the exercise, alternating left and right legs.

ARM ACCOMPANIMENTS • The Double Arm Pull-Down works best with this exercise.

REMEMBER • Initiate the crunch from the abdominals. Think of the stomach going back toward the spine to bring the two halves of your body together into the crunch.

DEVICES • *Poles:* Double-up the walking poles and raise them horizontally overhead. Instead of bringing your knee up to your chest, bring your poles down to your stomach and your knee up to touch the poles. *Cords:* Anchor the cords behind you at the waist or underneath your step-bench. Or, criss-cross them behind your back and up over your shoulders, holding on to them on either side of your head. Pull them straight down over your shoulders. *Weights:* Use ankle weights for both the in-place and on-the-move versions. *Bench:* For in-place walking, use a step-bench, stepping up with your stationary (right) leg to execute a left leg lift Crunch and then stepping down. Reverse this for your right leg.

TRANSITION • Do 25 repetitions of Pump 'N Walk. Then go to Lower Back Sets #1–5.

Lower-Back Routines

With lower-back pain listed as Americans' number-one medical concern, the lower back could be called the Achilles' heel of the human body. A true weak point, it's one of the most sensitive areas to develop and train. Because of the way we live, the lower-back muscles don't get enough exercise. The same can be said of the abdominal muscles, which support the lower back from the front side of your body. It will be difficult for you to support your body properly unless you give the proper attention to building, shaping, and stretching the muscles in this area.

The lower-back muscles consist primarily of the spinal erectors. The spinal erectors are two columns of muscles located in the center of your back along either side of your spine. They consist of several muscles that help to keep your spine erect and to protect the nerve channels that originate in this area.

Spinal erectors serve more as stabilizers or posture holders (like the triceps muscles are used to straighten out the back of the arm) than as muscles that move the body through a full range of motion. They can be strengthened with back-extension exercises.

The Lower-Back Routines are better than bodybuilding and traditional lower-back calisthenics, because they gradually increase in resistance and the range of movement and therefore strengthen your back.

You must be careful not to overload your lower back. The weight of your own upper body is usually more than enough. The angle at which you bend over will also affect the degree of workload. Always be careful not to arch or hyperextend your back when you straighten up.

Now that you have tightened your abdominals, you will be able to stretch them out by doing the series of Back Extension Exercises in this section.

You have strengthened your lower back indirectly already with exercises like Leg Lifts and Trunk Turns. Now you will concentrate directly on the lower back and lower lats. You will do the Lower Back Routines by bending and straightening your back while you exercise. But before doing this, you must stretch and strengthen your back.

If you have persistent back pain, skip this section until after you have had a doctor's evaluation. Once the pain subsides, try to start slowly by doing a single set of these exercises along with the Upper-Body Routines. Add no more than a set per week until your back is stronger.

Practice Levels

Level I: Do 5–12 repetitions for each torso movement (or 10–24 total); Level II: 12–15; Level III: 15–20; Level IV: 20–25; and Level V: 25–30.

ALTERNATIVES • Walkers who can't or shouldn't bend over, substitute:

- Buttocks/Hips Set #2: Leg Push-Back or Alternate Lower Back Set #2B: Look-Back Walk for Lower Back Set #2

- Alternative Lower Back Set #3A: Back Step for Lower Back Set #3

- Alternative Lower Back Set #4A: Back Cross-Over Step for Lower Back Set #4

- Abdominals Set #2: Trunk Turn or Alternate Lower Back Set #5B: Turn-Back for Lower Back Set #5.

Lower Back Set #1: Pelvic Tilt

This exercise shapes and strengthens the lower back. It also improves your posture by flattening the lower back when you walk or stand and lowering your center of gravity to allow you to take longer steps.

Fig. 10–29 • Lower Back Set #1: Pelvic Tilt, In Place

START • Keep your feet hip-width apart and your arms bent at a 90-degree angle. Use short- to medium-length strides and low- to medium-height Leg Lifts.

MOVE • *In Place:* Place your feet side by side. Pull in your stomach while tilting your pelvic girdle forward. Use your stomach to pull and your buttocks/hips to push. Reach back to feel the small of your back flatten out. Hold yourself in the forward-tilted position as you take two steps in place. Relax on the third (left) step, and initiate the Pelvic Tilt again on the fifth (left) step: you will be doing two steps tucked under and two steps relaxed (Fig. 10–29). *Advanced walkers:* Build up the counts so that you hold each Pelvic Tilt for twelve steps and relax for two steps.

On the Move: Use the same method of initiating the Pelvic Tilt on your left step forward, holding your torso in the tilted position for 2–12 counts, then releasing it for two counts (Fig. 10–30). Repeat the Pelvic Tilt exercise 5–12 times to complete the set.

ARM ACCOMPANIMENT • Use the Single Bent Arm Pump at chest to chin height. Pump your arms straight forward and straight back with the elbows turned in to your sides.

REMEMBER • Keep your upper body aligned with shoulders back and chin tucked in.

DEVICES • *Poles/Cords/Weights:* Use walking poles, cords, and weights with the standard Pump 'N Walk method. Keep your moves simple and the rest of your body as relaxed as possible while you concentrate on the Lower-Back Routines.

TRANSITION • Do 12–25 repetitions of the Pump 'N Walk, then go either to Lower Back Set #2 or to Calves and Shins Set #1.

Fig. 10–30 • Lower Back Set #1: Pelvic Tilt, On the Move

Lower Back Set #2: Bent-Over Walk

This exercise strengthens and shapes your entire lower spinal erectors and lower lats muscles.

START • Standing erect with feet hip-width apart, place your arms by your sides, bent at a 90-degree angle.

MOVE • *In Place:* As you slowly bend your body forward, take a left step and pump your right arm forward and your left arm back. *Beginners,* bend to up to 45 degrees forward (see Fig. 10–31). *Advanced walkers,* bend up to 90 degrees forward. Notice that at 90 degrees your upper body is almost parallel to the ground. Now pump your left arm forward and right arm back as you raise your torso back into the upright position.

On the Move: Bend over and straighten up your body while alternating your left and right steps (Fig. 10–32). Once you have mastered this basic movement, practice the Bend Over exercise using the Three- or Five-Count Step method, again accompanied by opposite-side forward Arm Pumps. To do this, take a left step as you bend forward, then a right and a left step as you straighten up. Take a right step as you bend forward, then a left and a right step as you straighten up again.

REMEMBER • When straightening up, stop when you are completely upright, to prevent arching your back.

ARM ACCOMPANIMENTS • Alternate Bent Arm Pumps.

Fig. 10–31 • Lower Back Set #2— Bent-Over Walk, 45-degree bend, In Place

Fig. 10–32 • Lower Back Set #2— Bent-Over Walk, 90-degree bend, On the Move

DEVICES • *Poles:* Double-plant the poles, placing them far enough in front of you (approximately 1–2 feet in front of your forward moving leg) that you have room to bend over. Support your weight by placing the poles in front of you. *Cords:* Anchor cords at your feet or waist and pump them to chest to chin height.

TRANSITION • Do 12–25 repetitions of the Pump 'N Walk, then go either to Lower Back Set #3 or to Calves and Shins Sets #1–3.

Alternative Lower Back Set #2A

Practice Buttocks/Hips Set #2: Leg Push-Back.

Alternative Lower Back Set #2B: Look-Back (Fig. 10-33)

This exercise strengthens and shapes the entire lower back.

START • Place feet hip-width to shoulder-width apart.

MOVE • *In-Place* and *On-the-Move Left Look-Backs:* As you lift your left leg or take a left step forward, pump your left arm back and right arm forward, while turning your head and body to your left and rotating your side. Feel the contraction of your left spinal erector muscles. As you lift your right foot and pump your left arm, turn your head and body back to face forward.

Beginners: Turn your body 45 degrees back.

Advanced walkers: You can rotate your body up to 90 degrees back.

Right Look-Backs: As you lift your right leg or take a right step forward, pump your right arm back and left arm forward while turning your head right and rotating your body to the right. Repeat 12 to 25 times.

REMEMBER • When walking on the move, keep your eyes focused in the direction of travel. When turning your head and body forward, don't over-rotate beyond your hip line. Keep your hips and shoulders squared and perpendicular with the direction of travel.

Fig. 10–33 • Alt. Lower Back Set #2B—Look-Back

Lower Back Set #3: Bent-Over Row Back (Fig. 10–34)

This exercise shapes and strengthens the whole back, but especially the spinal erectors and the lower lats. It also works your hand and forearm muscles as you tighten and loosen your grip. This is similar to the Row Back exercise in the Upper Back Set #1 on page 158, but here you bend over while doing it.

START • Place feet in the hip-width to shoulder-width stance. Extend your arms palms-down.

MOVE • *On the Move:* Reach forward with both of your hands in a loosened grip as you take a left step forward (or a Leg Lift upward). At the same time, bend your upper body forward up to a 45-degree angle from your hips so your back is straight, and make sure your navel is pulling toward your spine (Fig. 10–35). This will protect your lower back. Take a right step. Tighten your grip, and pull both arms straight back. Take a left step and begin to straighten your upper body. Take another right step as you continue to pull back. Take another left and a right step as you pull your arms straight back and rotate them inward, ending up with palms-in. Pull your arms way back and squeeze your fists until they are fully clenched as they reach the line of your hip joint, or just behind it. Take a right step to repeat the Bent Over Row Backs.

In Place: Use the same bending over, reaching forward, and straightening up Row Back motion, but march in place (Fig. 10–36).

Fig. 10–34 • Lower Back Set #3—Bent-Over Row Back

Fig. 10–35 • Lower Back Set #3—Bent-Over Row Back, On the Move

Fig. 10–36 • Lower Back Set #3—Bent-Over Row Back, In Place

ARM ACCOMPANIMENTS • Double Pole Plants with Arm Row Backs.

DEVICES • *Poles:* Push your arms out against resistance and relax as you pull them back for the Row Backs. Double up your poles and grip them horizontally to pull them straight back to your chest. *Weights:* Grip weights with palms-down and pull them back to your sides, palms-in. *Cords:* Wrap cords around your waist. Grip the cord handles with your hands at the front of your body.

TRANSITION • Do 25 repetitions of the Pump 'N Walk, then go either to Lower Back Set #4 or Calves and Shins Sets #1–3.

Alternative Lower Back Set #3A: Back Step

This exercise shapes and strengthens the lower back.

START • Place feet hip-width to shoulder-width apart.

MOVE • *In Place:* Step straight back with your left foot. Touch the ground with your forefoot. Straighten front and back legs. (This move makes this exercise different from the Back Lunge Step, where you bend your front knee.) Pump your left arm forward and your right arm back as you step back with your left foot. Then step back with your right foot while pumping your right arm forward and your left arm back. Repeat the exercise, alternating steps and arms (Fig. 10–37).

On the Move: Walk backward slowly as you alternate steps and arms. Take a left step back and pump your right arm forward and left arm back. Take a right step back as you pump your left arm forward and right arm back (Fig. 10–38).

REMEMBER • Look back over your shoulder as you walk so that you can see where you're going.

Lower Back Set #4: Bent-Over Row-Up

This exercise works the entire lower back, including the spinal erectors and the lower lats.

START • Place feet hip-width apart. Do an upright Row, bending the arms out as you pull your fists up with the palms facing your chest.

Fig. 10–37 • Alt. Lower Back Set #3A—Back Steps, In Place

Fig. 10–38 • Alt. Lower Back Set #3A—Back Steps, On the Move

Fig. 10–39 • Lower Back Set #4—Bent-Over Row-Ups: reach down and pull up

Fig. 10–40 • Lower Back Set #4—Pulled-Up position

MOVE • You can do the same Bent-Over Row-Ups whether walking in place or on the move. Use Five-Count Steps. Straighten your arms and reach down toward your knees as you bend forward 45 degrees from your hips (Fig. 10–39). Loosen your grip. Take a left step when your fists reach knee level and your arms are straight. Bend your arms and pull your fists up toward your chest, taking a right, a left, and another right step as you row your arms up. Clench your fists more tightly, and pull them down to either side of your chest as you fully straighten your body (Fig. 10–40). Begin with the next repetition of Bent-Over Row-Ups, starting on your left step.

REMEMBER • Keep your head in line with the rest of your spine as you bend over at the waist. Keep your chin tucked in and your eyes focused following the movement. You should feel your lower back muscles working as you bend over and straighten your body.

ARM ACCOMPANIMENTS • Use the double-arm rowing motion with hand weights and doubled-up walking sticks only. *Cords:* Pump forward with cords, stretching as you bend over and contracting as you straighten your body.

LEG ACCOMPANIMENTS • Use ankle weights if walking in place. March in place as you do the bend-over and row-up action.

TRANSITION • Do 25 repetitions of the Pump 'N Walk, then go either to Lower Back Set #5 or Calves and Shins Sets #1–4.

Alternative Lower Back Set #4A: Back Cross-Over Step

This exercise shapes and strengthens the lower back.

START • Place feet hip-width to shoulder-width apart.

MOVE • *In Place:* Take a left step back and straighten your left leg as you cross it over to the right side. Plant your left forefoot on the right side of your body. Pump your right arm forward and your left arm back. Repeat the exercise with your right foot (Fig. 10–41).

On the Move: Walk backward, alternating left and right Back Cross-Over Steps.

REMEMBER • Look over your left and right shoulders as you walk backward.

Lower Back Set #5: Bent-Over Raised Arm

This exercise works the whole back, especially the lower back.

START • Place your feet hip-width apart. Bend your arms at a 90-degree angle, then raise them up over your shoulders. Raise palms-in fists

Fig. 10–41 • Alt. Lower Back Set #4A—Back Cross-Over Steps

behind and on either side of your head. Use the Five-Count-Step method; each repetition cycle will start on alternating left and right feet.

MOVE • Practice this exercise while walking in place or on the move. Take a left and a right step as you bend over to 45 degrees (beginners) the first week, and to 90 degrees the second week. Keep your arms positioned on either side of your body (Fig. 10–42). Take three more steps: a left, a right, and a left again as you straighten up your body (Fig. 10–43). Begin the next repetition with your right foot.

REMEMBER • Try not to arch your back as you return your body to its fully erect position. Keep your pelvis tucked slightly and your stomach pulled up and in to lengthen and support your lower back throughout the exercise.

You will notice that the arms do not move during this exercise. This minimum of movement allows you to walk while concentrating on exercising the lower-back muscles with great resistance through a wide range of motions.

You do not have to bend completely to 90 degrees to get the benefits of this exercise. To be safe, practice at 45 degrees until you feel strong and comfortable with the exercise.

Fig. 10–42 • Lower Back Set #5— Bent-Over Raised Arm: 45 degrees (bent over)

Fig. 10–43 • Raised Up

Fig. 10–44 • Lower Back Set #5— Bent-Over Raised Arm: stretch cords 90 degrees (raising up)

DEVICES • Since your raised arms are already acting as an extra resistance device, it's best to try out this exercise freehanded in the beginning (the first few weeks). Then shift to light weights and resistance devices when you feel ready.

Poles: Double up your poles and hold them horizontally over and behind your head. *Cords:* In the beginning, stretch up the cords with elbows chest high. Later you can advance to elbows at shoulder height. *Weights:* Use ankle weights for walking in place. *Bench:* Step up and down with both feet, doing the exercise when both feet are on the step up bench.

TRANSITION • Do 25 repetitions of the Pump 'N Walk, then go to Calves and Shins Sets #1–5.

Alternative Lower Back Set #5A

Practice Abs Set #2: Trunk Turn instead of Lower Back Set #5.

Alternative Lower Back Set #5B: Turn-Back (Fig. 10–45)

This exercise works the whole back, but focuses especially on the lower back. It differs from Set #5A Trunk Turns in that you rotate your body behind rather than in front of your body or hip line. Turn-Backs also resemble Set #2B Look-Backs, except they are done with both arms raised.

START • Feet should be hip-width to shoulder-width apart. Raise both arms to shoulder height and bend them both at a 90-degree angle.

MOVE • *In Place* and *On the Move:* As you take a left step, keep your head up and rotate your body 45 degrees (beginners) to 90 degrees (advanced) to the left. As you take a right step, rotate your body forward until it is parallel to the direction of travel. Keep your head and eyes facing straight forward as you turn. Practice the Left-Sided Turn-Backs for 12–25 repetitions and then repeat the movement on the opposite side. Step with the right foot as you do 12–25 Right-Sided Turn-Backs.

Fig. 10–45 • Alt. Lower Back Set #5B—Turn-Back

REMEMBER • Start each Turn-Back with your shoulders squared. Avoid over-rotation, which will turn this into an abdominal exercise.

ARM ACCOMPANIMENTS • *Weights:* Hold weights with your palms up. *Cords:* Stretch the cords from the waist or from under-foot attachments. Keep them stretched in the raised-arm position. *Poles:* Double-up the poles over your head.

Calves and Shins Routines

The calves and shins are used to flex your feet forward, back, and side to side and to rotate your ankle.

The calf, at the back of your lower leg, includes three muscles: the soleus, the plantaris, and the two-headed gastrocnemius. You work these muscles when you "toe-off," or raise your heels off the ground and go up onto your toes while walking.

The shin, at the front of your lower leg, has one major muscle, the tibialis anterior. You use your shin to raise up your forefoot until your weight is shifted to your heel. In addition, there are tendon link muscles, which include: the peroneus (longus and brevis), the extensors (hallucis longus and digitorum longus), the tibialis exterior, and the flexors (hallucis longus and digitorum longus). These run along the sides and front of your lower leg. The tibialis exteriors and the flexors are more difficult to train than the first two muscles, but they are still important to the function of the foot in Walkshaping and need to be stretched and strengthened.

Calves and shins can be worked more naturally and continuously by walking than by any other movement. Needed for the heel strike and the toe push-off, they are worked even more when going up and down inclines.

However, because many of us walk flat-footed and without parallel foot placement, our lower leg muscles are not as developed as they could be.

Walkshaping exercises put your feet through a greater range of movement and therefore add the necessary "stress" to make your lower legs stronger. Using step-up benches and ankle weights adds the extra resistance that you will need to shape and develop your lower legs.

Practice Levels

Level I: Do 5–12 repetitions with each leg (or 10–24 total); Level II: 12–15; Level III: 15–20; Level IV: 21–25; and Level V: 25–30.

Calves and Shins Set #1: Toes-Raised Walk

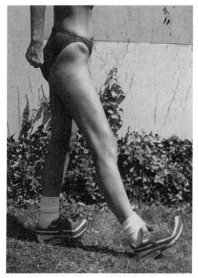

Fig. 10–46 • Calves and Shins Set #1—The Toes-Raised Walk, In Place

This exercise strengthens and develops the shin muscles, especially the soleus, while also stretching the calves.

START • Stand with your feet parallel and hip- to shoulder-width apart. Raise your forefeet 45 degrees from the ground and shift your weight back to your heels. Bend your body slightly forward (about 5 degrees). Keep your knees slightly bent. Bend your arms to 90 degrees, with your elbows by your sides.

MOVE • *In Place:* Take short to medium steps forward and back, or walk around in small circles. Take 5–25 Toes Raised steps before resuming your regular heel-toe action (Fig. 10–46). Pump your right arm forward, chin- to chest-high, and your left arm back behind the line of your hip.

On the Move: Take a left step forward and land on your heel, keeping your front and back knees slightly bent. Roll your left foot slightly forward, but do not shift your weight. You should be pulling back your forefoot continually and holding it in the Toes Raised position to allow you to start walking on your heels. Take a right-heel step as you pump your left arm forward and right arm back. Repeat the left-right Toes-Raised Walk steps 12–25 times.

DEVICES • Alternate Arm Pumps with *weights* and *cords*. You can also use ankle weights. Use *poles* to maintain your balance during the Toes-Raised Walk, allowing you to pull back your forefoot more fully. *Bench:* Step off the step-up bench with your left foot, landing on your heel. Step back up again with your left foot. Then step off with your right foot, landing on your heel. Step back up onto your right foot.

VARIATIONS • *Advanced walkers:* In place, stand with your heels on the step-up bench. Lower your forefoot with your toes going as far down as they can. Then raise your forefoot as far up as your toes can go. You can strap your ankle weights to your forefoot to get extra resistance.

TRANSITION • Do 12–25 repetitions of the Pump 'N Walk, then go either to Calves and Shins Set #2 or to the Cool-Down Walk.

Calves and Shins Set #2: Heels-Raised Walk (Fig. 10–47)

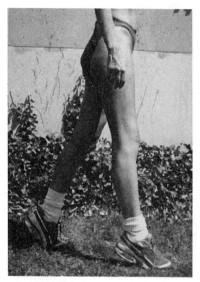

Fig. 10–47 • Calves and Shin Set #2—Heels-Raised Walk, In Place

This exercise strengthens your calves and stretches your shins.

START • With your feet hip- to shoulder-width apart, raise your heels as you shift your weight to your forefoot. Use the chin- to chest-height 90-degree Bent Arm Pump. In place, use short Leg Lifts; on the move, use medium to long Strides.

MOVE • *In Place:* Step forward with the left forefoot. As you land, raise both heels off the ground and flex your calf muscles. Step back with your left foot, and repeat the action by stepping forward with your right forefoot while pumping your arms in opposition. Do 12–25 left-right Heels-Raised Steps.

On the Move: Pump your right arm forward and your left arm back as you take a left step forward and land on your left forefoot. As your left forefoot strikes the ground, raise both of your heels as far off the ground as they can go and flex your calf muscles. Lower your left heel slightly, without letting it touch the ground. As you balance yourself on your left forefoot, bring your right foot forward, and toe off with your right forefoot to propel your right leg forward. Repeat on the right. Repeat the exercise 12–25 times.

REMEMBER • Keep yourself up on your toes: avoid shifting your weight back to your heels.

DEVICES • Alternately pump arms with *hand weights, stretch cords,* and *walking sticks. Poles:* Use the poles to keep yourself balanced and up on your toes through the repetitions. *Bench:* With both heels hanging over the edge of the bench, use your calves to lower your heels and raise them. This gives you the maximum range of motion for this muscle group.

Alternatively, start with both feet on the ground next to the bench. Step up with the left forefoot and raise your heel. Then step down with the left forefoot. Now step up with the right forefoot and raise the heel. Then step down with the right forefoot. Try to keep your weight in the balls of your feet, just letting your heels touch down briefly.

TRANSITION • Do 12–25 repetitions of the Pump 'N Walk. Then go either to Calves and Shins Set #3 or to the Cool-Down Walk.

Calves and Shins Set #3: Heel-Toe Rock (Figs. 10–48, 49)

Fig. 10–48 • Calves and Shin Set #3—Heel-Toe Rock, In Place

This exercise shapes, strengthens, and stretches the entire lower leg. It also improves the heel-toe action that is used in all of the Walkshaping exercises.

START • *In Place:* Keep feet parallel, side by side, and hip- to shoulder-width apart. You will do the exercise with your feet side by side. *On the Move:* Assume the Stride Stretch parallel foot stance. Use the 90-degree bent Double Arm Pump at chin to chest height. Start with your arms raised forward to shoulder height, with your fists on either side of your head.

MOVE • *In Place:* Roll forward on the outer edges of your feet until you're up on your forefeet. As you do this, pump your arms straight down and back until your fists pass the line of your buttocks/hips joints. Push your arms back to maintain your balance as you go all the way up onto your toes and straighten out your legs. Flex your calf muscles. Avoid the urge to arch your back while balancing on your toes.

Now roll back down along the outer edges of your feet. Pull up your forefeet 45 degrees from the ground as you shift the weight back to your heels. Straighten your legs without locking and bend forward slightly. At the same time, pump your arms forward until they are at shoulder height. Feel the stretch in your calves. Repeat the Heel-Toe Rock exercise 12–25 times.

On the Move: Take a left Stride Stretch Step and roll up onto both forefeet, making sure to maintain a hip- to shoulder-width stance. As you roll up, pump your arms back with your fists behind the line of your buttocks/hips. Flex the muscles in both of your calves as you straighten your legs. Now roll back onto both of your heels, raising up your forefeet 45 degrees. Pump both of your arms forward. As your elbows reach shoulder height, your calves should be fully stretched out and your legs almost fully straightened.

If you have difficulty pulling your back forefoot up from this front-back position, know that it will become easier as your calf muscles become more flexible. Step forward with your back (right) foot, putting it in front of your left foot. Repeat the Heel-Toe Rock exer-

Fig. 10–49 • Calves and Shin Set #3—Heel-Toe Rock, On the Move

cise with the right foot forward, alternating left and right feet forward until you complete 12–25 Heel-Toe Rocks.

REMEMBER • Straighten your legs fully without locking your knees in the heels-up part of the exercise.

DEVICES • Use *weights*, *poles*, and *stretch cords* with the Double Arm Pump exercise. *Poles:* Double-plant your walking poles 2–3 feet in front of you. Be sure to plant them wide for maximum stability. Press down on both poles as you roll up onto your toes, and bend the poles back slightly as you roll up onto your heels.

WEIGHTS • Ankle weights work well for the heel-raise part of the exercise, because they add more stress to your calf muscles. They don't, however, stress the shins: To do this, add the weight to your forefoot. This is done most comfortably in the Toe-Raised Walk or the in-place Toe Raises from a step-bench.

TRANSITION • Do 12–25 repetitions of the Pump 'N Walk, then go either to the Calves and Shins Set #4 or to the Cool-Down Walk.

Calves and Shins Set #4: Toeing-Out and -In

This two-part exercise shapes the outer calves by turning your toes inward and the inner calf muscles (the soleus) by turning the toes outward. The exercise is the same as the Heels-Raised Walk, but here you turn your toes inward.

START • Your feet should be hip- to shoulder-width apart. Pump your arms, bent to 90-degrees, to chest to chin height.

MOVE •

PART ONE: TOES INWARD   Pump your right arm forward and left arm back while taking a left step forward and landing on your left heel (Fig. 10–50). As you do, turn your foot with toes facing inward (toes-in) at a 20 to 45-degree angle from the line along which you're traveling. Then roll up your foot to your forefoot, raising your heel off the ground. Feel the flex in your left outer calf. As you raise your forward heel, you should also raise your back foot, turning it inward and raising your back heel. Feel the flex in the outer calf of the back leg. Repeat the same movement by bringing your right foot forward.

In Place: Bring your left foot back and get ready to take a right step forward onto your right heel (Fig. 10–51). Repeat, alternating the left-right Toes Inward Heel Raises 12–25 times.

PART TWO: TOES OUTWARD HEELS RAISED   *On the Move:* Take a left step forward and strike with your heel. Turn your forefoot outward and roll up your foot to your toes. At the same time, roll up along the outward edge of your back foot and feel the flex on your back inner calf (Fig. 10–52).

In Place: Step back with your left foot and get ready to put your right foot forward. Plant your right heel and turn out your forefoot. Then roll up to your forefoot and toes and raise your heel off the ground, feeling the flex in your inner calf. Your left (back) foot should also be turned outward; simultaneously roll up onto your toes to raise up your back heel. Feel the flex in your inner calf. Step back with your right foot and get ready to take a left step forward. Repeat the left-right Outward Heel Raises 12–25 times.

DEVICES • Practice 90-degree Bent Arm Pumps with *weights, cords,* and *poles. Poles:* Alternate opposite-arm plants to keep balanced, so that you can fully raise your heels.

WEIGHTS • Ankle weights work well to stress your calves if you are walking in place. *Bench:* Stand with feet side by side, with the heels hanging off the edge of the step-up bench. Turning your feet inward,

Fig. 10–50 • Calves and Shin Set #4—Toeing-In, On the Move: toes inward

Fig. 10–51 • Calves and Shin Set #4—Toeing-In, In Place: toes inward

Fig. 10–52 • Calves and Shin Set #4—Toeing-Out, On the Move: toes outward

raise and lower your heels to the ground and up above the height of the step bench 12–25 times. Feel the flex in your outer calves. Next, turn your feet outward and raise and lower your heels 12–25 times as you feel the flex in your inner calves.

TRANSITION • Do 25 repetitions of the Pump 'N Walk. Then go either to Calves and Shins Sets #1–4 or to the Cool-Down Walk.

Calves and Shins Set #5: One-Leg Heel Raise (Fig. 10-53)

Fig. 10–53 • Calves and Shin Set #5—One-Leg Heel Raises, On the Move

This exercise allows you to further isolate each calf muscle, using the whole weight of your body to stress it.

START • Keep your feet rolled to each other in the hip- to shoulder-width stance. Use the 90-degree Bent Arm Pump at chest to chin height.

MOVE • Pump your right arm forward and your left arm back as you take a left step forward. Plant your left heel and roll up along the outer edge of your foot onto your toes. As you do so, toe-off with your back foot and lift it 2–6 inches off the ground. Flex your left calf muscle.

On the Move: Bring your back (right) foot forward without placing it back down. *In Place:* Roll your right forefoot back down and shift your weight to it. Step back to bring your left foot back in line and side by side with your right foot. Get ready to step forward with your right foot. Now, pump your left arm forward and right arm back. Repeat the left-right One-Leg Heel Raises 12–25 times.

REMEMBER • Lean forward slightly as you straighten your forward leg and raise up your heels. Also, straighten out your back leg as you lift your back foot completely off the ground.

ARM ACCOMPANIMENTS • Alternately pump weights, poles, and cords at chest to chin height. *Poles: Beginners:* double-plant your poles for more stability; *Advanced walkers*, use single-pole plants to effect the most stress on the calf muscle of your forward leg.

LEG ACCOMPANIMENTS • *Weights:* Ankle weights work well for in-place walkers to add extra resistance. Because of the slow guided movement, ankle weights can also be used by on-the-move walkers. *Bench:* Advanced in-place walkers, step forward and up onto the step-bench. Raise your forward heel up and lift your whole body's weight 2–6 inches as you lift your back leg off of the ground.

TRANSITION • Do 25 repetitions of the Pump 'N Walk, then go to the Cool-Down Walk.

Cool-Down Walk (1–5 minutes)

Continue walking at a slow to moderate pace (2–3½ miles per hour on the move; 30–60 steps per minute walking in place). Practice the chest- to chin-height Arm Pumps with medium Strides or low to medium Leg Lifts. After completing the Cool-Down Walk, go back to the Four Basic Stretches, on page 118.

The Walkshaping Program Summarized

A. Posture-Shaping Routines

Posture Set #1:   Hip-Width Parallel Foot Placement

Posture Set #2:   Pelvic Tilt

Posture Set #3:   Head Centering (Left, Right, Down, Back)

Posture Set #4:   Chin Tuck

Posture Set #5:   Bent Arm Pump Stretch (Deltoids, Chest, Chin, Head, Overhead, Behind Head)

Posture Set #6:   Stride Stretch Step

Posture Set #7:   Knee-Up Stretch

Posture Set #8:   Raising Your Step

Posture Set #9:   Heel-Toe Rock

Posture Set #10:   Synchronized Breathing/Pump 'N Walk Steps in Place (Two-Two, Three-Three, Four-Four)

B. 12 Minutes-a-Day Walkshaping Sets (Level I)

I.   Warm-Up Walk   1 minute
II. Stretching   1 minute
       Stretching Set #1: Calf and Achilles Heel Stretch
       Stretching Set #2: Quadriceps and Ankle Stretch
       Stretching Set #3: Lunge Stretch

Stretching Set #4: Hamstring Stretch
Stretching Set #5: Heel-Toe Rock

III. Whole-Body Routines   3 minutes

IV. (A) Upper-Body Routines—Day One   6 minutes

Do 12 to 25 reps of each of the following body-parts sets while walking in place or on the move.

1. Biceps Set #1: Hammer Curl
2. Chest Set #1: Bent Arm Cross-Over
3. Triceps Set #1: Elbow-Down Extension
4. Shoulders Set #1: Front Lateral
5. Upper Back Set #1: Row Back

OR

(B) Lower-Body Routines—Day Two   6 minutes

Do 12 to 25 reps of each of the following body-parts sets while pumping your arms using the 90-degree Bent Arm Pump.

1. Thighs Set #1: Lunge Step
2. Buttocks/Hips Set #1: Heel Dig
3. Abdominals Set #1: Belly Breathing
4. Lower Back Set #1: Pelvic Tilt
5. Calves and Shins Set #1: Toes-Raised Walk

V. Cool-Down Walk (stretching)   1 minute

C. 20 Minutes-a-Day Walkshaping Sets (Level II)

I. Warm-Up Walk   2 minutes

II. Stretching   2 minutes

Stretching Set #1: Calf and Achilles Stretch
Stretching Set #2: Quadriceps and Ankle Stretch
Stretching Set #3: Lunge and Groin Stretch
Stretching Set #4: Hamstring Stretch
Stretching Set #5: Heel-Toe Rock

III. Whole-Body Routines   4 minutes

IV. (A) Upper-Body Routines—Day One   10 minutes

(2 sets per body part)

Do 12 to 25 reps of each of the following body-parts sets while walking in place or on the move.

1. Biceps Set #1: Hammer Curl
   Biceps Set #2: Palm-Up Curl
2. Chest Set #1: A. Bent Arm Cross-Over

          B. Straight Arm Cross-Over

          C. Double Arm Cross-Over

     Chest Set #2: Fly Pump with Twist

  3. Triceps Set #1: Elbow-Down Extension

     Triceps Set #2: Elbow-Back-of-Hip Joint Extension

  4. Shoulders Set #1: Front Lateral

     Shoulders Set #2: Side Lateral

  5. Upper Back Set #1: Row Back

     Upper Back Set #2: Modified Upright Row

     OR

(B) Lower-Body Routines—Day Two   10 minutes

Do 12 to 25 reps of each of the following body-parts sets while pumping your arms using the 90-degree Bent Arm Pump.

  1. Thighs Set #1: Lunge Step

     Thighs Set #2: Cross-Over Step

  2. Buttocks/Hips Set #1: Heel Dig

     Buttocks/Hips Set #2: Leg Push-Back

  3. Abdominals Set #1: Belly Breathing

     Abdominals Set #2: Trunk Turn

  4. Lower Back Set #1: Pelvic Tilt

     Lower Back Set #2: Bent-Over Walk

  4A. Lower Back #1: Pelvic Tilt*

     Alternate Lower Back Set #2A: Leg Push-Back

                    B: Look-Back Walk

  5. Calves and Shins Set #1: Toes-Raised Walk

     Calves and Shins Set #2: Heels-Raised Walk

V. Cool-Down Walk (stretching)   2 minutes

30 Minutes-a-Day Walkshaping Sets (Level III)

I. Warm-Up Walk   3 minutes

II. Stretching   3 minutes

     Stretching Set #1: Calf and Achilles Heel Stretch

     Stretching Set #2: Quadriceps and Ankle Stretch

     Stretching Set #3: Lunge Stretch

     Stretching Set #4: Hamstring Stretch

     Stretching Set #5: Heel-Toe Rock

III. Whole-Body Routines   6 minutes

*Back Savers Routines

IV. (A) Upper-Body Routines—Day One   16 minutes
(3 sets per body part)

Do 12 to 25 reps of each of the following body-parts sets while walking in place or on the move.

1. Biceps Set #1: Hammer Curl
   Biceps Set #2: Palm-Up Curl
   Biceps Set #3: Palm-Down Curl
2. Chest Set #1: A. Bent Arm Cross-Over
                B. Straight Arm Cross-Over
                C. Double Arm Cross-Over
   Chest Set #2: Fly Pump with Twist
   Chest Set #3: Press-Out (double arm)
3. Triceps Set #1: Elbow-Down Extension
   Triceps Set #2: Elbow-Back-of-Hip Extension
   Triceps Set #3: Fists Behind Hipline Arm Extension
4. Shoulders Set #1: Front Lateral
   Shoulders Set #2: Side Lateral
   Shoulders Set #3: Back Lateral
5. Upper Back Set #1: Row Back
   Upper Back Set #2: Modified Upright Row
   Upper Back Set #3: Row-Out

OR

(B) Lower-Body Routines—Day Two   16 minutes

Do 12 to 25 reps of each of the following body-parts sets while pumping your arms using the 90-degree Bent Arm Pump.

1. Thighs Set #1: Lunge Step
   Thighs Set #2: Cross-Over Step
   Thighs Set #3: Leg Curl
2. Buttocks/Hips Set #1: Heel Dig
   Buttocks/Hips Set #2: Leg Push-Back
   Buttocks/Hips Set #3: Buttocks/Hips Squeeze
3. Abdominals Set #1: Belly Breathing
   Abdominals Set #2: Trunk Turn
   Abdominals Set #3: Leg-Raise Step
4. Lower Back Set #1: Pelvic Tilt
   Lower Back Set #2: Bent-Over Walk
   Lower Back Set #3: Bent-Over Row Back
4A. Alternate Lower Back Set #1A: Pelvic Tilt*

*Back Savers Routines

Alternate Lower Back Set #2A: Leg Push-Back
B: Look-Back Walk
Alternate Lower Back Set #3A: Back Step
5. Calves Shins and Set #1: Toes-Raised Walk
Calves Shins and Set #2: Heels-Raised Walk
Calves Shins and Set #3: Heel-Toe Rock
V. Cool-Down Walk (stretching)   3 minutes

45 Minutes-a-Day Walkshaping Sets (Level IV)

I.   Warm-Up Walk   4 minutes
II. Stretching   4 minutes
Stretching Set #1: Calf and Achilles Stretch
Stretching Set #2: Quadriceps and Ankle Stretch
Stretching Set #3: Lunge and Groin Stretch
Stretching Set #4: Hamstring Stretch
Stretching Set #5: Heel-Toe Rock
III. Whole-Body Routines   9 minutes
IV. (A) Upper-Body Routines—Day One   24 minutes
(4 sets per body part)
Do 12 to 25 reps of each of the following body-parts sets
while walking in place or on the move.
1. Biceps Set #1: Hammer Curl
Biceps Set #2: Palm-Up Curl
Biceps Set #3: Palm-Down Curl
Biceps Set #4: Palm-Out Curl
2. Chest Set #1: A. Bent Arm Cross-Over
B. Straight Arm Cross-Over
C. Double Arm Cross-Over
Chest Set #2: Fly Pump with Twist
Chest Set #3: Press-Out (double arm)
Chest Set #4: Elbow Squeeze
3. Triceps Set #1: Elbow-Down Extension
Triceps Set #2: Elbow-Back-of-Hip Joint Extension
Triceps Set #3: Fists Behind Hip-Line Arm Extension
Triceps Set #4: Side-Cross Extension
4. Shoulders Set #1: Front Lateral
Shoulders Set #2: Side Lateral
Shoulders Set #3: Back Lateral
Shoulders Set #4: Clean and Press-Up

5. Upper Back Set #1: Row Back
Upper Back Set #2: Modified Upright Row
Upper Back Set #3: Row-Out
Upper Back Set #4: Back Row-Up

OR

(B) Lower-Body Routines—Day Two   24 minutes

Do 12 to 25 reps of each of the following body-parts sets while pumping your arms using the 90-degree Bent Arm Pump.

1. Thighs Set #1: Lunge Step
Thighs Set #2: Cross-Over Step
Thighs Set #3: Leg Curl
Thighs Set #4: Leg Extension Step

2. Buttocks/Hips Set #1: Heel Dig
Buttocks/Hips Set #2: Leg Push-Back
Buttocks/Hips Set #3: Buttocks/Hips Squeeze
Buttocks/Hips Set #4: Side Leg Lift

3. Abdominals Set #1: Belly Breathing
Abdominals Set #2: Trunk Turn
Abdominals Set #3: Leg-Raise Step
Abdominals Set #4: Elbow-to-Knee Step

4. Lower Back Set #1: Pelvic Tilt
Lower Back Set #2: Bent-Over Walk
Lower Back Set #3: Bent-Over Row-Back
Lower Back Set #4: Bent-Over Row-Up

4A. Lower Back Set #1: Pelvic Tilt*
Alternate Lower Back Set #2A: Leg Push-Back
    B: Look-Back Walk
Alternate Lower Back Set #3A: Back Step
Alternate Lower Back Set #4A: Back Cross-Over Step

5. Calves and Shins Set #1: Toes-Raised Walk
Calves and Shins Set #2: Heels-Raised Walk
Calves and Shins Set #3: Heel-Toe Rock
Calves and Shins Set #4: Toeing-Out and -In

V. Cool-Down Walk (stretching)   4 minutes

60 Minutes-a-Day Walkshaping Sets (Level V)

I. Warm-Up Walk   5 minutes
II. Stretching   5 minutes

*Back Savers Routines

Stretching Set #1: Calf and Achilles Heel Stretch
Stretching Set #2: Quadriceps and Ankle Stretch
Stretching Set #3: Lunge Stretch
Stretching Set #4: Hamstring Stretch
Stretching Set #5: Heel-Toe Rock

III. Whole-Body Routines   15 minutes

IV. (A) Upper-Body Routines—Day One   30 minutes
(5 sets per body part)
Do 12 to 25 reps of each of the following body-parts sets while walking in place or on the move.

1. Biceps Set #1: Hammer Curl
   Biceps Set #2: Palm-Up Curl
   Biceps Set #3: Palm-Down Curl
   Biceps Set #4: Palm-Out Curl
   Biceps Set #5: A. Double Arm Curl
                    B. Raised Arm Curl
                    C. Concentration Curl

2. Chest Set #1: A. Bent Arm Cross-Over
                  B. Straight Arm Cross-Over
                  C. Double Arm Cross-Over
   Chest Set #2: Fly Pump with Twist
   Chest Set #3: Press-Out (double arm)
   Chest Set #4: Elbow Squeeze
   Chest Set #5: Fist Turn
   Chest Set #6: Pull-Over Pump (double arm)

3. Triceps Set #1: Elbow-Down Extension
   Triceps Set #2: Elbow-Back-of-Hip Joint Extension
   Triceps Set #3: Fists Behind Hipline Arm Extension
   Triceps Set #4: Side Cross Extension
   Triceps Set #5: Elbow-Up Extension

4. Shoulders Set #1: Front Lateral
   Shoulders Set #2: Side Lateral
   Shoulders Set #3: Back Lateral
   Shoulders Set #4: Clean and Press-Up
   Shoulders Set #5: Upright Row and Shrug

5. Upper Back Set #1: Row Back
   Upper Back Set #2: Modified Upright Row
   Upper Back Set #3: Row-Out
   Upper Back Set #4: Back Row-Up
   Upper Back Set #5: Pull-Down/Pull-Over

OR

(B) Lower-Body Routines—Day Two   30 minutes

Do 12 to 25 reps of each of the following body-parts sets while pumping your arms using the 90-degree Bent Arm Pump.

1. Thighs Set #1: Lunge Step
    Thighs Set #2: Cross-Over Step
    Thighs Set #3: Leg Curl
    Thighs Set #4: Leg Extension Step
    Thighs Set #5: Squat
2. Buttocks/Hips Set #1: Heel Dig
    Buttocks/Hips Set #2: Leg Push-Back
    Buttocks/Hips Set #3: Buttocks/Hips Squeeze
    Buttocks/Hips Set #4: Side Leg Lift
    Buttocks/Hips Set #5: Side Lunge Step
3. Abdominals Set #1: Belly Breathing
    Abdominals Set #2: Trunk Turn
    Abdominals Set #3: Leg-Raise Step
    Abdominals Set #4: Elbow-to-Knee Step
    Abdominals Set #5: Crunch
4. Lower Back Set #1: Pelvic Tilt
    Lower Back Set #2: Bent-Over Walk
    Lower Back Set #3: Bent-Over Row Back
    Lower Back Set #4: Bent-Over Row-Up
    Lower Back Set #5: Bent-Over Arm Raise
4A. Lower Back Set #1: Pelvic Tilt*
    Alternate Lower Back Set #2A: Leg Push-Back
                            B: Look-Back Walk
    Alternate Lower Back Set #3A: Back Step
    Alternate Lower Back Set #4A: Back Cross-Over Step
    Alternate Lower Back Set #5A: Trunk Turn
                            B: Turn-Back
5. Calves and Shins Set #1: Toes-Raised Walk
    Calves and Shins Set #2: Heels-Raised Walk
    Calves and Shins Set #3: Heel-Toe Rock
    Calves and Shins Set #4: Toeing-Out and -In
    Calves and Shins Set #5: One-Leg Heel Raise

V. Cool-Down Walk (stretching)   5 minutes

*Back Savers Routines

PART FOUR

Going the Distance

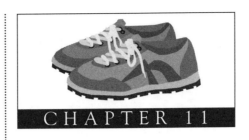

CHAPTER 11

Choreography

Once you've mastered the basic Walkshaping routines, you'll be stronger, fitter, and ready to handle a greater workload. Mastery will come after Week One for some and after Week Six for others. You'll know that you're ready to move ahead when you have the strength and endurance to practice the basic routines at a steady pace while synchronizing arm, leg, and torso movements.

In this chapter, you will learn to supplement your basic workout by adding choreographed arm moves and/or steps to your Warm-Up and Whole-Body Walks to burn more calories. You'll also learn how to split up the routines in your Upper- and Lower-Body Workouts over several days, so that you work your whole body every day while adding variety to your workout. The combination routines and step/arm accompaniments outlined here will increase your calorie burn during a Walkshaping workout by 50–100 percent.

When a Routine Is Too Difficult to Do

If you find it difficult to do a particular set, especially one that is done on the move, practice it in place first without weights or resistance. If a set is still too difficult for you, substitute another set from the same Body-Parts Routines; the set directly before or after the problematic one will usually do. Eventually, your Walkshaping routines will fit together like a dance routine, linked with smooth transitions from one exercise to the next.

Pace Yourself

Use the rate of your heartbeat, pulse, or breathing to measure the pace of your exercise intensity. Remember to go more slowly during the Warm-Up and Cool-Down Walks and to hold your stretches in one position rather than bouncing. Slow down if your pulse rate is too high or when you're breathing too hard to maintain a conversation, and speed up if your pulse rate drops, your breathing becomes too regular, or you haven't broken a sweat.

To link your pulse rate to your exercise pace: subtract your age from 220 (the maximum heartbeats per minute that a child can have) to find out your maximum heartbeat based on age. Now, multiply this number by 0.6 for your low-end heartbeat, and by 0.8 for your high-end. For example, if you're 40 years old, your maximum rate is 220 minus 40, or 180 beats per minute (BPM). Your lower limit for exercising is 180×0.6, or 108 BPM. Your upper limit for exercising is 180×0.8, or 144 BPM.

Your resting pulse is about ⅛ to ¼ of your maximum rate. (If your resting pulse is higher, you will notice a decline in BPM as your heart gets fitter and your endurance increases.)

Does Age Count?

Readers over age 35 should pay close attention here. With Walkshaping, you can have the body of a person up to 20 years younger than your chronological age, as measured by average strength and fitness scales.

PULSE-RATE MONITORING FOR A 40-YEAR OLD	
1 Resting Pulse	15% (30BPM) to 45% (81 BPM) of your maximum heart rate
2 Warm-Up Walk	25% to 60% of max., or up to 108 BPM
3 Whole-Body Walk and	60% to 80% of max., or 108–144 BPM
4 Body-Parts Routines	
5 Cool-Down	25% to 60% of max., or 45–108 BPM
6 Resting Pulse	15% to 25% of max., or 27–45 BPM

Your age, however, will affect the speed of your progress on the program and the time it takes for your sore muscles to recover. Most people progress more slowly after age 35. If you're in this age category, take great care in choosing the level at which you start to exercise. When in doubt, start with Level I, or return to Level I if you find that your original choice was too ambitious. (If you're over 55 and out of shape, you may need to spend the full six weeks at Level I.) If you're over 35 or haven't exercised in the last three months, consult a doctor before starting any new exercise program.

Your muscles begin to atrophy after age 35, often losing their shape and size. Try using no weights or lighter weights (½ to 3lbs.), especially if you haven't done strength training before. The older you are, the more time for recovery your muscles may need. Using the suggestions detailed below, split up your Body-Parts Routines to allow a full 48 hours of rest for each area. You may need even more rest when you first start out. Feel free to continue your Whole-Body Walk on your days off from your Body-Parts Workout.

Adding More Arm and Step Accompaniments

Before you combine routines, here are a series of arm and step accompaniments you can add to your basic Stride Stretch Step and Leg Lifts. Remember that a "step" is any movement that you take with your leg forward, to the side, back, or up. A "left step in place" generally means that you raise your knee and foot 3–8 inches; a "left step on the move" means that you place your left leg forward. Along with your Stride Stretch Steps and Leg Lifts, practice Heel Digs and Quick Steps, alternating left and right sides:

1. Heel Digs (see page 176, Buttocks/Hips Set #1)
   Steps where you touch down with your heel first, involving a more forceful plant and push down into the ground.

2. Leg Curl Steps (see page 171, Thighs Set #3)
   Steps where you raise your heel back to your buttocks/hips.

3. Cross-Over Steps (see page 169, Thighs Set #2)
   Alternate with your left side forward for 12 steps, then your right side forward for 12 steps.

More Arm Accompaniments

Instead of the chin-height Bent Arm Pump, the following easy arm accompaniments can be used with your Lower-Body Workout:

Straight Arm Pump

Like the Bent Arm Pump (see page 106), but here you bend your arm only slightly. Avoid locking your elbow joint because it tends to cut off the blood flow to your hands and forearms, which is bad for your joints. Pump your arm straight forward and straight back just as you did with the 90-degree Bent Arm Pump.

The Straight Arm Pump lengthens the distance your fists must travel, and goes well with slow-paced and large steps such as Stride Stretch and Lunge Steps. If you increase your speed, revert to the Bent Arm Pump.

45-Degree Cross-Over Pump (See page 135, Chest Set #1)

A shorter version of the 90-degree Bent Arm Cross-Over, but with arms bent to form 45-degree angles, this is the Arm Pump preferred by race-walkers. It shortens the distance your fists must travel and therefore makes a good accompaniment to short quick steps, including Heel Digs. Also, it allows you to pump your arms straight forward, straight back, or even across your chest as race-walkers do.

The single-arm version accompanies all of the Lower-Body Routines. The double-arm version (aka the Cradle Pump) goes well with Cross-Over Steps, Leg Extension Steps, Leg Push-Backs, Side Leg Lifts, Side Lunge Steps, and all exercises in the Abdominals Sets.

Press-Out and Row Back with Lunge Step, Leg Extension Step, and Squat Step (See page 139, Chest Set #3, and page 158, Upper Back Set #1)

As you step forward, press out both of your arms. Row them back as you shift your weight to take the next step. Be sure to keep your arms moving horizontally to your chest in line with your waist. For better balance, move your arms in opposition to, or opposite from, the direction your legs are moving. Beginner walkers, use single-arm versions; advanced walkers, use double-arm versions. For the single-arm version, press out your right arm and row back your left arm as you step with your left leg. As you step right, press out your left arm and row back your right arm.

Upper-Body Workout: More Step Accompaniments

In addition to the Stride Stretch Step and the Knee-Up Leg Lift, the previously listed steps go particularly well with the in-place version of the Upper-Body Workout.

Quick Step (See page 108, Stride Stretch Step)

This very short step—1–6 inches high in place and 6–18 inches long on the move—moves at 120–160 steps per minute. Practice the Heel-Toe Rock with each step to give all of your leg muscles a thorough workout.

Medium Step (See page 108, Stride Stretch Step)

Taking you back to a normal-size step, this movement is 18 inches high for the Leg Lift and 18–36 inches long for the Stride Step. In Walkshaping, the medium step is performed vigorously and is always practiced with the heel-toe rolling motion.

Combining Upper- and Lower-Body Routines

Many of the arm moves and steps contained in Walkshaping's Upper- and Lower-Body Workouts can be incorporated into the Warm-Up and Whole-Body Walks, provided you keep in mind the following rules:

IN OPPOSITION • When combining arm and leg routines, it's best to work "in opposition," working the arm on the side of the body opposite to the working leg. The "left-step-and-right-arm pump" best exemplifies this. It is easiest to work in opposition while walking in place.

Now expand the opposite arm/opposite leg rule to all of your body moves to do double-arm movements and stepping as follows: if you step back, move your arms forward; if you step to the left side, rotate your arms and torso to the right side.

WARM-UP WALK • Practice full-range arm and leg movements, which distribute the workload over a number of muscles, so as to avoid stressing any particular muscle group.

WHOLE-BODY WALK • Use arm and leg movements that can be practiced at a faster pace, but be sure not to place too much stress on any one body area.

BODY-PARTS ROUTINES • Stick with the exercises in the Upper- and Lower-Body Routines. Unlike in the Warm-Up and the Whole-Body Walks, you now want to isolate and work individual muscle groups.

EASY ARMS/HARD STEPS • Use this rule to add arm accompaniments to the Lower-Body Workout.

EASY STEPS/HARD ARMS • Use this rule to add step accompaniments to the Upper-Body Workout.

Try out and practice new arm or step combinations during the slow-paced Warm-Up Walk so that you'll have time to think about them. Once you feel comfortable, practice them during the faster-paced Whole-Body Walk.

Continue to use a Stride Stretch Step or Knee-Up Leg Lift for your Warm-Up Walk. Use smaller steps in the beginning (Levels I and II), because the double-arm movements will add to your workload considerably. How quickly you progress to larger steps will depend on your fitness level: Levels I–II, use small steps; Level III, medium-sized steps; and Levels IV-V, large steps.

Adding More Stretching Exercises

After you have mastered the basic four stretches, add the following stretching exercises to increase flexibility (see page 226, Figs. 11–1 to 11–8).

Choreographing Your Indoor Routines

With practice you can more creatively apply both on-the-move and in-place Walkshaping routines to walking indoors.

Small Spaces

To maximize the use of a small indoor space, reverse the direction of your walk. Here are two step routines that will make Walkshaping into a more continuous dancelike movement.

Fig. 11–1 • Bent Arm Shoulder Stretch (Beginners): Just above the elbow, gently press your bent arm across your chest until you feel the stretch in your shoulder muscles. Avoid hunching your shoulders. Repeat on the other side.

Fig. 11–2 • Straight Arm Shoulder Stretch (Advanced): Just above the elbow, press your slightly bent straightened arm against your chest for a greater stretch.

Fig. 11–3 • Triceps and Shoulders Stretch: Raise your arm above your head. With the other arm, grab your raised arm above the elbow and gently pull it behind your head. Avoid arching your back. Repeat on the other side.

Fig. 11–4 • Biceps and Chest Stretch: Stand at arm's-length from and perpendicular to a wall. Extend your arm sideways and place your palm against the wall at shoulder height. Taking small steps, slowly turn away from the extended arm until you feel a stretch in your chest and biceps. Avoid hunching your shoulders or arching your back. Slowly rotate back toward your arm and repeat on the other side.

Fig. 11–5 • Neck Stretch: Place your palm on the opposite side of your head with the fingers touching your ear. Gently pull your head sideways, keeping the opposite shoulder pressed down, until you feel the stretch in your neck. Repeat on the other side.

Fig. 11–6 • Spinal and Lower Back Stretch: With feet shoulder-width apart, place hands on your thighs as you bend slightly from the hips, bracing yourself as you lower your torso. Inhale deeply; as you exhale, hollow out your torso, pull your stomach in toward your spine, and let your back curve out. Feel the stretch in your spine and lower back.

Fig. 11–7 • Side Stretch: Brace yourself with your hand on your hip as you place your feet shoulder-width apart. Slowly bend to the side while raising your opposite arm toward your ear. Feel the stretch in your hips and spine.

Pivot Step

After taking two or three steps forward, with your right foot forward take a Pivot Step to reverse your direction by turning your body 180 degrees counterclockwise. Execute a Pivot Step by rolling onto the balls of your feet and turning your body while shifting your weight onto the balls of your front and back foot (Fig. 11–8) and turning around to face the other direction. Once around, roll your foot back down onto your heels before taking the next step. In one quick move your back foot becomes your front foot and your front foot, your back foot (Fig. 11–9). Now continue your stepping routines. You can also take a left Pivot Step by rotating in the clockwise direction.

360-Degree Turn-Around Walk

To add variety to your stepping routine and improve your posture, try turning your body completely around. Turning your body counterclockwise, take a right Cross-Over Step (Fig. 11–10) followed by a left

Fig. 11–8 • Pivot Step Right First Position

Fig. 11–9 • Pivot Step Final Position

Fig. 11–10 • Start again with Right Cross-Over Step for a Counter-clockwise Turn-Around Walk

Back Cross-Over Step (Fig. 11–11). You have now turned 180 degrees. Continue with another right Cross-Over Step (Fig. 11–12) and another left Back Cross-Over Step and you will be back again where you started. For a smoother transition, angle your toe in the direction you are going. Make sure your knees stay in line with your ankles. Practice the Turn-Around Step in place first, with your right foot leading. Next, try it in the clockwise direction with your left foot leading. It's important to hold your posture erect and keep your arms pumping for good balance. Try adding the stepping routine to your on-the-move walk.

The Pivot Step and Turn-Around Walking Routine can also be used while walking on the move fast for fun. For example, the Turn-Around Walk is a great way to leave a room. It gives you a graceful way to turn, say good-bye halfway through the turn, and continue turning to leave.

Aerobics Class

Try out your Walkshaping routines in a beginners' low-impact aerobics class. Low-impact aerobics is done by walking, marching, and stepping up and down on a step bench. You'll be able to use a variety of the arm movements right away. Show your instructor this book and ask him or her to help you integrate more of the routine into the class routine.

Malls and Tracks

Walking on the move on indoor tracks or indoor malls is similar to outdoor walking except for the need to turn sharp corners. Also, you should reverse the direction of any walking path that is circular so that you will put equal stress on your muscles.

Treadmills and Stepping Machines

You can apply the On-the-Move Walkshaping routine to a treadmill or stepping machine, but follow these guidelines (Fig. 11–13, 14):

1. Set the treadmill on a 1 percent incline for more comfortable walking.

2. Use a low treadmill speed (1–2 mph) to master the stepping and arm movements and to practice all complicated moves like Cross-Over Steps.

3. Slow down the steps and hold on to the railings when doing lunge steps, squat steps and back steps.

4. The Lower Body Workout should generally be done at a lower speed (never more that 3 mph).

5. The Upper Body Workout can be done at higher speeds using Quick, medium, and Stride Stretch steps as accompaniments.

Combination Arms: Warm-Up and Whole-Body Walks

Substitute or intersperse the basic Bent and Straight Arm Pumps with the following arm combinations during the Warm-Up Walk. Notice that by evenly distributing the workload over a number of muscle

Fig. 11–11 • Left Back Cross-Over Step

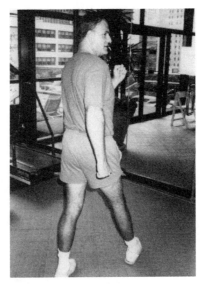

Fig. 11–12 • Right Cross-Over Step

Fig. 11–13 • Treadmill Walkshaping (Lunge Step)

groups, you increase your total amount of work while exercising your upper body. Here are lists of arm/step combinations for the Warm-Up and Whole-Body Walks. Practice the Warm-Up Walk routines at a 30–60-step-per-minute pace, and the Whole-Body Walk routines at a 90–120-step-per-minute pace.

BEGINNERS (LEVELS I–II) • Increase your calorie burn by increasing the range of motion of your arms and the size of your steps. These greater-range movements will also warm up your body faster.

Beginners: Warm-Up and Whole-Body Walk Arm/Step Combinations

1. Head-height Bent Arm Pump and Short or Quick Step

2. Head-height Double Bent Arm Pump and Stride Stretch Step

3. Chest- to chin-height Bent Arm Pump and Stride Stretch Step

4. The chest-height Bent Arm Pump and Quick Step

5. Handshake or Row Back Pump and Stride Stretch Step

Fig. 11–14 • Treadmill Walkshaping

Fig. 11–15 • Combination Biceps Curl and Triceps Extension

ADVANCED (LEVELS III–V) • Increase your calorie burn by combining sets of arm and leg routines. These double-arm variations will warm up your body faster. This is important, since you need more exertion to warm up your muscles as you become fitter.

Advanced Warm-Up Walk and Whole-Body Walk Arm/Step Combinations

Note: Practice each arm combination continuously, following one arm movement with another. For example, in the Double Biceps Curl—Double Arm Press-Ups that follows, first curl up both arms, then curl them down. From the down position, raise your arms up over your shoulders, then lower them back down to your sides and execute another Biceps Curl. Or do any and all of the combinations in the set series with the Bent Arm Pump as your first set. Repeat each one 5–25 times before going on to the next one.

1. Double Biceps Curls, followed by Double Arm Press-Ups

2. Double Arm Front Laterals, followed by Double Arm Side Laterals

3. Double Fly Pumps, followed by Double Triceps Extensions

4. Double Arm Row-Ups and Row-Downs, followed by Double Arm Side Laterals or Front Laterals

5. Double Arm Press-Outs, followed by Double Arm Row-Backs or Double Arm Elbow-Down Triceps Extensions

6. Double Arm Row-Backs, followed by Straight Arm Cross-Overs.

7. Double Arm Cross-Overs, followed by Double Arm Side Cross Triceps Extensions or Double Arm Pull-Overs

8. Alternating Biceps and Triceps Curls (Fig. 11–15). This requires some explanation. Do a right Palm-Up Biceps Curl with a left Elbow-Down Triceps Extension, then a left Palm-Up Biceps Curl with a right Elbow-Down Triceps Extension (e.g., Single Arm Row-Out). Keep elbows down and start each movement with arms bent to 90 degrees.

Step Accompaniments

Practice the above combination arm routines with small to medium-size steps for the Whole-Body Walk. For the Warm-Up Walk, practice any number of medium- to big-size steps such as Stride Stretch Steps, Knee-Up Leg Lifts, or Lunge Steps.

Combination Steps: Warm-Up Walk and Whole-Body Walk

Like arm moves, steps can be combined and alternated to add variety and vigor to your workout, making your Warm-Up and in-place Whole-Body Walks much more interesting and effective. Alternate the basic in-place Knee-Up Leg Lifts with one of the following steps forward and back, and side to side as well:

1. Stride Stretch Steps followed by Back Steps

   Alternative #1: Take a left Stride Stretch Step forward and step back with your left foot. Then take a right Stride Stretch Step forward and step back with your right foot. Begin the series again.

   Alternative #2: Take a left Stride Stretch Step forward and step back with your left foot.

   Then take a left Stride Stretch Step back and step forward with your right foot. Next, take a right Stride Stretch Step forward and step back with your right foot. Then, take a right Stride Stretch Step back and step forward with your right foot. Repeat the series.

2. Heel Digs with Back Steps

3. Heel Digs with Back Cross-Over Steps

4. Heel Digs with Leg Curls

5. Heel Digs with Back Cross-Over Steps

6. Side-to-Side Steps with forefoot plants

7. Side Steps with Cross-Over Steps, left and right

8. Side-to-Side Step Leg Curls Step left, curl up your right leg. Then step right and curl up your left leg.

Do 12 to 25 repetitions of each kind of step before switching to another step technique.

When Your Muscles Get Sore

It will take some of you longer than others to recuperate between Body-Parts Routines. If your muscles are too sore to move, skip over the sets that hurt and resume practicing them once the soreness subsides. This is usually the following day, although it sometimes take a few days for muscles and joints to recuperate.

Expect some muscle soreness as you reshape your body. Your muscles are growing and must recuperate from the stress of being exercised. Muscle soreness from a strained or pulled muscle may take longer—up to 1–2 weeks—to heal. Therefore, it is important to avoid overstressing your muscles by adding too much weight or by doing too many repetitions or sets of the same Body-Parts Exercise before you are strong enough. It is difficult to incur this kind of damage through Walkshaping because the program keeps your weight load much lighter than with static bodybuilding. But it is still possible to strain or pull a muscle if you exceed your skill and strength level, stray from the prescribed exercise schedule, or fail to warm up sufficiently before working out.

If you're feeling sore while doing an exercise, even after a rest day, check to see if you are doing too much too soon, haven't completed a long enough warm-up or cool-down, or need more stretching time to increase your muscle flexibility.

Another phenomenon is the soreness of muscles that are ancillary to an exercise. For example, your triceps may become sore from doing chest or shoulder press-ups, leaving you too sore to do the Triceps Sets on the same or even the next day. If this problem persists, consider performing your Triceps and Shoulder Routines on alternate days.

Splitting Up Your Routines

You may want to alternate your Upper- and Lower-Body Routines, as discussed earlier. But if you'd like to get more of a full body workout each day, try the following suggested schedules to split up your routines to allow a 24–48-hour rest between concentrated muscle group workouts:

Two-Day Split

Day One: Upper-Body Workout: Upper Back and Biceps Sets
Lower-Body Workout: Thighs and Buttocks/Hips Sets
Day Two: Whole-Body Walk
Day Three: Upper-Body Workout: Triceps, Chest, and Shoulders Sets
Lower-Body Workout: Calves, Lower Back, and
Abdominals Sets
Day Four: Whole-Body Walk
Day Five: Upper-Body Workout: Upper Back and Biceps Sets
Lower-Body Workout: Thighs and Buttocks/Hips Sets
Day Six: Whole-Body Walk
Day Seven: Upper-Body Workout: Triceps, Chest, and Shoulders Sets
Lower-Body Workout: Calves, Lower Back, and
Abdominals Sets

Three-Day Split

If you like to spread your Upper- and Lower-Body Workouts over three days, try the Three-Day-Split routine:

Day One: Chest and Triceps Sets; Abdominals and Lower Back Sets

Day Two: Upper Back and Biceps Sets; Thighs and Buttocks/Hips Sets

Day Three: Shoulders Sets; Calves and Shins Sets

Day Four: Day of rest or continue to repeat Day One

Four-Day Split

Day One: Upper Back and Biceps Sets; Thighs, Buttocks/Hips and Abdominals Sets

Day Two: Chest and Triceps Sets; Calves, Shins, and Lower Back Sets

Day Three: Shoulders Sets; Thighs, Buttocks/Hips and Abdominals Sets

Day Four: Upper Back and Biceps Sets; Abdominals and Lower Back Sets

Moving Out

After you've practiced the in-place version of the Walkshaping sets, take them with you on your daily walk in a covered mall, an indoor walking track, or outside.

To help yourself remember the order of the 5–25 Upper- and Lower-Body Sets you'll be practicing, make a copy of or tear out the Walkshaping Lists on pages 209–216. The exercises are named after the movements, so if you've practiced them at home, their names should bring them to mind.

The First Day on the Move

The first day out, practice the routine without weights or other resistance devices, in order to focus on the movements themselves. When you're ready to bring along a device, I suggest you start by using a single device for the entire workout period. This way you won't confuse yourself by having to switch devices. For example, start with either the weights or stretch cords, since they are maneuvered as easily as your free hands. Once you've become more skilled at doing the exercises, take two devices such as stretch cords (which are light and compact) and weights, or ski poles and weights with you. If you opt to use more than one device, you may need to carry the equipment you're not currently using in a backpack. When you get to the point where you use three devices, limit your hand weights to 2½ lbs. and use collapsible ski poles, as well as a waist belt to hold your stretch cords. In doing so, you will gain the flexibility to change devices during a workout set. If you adopt this method, stick to one device per body part.

A Mental Picture of Your Muscles Working

When attempting to combine Lower- and Upper-Body Routines, it helps to visualize your muscles working. One insight is to see your arms and legs as performing equivalent functions for each half of your body. For example, your hips are the shoulders of your lower body, just as your knees are your lower body's elbows, your thighs are the lower body's upper arms, and so on.

With this in mind, it is easy to see that the Leg Curl is similar to the Biceps Curl, since they exercise the equivalent biceps and hamstrings muscles. Likewise, the Triceps and Leg Extensions perform comparable functions, exercising the similar triceps and quadriceps

ANTAGONISTIC FORWARD AND BACK MUSCLES	
Forward	Back
Biceps	Triceps
Chest	Upper Back
Hip Flexors	Hip Extensors
Abdominals	Lower Back
Quadriceps	Hamstrings
Calves	Shins

ANTAGONISTIC SIDE TO SIDE MUSCLES	
Left Side	**Right Side**
Left Oblique	Right Oblique
Left Arm	Right Arm
Left Shoulder	Right Shoulder
Left Leg	Right Leg

muscles. The hip flexors function as the deltoid muscles; hip flexors raise your legs and hold them in place, while the deltoids do the same for your arms. Thus, the Straight Leg Raises resemble the Straight Arm Raises, and the Leg Push-Backs work the buttocks/hips like the Front Laterals work the deltoids.

Another useful mental picture sets up your muscles as antagonistic pairs that combine to move your body parts in two opposing directions—usually forward and back or side to side. According to this explanation, the buttocks are like the deltoids and the hip flexors are like the lats. Because the chest muscles are like the inner thighs, you can train them with Cross-Over Arms just as you train the inner thigh muscles with Cross-Over Steps. In this way, Squats function as Push-Ups, the Buttocks Squeeze as the Shoulder Shrug, and the Side Leg Lifts as the Side Laterals (or Straight Arm Raises). A list of antagonistic muscles follows, divided into forward-back and side-to-side moving pairs.

CHAPTER 12

Managing Your Program

The best way to manage your Walkshaping Program is to keep daily and weekly logs of your progress. This is a great motivator, moving you forward to reach the goals you set for yourself.

Keep Moving: Calorie Output

It's true that after you complete a daily workout, you continue to burn calories for the rest of the day. But your total calorie and fat burn will be higher and faster if you also lead an active life and learn to manage what you eat and drink.

Don't rest on your laurels just because you've finished your daily Walkshaping workout, even if it's a 60-minute workout. It's important that you keep moving during other parts of your day as well, particularly if you want to lose 5 lbs. or more. Choose hobbies and forms of recreation that involve physical activity.

A pound of fat consists of 3,500 unused calories. A 12-minute Walkshaping workout burns 100–300 calories; a 60-minute session burns up to 900 calories. Thus, you will need to Walkshape for 2–6 hours in order to lose a pound of fat. Of course, your body will keep burning calories even after you finish your workout, because exercise raises your resting metabolic rate. As your body becomes more muscular, your movements will burn more calories than they did before. This can add up to a fat loss of 7,000 calories (or 2 lbs.) a week as your body converts its fat to muscle.

Even if you're not practicing the Walkshaping workout, walk every day, whenever and at whatever pace you can, to keep your body burning calories of fat. Once you start Walkshaping, this daily walk will feel like a stroll in the park.

To keep your metabolism, or fat-burning machine, in high gear, practice other low-impact/low-ballistic-motion sports and activities, such as bicycling, swimming, stepping or stair-climbing on machines, cross-country skiing (or ski machines), skating, and low-impact aerobic dancing.

Avoid regular exercise that involves a lot of running, jumping, or other high-impact/high-ballistic motions, such as power lifting, jogging, jumping rope, basketball, and boxing. It's all right if you occasionally play a game of tennis or basketball or take a run on a dirt path. But if you engage in these activities as your regular (3 or more times a week) exercise, you will probably experience joint and back injuries, especially after three years of regular practice. This may be unwelcome, harsh-sounding advice, but the fact is that many runners and other high-impact exercisers are switching from these activities to walking (and now Walkshaping) in order to save their backs and joints from permanent damage, or to reduce the pain they experience in exercising already injured joints and vertebrae.

Clubs and Trainers

If you have a physical trainer or are a health-club member, incorporate the in-place Walkshaping workout into your current exercise program. Many physical trainers and aerobics class leaders have already started to practice some form of Walkshaping as a low-impact aerobics routine, and for many of you, exercising with the assistance of a trainer or a group of walking friends will help you stick with the program. Also, a trainer or leader can watch to make sure that you perform the exercises correctly.

Variation and Travel

Walkshaping is an exercise for all seasons and all spaces. It is portable, since you can take your walking body and compact resistance devices with you on any trip. With the in-place version, you can exercise in the small space between beds in a motel.

One of the best places to practice Walkshaping is a sandy beach. Your bathing suit allows you a full range of motion, and the sand adds extra resistance.

Eating Mechanics: Calorie Intake

Since Walkshaping's shape-up program is activity-based, not diet-based, I focus on using mechanics, such as exercise, to manage your diet. Despite the "come-ons" that make losing weight sound easy, eating for weight control requires significant effort and discipline, just as exercise does. Although diet programs continue to preach that how and what you eat is the solution, managing what you eat is, at best, only half of the equation. Physical activity is essential to weight loss: if you diet without exercising, most of the weight you lose is muscle, not fat, and is gained back anyway. With Walkshaping, I ask only that your level of food intake not increase as you raise your activity level. A balanced, low-fat, low-sugar, high-protein diet will accelerate the rate at which you lose fat.

Dieter's Myths

For every dieters' aphorism you've heard, there is a real exercise or Walkshaping solution. Here are the common dieting myths and facts:

"EAT MORE, WEIGH LESS" Yes, if you reduce your fatty food intake you will be able to eat more of other foods and still weigh less. But these "other foods" must be bulky foods like salads (without dressing), which contain water and fiber to make you feel full. This isn't an open invitation to stuff yourself or permission to binge on carbohydrates, sweets, proteins, or other high-calorie foods. You can still gain weight if you eat too much of something that contains a lot of calories, even if it's pasta and vegetables.

"PERMANENT WEIGHT LOSS, OR, 'FOREVER THIN'" Most follow-up studies of rapid-weight-loss diets show a 99 percent failure rate. This yo-yo pattern of crash dieting followed by rapid weight gain leaves the body weaker and flabbier than when you started.

It takes work to keep off weight. The larger or fatter you are, the greater your appetite. If you haven't been overweight your whole life, then the easiest part will be your initial big weight loss. If you have, you will always retain fat cells, which will keep your appetite higher. To achieve effective long-term weight control, you must learn to be very physically active—in effect, to crave physical activity as much as you now crave food. Since it will be easier to consume fewer calories than to exercise them off afterward, you must continue to monitor what you eat.

"THROW OUT YOUR SCALE" While guarding against a weight obsession is certainly good advice, your scale and tape measure will help you monitor your progress. A 1–5-lb. weight gain from a weekend buffet will show up on your scale before it hits your hips, so weigh yourself as a reminder not to skip any workout days for a while. Use your scale as an early warning system to alert you to a relapse before it gets out of control.

Your body shape is a function of how active you are on a daily and a weekly basis. A week of inactivity can easily lead to a gain of 2 lbs., so it's important to avoid the downtime that results from athletic injuries or laziness. If you're bored or tired or your muscles are too sore to do your Walkshaping workout, then just stroll. Your minimum level of activity should be the completion of your weekly mileage quota at the stroller's or brisk walker's pace.

"THINK THIN, BE THIN" Thinking is only the beginning. Without following through on these good thoughts with daily exercise, only those who are already thin will be thin just by thinking about it. If you are a mesomorph (your body tends toward muscular) or an endomorph (your body tends toward fatty), then you must work to be thin, monitoring your food intake and keeping up your exercise and activity program.

"YOU ARE WHAT YOU EAT" "If you eat fat, you'll be fat." It is true that if you consume too many fatty foods, you will gain weight quickly. But you will also get fat by eating or drinking a lot of sweets, breads, or

		MILEAGE QUOTAS FOR STROLLING AND BRISK WALKING		
Level	Daily Mileage	Total Walkshaping Mileage	Total Weekly Mileage	Total Walkshaping Weekly Mileage
I	½–1 mile	¼–¾ mile	3.5–7	2–5
II	1–2 miles	½–1 mile	7–14	3.5–7
III	3–4 miles	1–2 miles	21–28	7–14
IV	4–5 miles	2–3 miles	28–35	14–21
V	5–10 miles	3–5 miles	35–70	21–35

alcohol. Regardless, the shape of your body is determined more by your level of activity than your level of food intake. Particularly after the age of 25, you have the shape that you've earned through exercise and physical activity. As you age, you lose your natural ability to keep in shape and must compensate for this loss through increased physical activity. The best way to look, feel, and act younger than your age is to burn fat calories daily and maintain toned muscles.

"NEVER BE FAT AGAIN" It's easy to make promises that can't be proven until far into the future. As you become older, your percentage of body fat is determined by your average daily activity level. If you're overweight, it is because your body burns fewer calories than you consume or than exist in your body's accumulated fat stores. When trying to lose excess body fat, you must be more physically active than when you're merely maintaining your ideal body weight.

Exercises such as Walkshaping represent a concentrated amount of activity. If you practice the program daily, or even every other day, you will have the extra edge you need to burn off the accumulated body fat that intermittent sports, physical work, and regular walking can't do.

Eating Exercises

Practice these eating and drinking "exercises."

BEVERAGES • Keep fresh water on hand, and drink plenty of it throughout the day, even when you're not thirsty. When you're hungry between meals, drink water instead of snacking. This will give you a full feeling, which will help to curb your appetite for food. Likewise, before consuming high-calorie alcoholic beverages, drink 8 ounces of water to limit your capacity for liquids. Avoid beverages with sugar and artificial sweeteners; sugar adds 150–200 calories per glass, can, or bottle of a typical drink, and artificial sweeteners stimulate your appetite for food. Add water to fruit juices, and substitute skim milk for whole milk.

SNACKS • There are two schools of thought on the frequency of eating. The French school prescribes that you stick with three daily meals and refrain from in-between-meal snacking. The idea is that your stomach should rest between meals, and snacks overstimulate the digestive juices. On the other hand, the New American school prescribes frequent small meals, or "grazing." The advantage of this approach is that you control your appetite with smaller portions, so you may be less likely to overeat. If you are highly disciplined or not often hungry, the French approach may work for you. But if you get hungry often, you should learn to manage how and what you eat. Avoid high-fat, high-sugar, and low-fiber snacks; they do little to quell your appetite.

FOOD • Fibrous foods such as salads, vegetables, fruits, and grains add bulk to your diet and make you feel full more quickly. Substitute whole fruits and skim-milk-based foods for high-fat foods such as whole milk, cheeses, baked goods, and potato chips. Avoid high-fat red meats such as sausages, spare ribs, and hot dogs.

Limit your fat intake to 20–30 grams per day if you're trying to lose weight, and 35 grams if you're maintaining your weight. Remember to count calories as well as fat. Many low-fat foods (such as yogurt, ice cream, and no-fat baked goods) are high in calories because they are heavily sweetened. It's better to prepare or order food in its natural state, then add butter and sauces sparingly. If you eat more than 30 or 35 grams of fat in a day, do 9 calories (approximately 1/10 of a mile) of extra exercise for each extra gram.

Computing Your Daily Caloric Intake

Keep track of what you eat and drink on your daily Log Sheets. If you have regular eating habits, fill out in detail what you eat on a typical day, showing the portion size and caloric value for each item, then use these numbers to estimate your weekly intake.

While practicing the Walkshapers™ Program, keep track of your daily caloric intake, noting whether you increase your food and drink intake as a result of your increased exercise activities. If you don't know the caloric value of certain foods or the exact size of your portions, refer to the *Nutrition Almanac* (John Kirschbaum [ed.], McGraw-Hill 1989) or other calorie-counter books. You needn't restrict your caloric intake, but do try to keep it constant. Your increased level of activity should ultimately function as an appetite suppressant; at most, you will eat a little more during the first week or two of the program and level off thereafter.

If you want to restrict your caloric intake while on the Walkshaping program, I recommend that you take in at least 1,200 calories per day if you weigh 150 pounds or more and at least 1000 calories per day if you weigh less. My book *Walking Medicine* (Book IV, Chapter 5) contains a complete menu plan for weight loss and maintenance.

TYPICAL-DAY FOOD LOG

Snack(s) _____
_____

Total Calories _____

Breakfast _____
_____

Total Calories _____

Lunch _____
_____

Total Calories _____

Dinner _____
_____

Total Calories _____

The Calorie System of Exercise

How many calories are burned when you walk a mile? A 1-mile walk without the use of Walkshaping's Pump 'N Stride technique burns an average of 100 calories. A 1-mile walk with the Walkshaping tech-nique burns approximately twice that amount, or 200 calories. A 1-mile walk using the technique and hand-held weights increases your calories burn by 20–50 percent, up to a total of 300 calories.

Monitoring Your Measurements

If you're practicing the Walkshaping workouts according to the pro-gram plan and find that you are gaining weight, check your girth mea-surements. If your waist and hips are the same, or smaller than when you started the program, you have probably gained muscle weight. Also check if you've consumed salty foods, which make you retain more water than usual and negatively affect mass or weight. If not, check to see if you're consuming more calories daily than you were before you started the program. If so, you must cut back your con-sumption or further reduce the fat in your diet. Or add extra miles of walking and allow yourself 100 extra calories per mile. Monitor your weight and girth measurements over the next five days.

After Six Weeks

Walkshaping is not just a six-week shape-up program. It can be prac-ticed year-round as a primary health maintenance program. If your goal is to lose more than 10 lbs. or 3 inches from your waist and thighs, you will probably have to practice the Walkshaping program for 12, 18, or 24 weeks.

Eileen Hunt, Carlo Fiorletta, and Cindy Manion (see Introduc-tion) lost 10–25 lbs. on the program.

12 Minutes vs. 60 Minutes

If you started with the 12-minute program because you were out of shape or too busy to exercise, then Week Seven is the time to recon-sider your first-term strategy. If your body type is mesomorph (on the muscular side) or an endomorph (on the fatty side), your body may crave more than 12 minutes a day of exercise. Maybe it's time to make a greater commitment to exercising. My 60-minute-a-day goal gives me the leeway to skip days if I am sore or have conflicting commitments, but I still average three to five 60-minute sessions a week.

If you're still too busy to step up to a steady 20–60 minute program, try alternating between shorter and longer workout days. Shoot for the 30-minute program.

Even if you haven't set aside a formal period for Walkshaping, you can still practice select groups of the body-parts routines to tone up specific flabby areas. For example, in-place Lunge Steps and Torso Turns will help to keep your thighs and waist toned. Triceps and Biceps Curls and Triceps Extensions will keep your upper arms toned.

Showing Off

Your best reminder and motivator is the image of yourself in a full-length mirror in a bathing suit. Don't be shy to make a physical appraisal and strike a few body-shaping poses to show off your muscles to yourself. A mental image of the shaped-up you will keep you going on the Walkshaping Program.

Problem Areas

You may have identified your flabbiest or weakest body areas already when you set your personal shape goals. Practice extra reps or sets of Body-Parts Routines to further tone them up, building up to 50–100 reps of an exercise with no weights or resistance devices and 25–50 reps with light weights. Performing a large number of reps with a light weight will help you burn off more fat and develop a "sculpted" rather than "overbuilt" look in a particular body area.

When All Else Fails

If you've read this far, you're obviously concerned about finding a solution to being out of shape. To get and stay in shape, you must invest time and effort; when you fall down on the job, you must try again.

If you make an investment in this book and my program, I want to see that it pays off for you. So if you have questions about or problems with the program, or if you need local support, write to me:

The Walkshaping™ Program

P.O. Box K
Gracie Station
New York, NY 10028

Appendix

You can do the Walkshaping™ Program without any special weights or devices. However, if you want to add extra weight or resistance, standard hand and wrist weights are available at gyms and health clubs, and at any sporting goods store. Buy "surgical tubing" at medical-supplies stores to use as stretch cords. Find ski poles at ski shops, or make your own walking sticks from broomsticks or carved dead branches. Construct a step-bench out of a cinder block and a 1′ × 4′ × 3″ piece of wood.

If you wish to order the special weights and devices featured in this book, send a check or money order in the amount of the price listed on page 246, adding $8.00 for postage and handling:

Devices

Power Poles (collapsible)	$ 69.95
Pedometer	$ 20.00
Carrying Case	$ 20.00
Walk 'N Tone Cords	$ 19.95
Exertube (44″ long)	
x-light	$ 3.75
light	$ 4.00
medium	$ 5.00
heavy	$ 6.00
Step-Benches	$ 59.95

Hand Weights

(For hand weights please add an additional $2.00 for each pound over 2.5 pounds.)

Strong Puts (includes video, workout chart, pads)

(circle weight)	
2.5 lbs.	$31.00
5 lbs.	$31.00
7.5 lbs.	$36.00
10 lbs.	$36.00
Swing Weights (stick)	$19.95

Exercise Bands	
9″ × ¼″	$ 1.00
9″ × ⅜″	$ 1.25
9″ × ⅝″	$ 1.75
9″ × ¾″	$ 2.00
9″ × 1″	$ 2.50
9″ × 1½″	$ 3.25

Big Bands	
12″ × ½″	$ 2.00
12″ × ¾″	$ 2.50
16″ × ½″	$ 2.75
16″ × ¾″	$ 3.00

Step II	
light	$ 5.00
medium	$ 6.00
Ultratoner tubing	$ 14.95
Exerbar	$ 19.95

Books and Tapes

For books, please add $4.00 for postage and handling for the first book or tape and add $1.00 for each additional book or tape per order. For Walkshapers: 180-minute audio accompaniment (includes music), $19.00

Exercise Books and Tapes

For Beginners:

Exercisewalking Book	$12.95
Exercise Walking Audio	$ 9.95

For Aerobic or Intermediate Level Walking:

Walking Workouts Book	$14.95

For In-Place—Beginner and Intermediate:

Walking Workout Video	$19.95

For Hiking, Long-Distance Walking, or Racewalking:

Sportwalking	$12.95

For Walkshapers:

Book	$20.00
Audio	$19.00

Travel Books

America's 100 Greatest Walks	$12.95
Walking Atlas of California	$14.95
Walking Atlas of New England	$14.95
Walking Atlas of Mid-America	$14.95

Send all orders and payments to:

WALKING WORLD
P.O. Box K
Gracie Station
New York, NY 10028

Allow 4–6 weeks for delivery.

Acknowledgments

I would also like to thank the following contributors the the Walkshaping Program:

Consultants

Choreographers

Carlo Fiorletta
Derek Grier
Elizabeth Silon

Editors/Researchers

David Bowman
Richard Levine
Wendy MacKenzie
Claire Olivia Moed
Betty Ouyang
Lea-Beth Shapiro
Lisa Siegel
Alisha Tonsic
Will Wilkinson

Photographers

Avis Boone
Heather Cadwalader
Lauren Fessenden
Lorri Galarza
Derek Grier
Polly Hewson
Eileen Hunt
Manfred Jahreiss
Kelly Kane
Pam Kobrin
Britt Kurtz
Chris Magro
Cindy Manion
Catherine McDonald
Katia McElhanon
Nicolina Pitruzzella
Kara Rekeda
Polina Rozc
Faith Sanford
Alexa Servodidio
Lisa Siegel
Elizabeth Silon
Sheila Simmons
Marian Voetberg
Stacey Wolf
Gary Yanker

Cover Models

Avis Boone
Britt Kurtz
Alexa Servodidio
Elizabeth Silon
Gary Yanker

Model Walkers

Avis Boone
Linda Cassens
Peggy Cawley
Marietta Clark
Gary Croxton
Jodi DeCrenza
Tracy Dillon
Melanie Ferrel
Julianne Feuerstein
Joe Figueroa
Kate Flanigan
Colleen Fleming
Lorri Galarza
Michael Garrido
Derek Grier
Rita Gutowski
Sylvia Hollweck
Eileen Hunt
Pam Kobrin
Britt Kurtz
Christina Lambertson
Christopher Magro
Cindy Manion
Jeanette Martinez
Catherine McDonald
Katia McElhannon
Andrea Morese
Zoie Michaels
Marina Morgan
Nanci Mulholland
Kelly O'Neil

Nicolina Pitruzzella
Valencia Ramos
Kara Rekeda
Renee Robertson
Ellen Rooney
Alexa Servodidio
Elizabeth Silon
Sheila Simmons
Angela Simpson
Christina Stiegelmeyer
Marian Voetberg
Will Wilkinson

The author also wishes to thank the Excelsior Athletic Club for providing its facilities and trainers in the development of the Walk-shaping Program.

Biographies of Contributors

AUTHOR

Gary Yanker, America's foremost authority on walking, is the author of eight books and two tapes on walking, with over 1 million copies in print. His writing has appeared in *The New York Times*, *Reader's Digest*, *Modern Maturity*, and numerous other popular publications. He has also served as the walking editor of both *Prevention* and *American Health* magazines. He leads walking clinics all over the country. Yanker is also an attorney and holds a Juris Doctor and master's degree in business administration from Columbia University.

SANDRA V. ABRAMSON, P.T.

Ms. Abramson is a physical therapist. She holds a B.S. in physical therapy from Ithaca College. She prescribes walking to her patients in her physical therapy practice and walks at least one mile a day. Ms. Abramson lives in New York City.

DAVID AMUNDSEN, D.C.

Dr. Amundsen emphasizes preventive health care in his practice. He is a graduate of the Palmer College of Chiropractic. Dr. Amundsen walks 9 miles a week. He lives near Petaluma, California.

JOHN BALL, M.D.

Dr. Ball is an internist who specializes in endocrinology and metabolism. A graduate of Princeton and the University of Nebraska Medical School, he walks on hills with Heavy Hands nearly every day of the week. Dr. Ball prescribes walking to his patients who have a strong genetic predisposition for diabetes. He lives near Seattle.

EDMUND BURKE, PH.D.

Edmund Burke is an associate professor at the University of Colorado. He is also a highly prolific writer, and a consultant to the fitness industry. Dr. Burke received his doctorate in exercise physiology from the Ohio State University, in Columbus. A 30-mile-a-week walker, he lives in Colorado Springs, Colorado.

SUSAN CABLE, R.P.T.

Ms. Cable is a physical therapist who presently works with children but who has treated patients of all ages. She walks 3 to 5 days a week, 3 miles a day. Ms. Cable lives near Boston, Massachusetts.

DEEPAK CHABRA, M.D.

Dr. Chabra's patients facing major cancer surgery are put on a deep-breathing/walking program. He finds that the walking works wonders for successful postoperative recovery, inducing minimal complications and a shorter hospital stay. Dr. Chabra enjoys walking with his family and hikes 1 to 2 miles a day, 2 to 3 days a week. He lives near Sacramento, California.

HOWARD FLAKS, M.D.

Dr. Flaks is the public-relations chairman of the American Society of Bariatric Physicians (specializing in the treatment of obesity). He enjoys walking on all sorts of terrain and does so daily, logging 20 miles a week. He lives near Los Angeles, California.

BARRY FRANKLIN, PH.D.

Dr. Franklin holds a Ph.D. in physiology, with a specialization in exercise. He is director of cardiac rehabilitation at the William Beaumont Hospital in Royal Oak, Michigan, and is an associate professor of physiology at the Wayne State University School of Medicine in

Detroit. He walks 3 to 4 miles a day, 3 to 4 days a week. He lives near Detroit, Michigan.

AVRUM FROIMSOM, M.D.
Dr. Froimsom is director of orthopedic surgery at the Mt. Sinai Medical Center in Cleveland. An avid jogger for 40 years, he switched to walking because of sore legs. He now walks 6 days a week for a total of 20 miles. Dr. Froimsom lives near Cleveland, Ohio.

ROBERT GLICK, M.D.
Dr. Glick had to give up running, so he started walking 45 to 60 minutes, 5 to 7 days a week. He sometimes recommends walking to his patients to alleviate tension. Dr. Glick lives near New York City.

HARLEN C. HUNTER, D.O.
Dr. Hunter is owner and founder of Hunter Medical, formerly St. Louis Sports Medicine Clinic. He graduated from the College of Ortheopathic Medicine and Surgery, Des Moines, and did his orthopedic residency at Des Moines Hospital, St. Louis. He prescribes walking to his patients for physical fitness, and walking in water for hip and joint arthritis. He's the author of *Motorsports Medicine*, 1992. Dr. Hunter walks a minimum of 3 miles a day and lives near St. Louis, Missouri.

JOSEPH KANSAO, D.C.
Dr. Kansao specializes in preventive and rehabilitative sports medicine. He is medical editor of *Running News* and author of a monthly article in *Athletic Magazine*. He walks 6 days a week, 6 miles a day. Dr. Kansao lives near New York City.

MARK LANDRY, D.P.M.
Dr. Landry is a board-certified podiatric surgeon and holds a master's degree in biomechanics and kinesiology. Dr. Landry walks 1 mile every day. He is a graduate of the Ohio College of Podiatric Medicine. Dr. Landry lives near Kansas City, Missouri.

MARK LA PORTA, M.D.
Dr. La Porta is an internist who practices preventive medicine, focusing on geriatrics, with a private practice in Miami, Florida. He has taught podiatric medicine and physical diagnosis at the Dr. William Scholl College of Podiatry in Chicago and has been a medical instructor at Rush Memorial College in Chicago. Dr. La Porta received the M.D. degree from Northwestern University Medical School in

Chicago ina 1978. Dr. La Porta walks 4 days a week and lives in Miami Beach, Florida.

KAREN P. LAUZE, M.D.

Dr. Lauze prescribes walking for her headache patients to reduce frequency and severity of headaches. She graduated from Boston University School of Medicine. She specializes in neurology. She walks 3 to 5 miles a day, 3 to 5 days a week. Dr. Lauze lives near Petoskey, Michigan.

RUTH LERNER, PH.D.

Dr. Lerner is a licensed clinical psychologist who incorporates walking into her therapy sessions and finds that exercise is especially helpful for depressed patients. Dr. Lerner walks 4 days, 16 hours a week, and lives in Los Angeles.

RALPH MARTIN, D.O.

Dr. Martin is certified in OB/GYN and past president of the Association of Osteopathic and OB/GYN Association. He is a graduate of the College of Osteopathic and Surgery Medicine, Des Moines. He is in private practice and prescribes walking for his overweight patients. Dr. Martin walks 2 miles a day and lives near Atlanta, Georgia.

ROGER MAZLEN, M.D., P.C.

Dr. Mazlen, who specializes in nutrition and preventive medicine, is a clinical assistant professor of medicine at Mt. Sinai School of Medicine. He walks 4 to 5 days a week, 3 miles a day. Dr. Mazlen lives near New York City.

SARAH MILLER, PH.D.

Dr. Miller, a clinical psychologist, works with very overweight individuals (40 pounds or more) and has helped them achieve their health goals with a walking program. Dr. Miller walks 3 miles a day, 5 to 7 days a week. She lives near Napa, California.

KENNETH MURKOWSKI, D.C.

Dr. Murkowski specializes in pediatrics and sports and industrial medicine. Because of past knee injuries, he took up walking and now logs 3 miles a day, 3 to 4 days a week. He also enjoys biking and swimming. Dr. Murkowski lives near Jackson, Mississippi.

THOMAS M. ORMSBY, P.T.

Mr. Ormsby is the program director at Gateway Health and Fitness in Newark, New Jersey. He is a graduate of Rutgers University, in New

Jersey, and holds a B.S. in Exercise Science and Sports Studies. He is also a Certified Personal Trainer by the American Council on Exercise. Mr. Ormsby walks 5 miles a day, 5 days a week. He lives in New Jersey.

TODD PELLESCHI, D.P.M.

Dr. Pelleschi is a graduate of the Ohio College of Podiatric Medicine and a board-certified foot and ankle surgeon. He has used walking to improve cardiovascular and lower-extremity circulatory efficiency in several of his patients. Biking is his primary exercise, but he also walks 3 days a week, 6 miles a walk. Dr. Pelleschi lives in Pennsylvania.

KATHLEEN PETRILLO, R.D.

Ms. Petrillo is a registered dietician and counsels on nutrition. She walks 3 days a week, 4 miles a day. Ms. Petrillo lives near Boston, Massachusetts.

RONALD PONCHAK, P.T.

Mr. Ponchak is a physical therapist with a private practice in New York City, treating orthopedic and sports-injured clients. He walks 10–12 miles a week.

MALCOLM RICE III, M.D.

Dr. Rice is Medical Director, Extended Care Center, Edward Hines, Jr. V. A. Hospital, Hines, Illinois. He received his M.S. in Biology from Roosevelt University, Chicago, and his medical degree from St. George's School of Medicine, Grenada, W.I. He completed his residency training in Internal Medicine at Methodist Hospital, Brooklyn, New York, and his fellowship training in Geriatrics at Mt. Sinai Medical Center, New York. He lives in a northern suburb of Chicago and walks daily for exercise.

ALBERT ROSEN, M.D., P.A.

Dr. Rosen is a staff member in pediatrics at Columbia Presbyterian Medical Center in New York and at Valley Hospital in Ridgewood, New Jersey. A long-time race-walker and hiker, Dr. Rosen has climbed many of the world's highest peaks. He lives in New Jersey.

ALLEN SELNER, D.P.M.

Dr. Selner specializes in sports medicine for women. He walks at least 1 mile every day. Dr. Selner lives near Los Angeles.

PAUL SHEITEL, D.P.M.

Dr. Sheitel graduated from Illinois College of Podiatric Medicine. He walks 8 miles a week and does bodybuilding 2 to 3 times a week.

ELIZABETH SILON, P.T.

Ms. Silon has been a fitness professional for over 6 years. A graduate of Syracuse University, she is ACE, AFAA certified. Currently she is an aerobics instructor and personal trainer at the Peninsula Spa in New York City. Ms. Silon walks 6 to 8 miles a week.

TERRY SPILKEN, D.P.M.

Dr. Spilken is on the adjunct faculty of the New York College of Podiatric Medicine and is the podiatrist consultant to the Alvin Ailey American Dance Theater and Light Opera Company of Manhattan. Dr. Spilken prescribes walking exercises to dancers and other athletes to rehabilitate foot problems. A 15-mile-a-week exercise-walker, he practices in New York City.

JACK STERN, M.D.

Dr. Stern is medical director of Canyon Ranch Health Resort in Tucson, Arizona, and coauthor of *The Home Medical Handbook*. Dr. Stern speed-walks 8 miles a day, 5 to 6 days a week, and lives in Tucson.

JAMES D. THOMAS, M.D.

Dr. Thomas is Director of Cardiovascular Imaging, Department of Cardiology, and Professor of Medicine and Biomedical Engineering at Ohio State University, Cleveland, Ohio. As a specialist in the medical and surgical treatment of valvular heart disease, he often prescribes walking as part of a cardiac rehabilitation program for his patients. He has served as a staff cardiologist at Massachusetts General Hospital and graduated first in his class from Harvard Medical School. Dr. Thomas walks between 6 and 8 miles per week and lives near Cleveland, Ohio.

ROBERT E. TOMPKINS, D.O.

Dr. Tompkins is resident in anesthesiology at University of Miami Jackson Memorial Hospital. He will become a fellow in pain management. He graduated from New York College of Osteopathic Medicine in Old Westbury, New York, and State University of New York at Oneonta, New York. Dr. Tompkins lives in Miami and walks 8 miles a week for exercise.

CHRIS VANCE, D.P.M.

Dr. Vance is a graduate of California College of Podiatric Medicine and is board certified in biomechanics and podiatric medicine. He prescribes walking for gait correction, exercise, and health maintenance. His prescription of regular walking reduces the insulin requirements of his patients. Dr. Vance is an active walker who covers 4 miles a day, 4 days a week. He lives near Seattle.

MARK YOUNG, M.D.
Dr. Young now specializes in physical medicine and rehabilitation at Johns Hopkins School of Medicine in Baltimore, Maryland, and previously taught at Albert Einstein College of Medicine in New York. He walks 25 or more miles a week and lives near Baltimore, Maryland.

Index